Puritan Spirits in the
Abolitionist Imagination

AMERICAN BEGINNINGS, 1500–1900

A Series Edited by Edward Gray, Stephen Mihm, and Mark Peterson

Also in the series:

Puritan Spirits in the Abolitionist Imagination

KENYON GRADERT

University of Chicago Press
Chicago and London

PUBLICATION OF THIS BOOK HAS BEEN AIDED BY A GRANT FROM
THE BEVINGTON FUND.

The University of Chicago Press, Chicago 60637
The University of Chicago Press, Ltd., London
© 2020 by The University of Chicago
Published 2020
Printed in the United States of America

29 28 27 26 25 24 23 22 21 20   1 2 3 4 5

ISBN-13: 978-0-226-69402-3 (cloth)
ISBN-13: 978-0-226-69416-0 (e-book)
DOI: https://doi.org/10.7208/chicago/9780226694160.001.0001

Library of Congress Cataloging-in-Publication Data

Names: Gradert, Kenyon, author.
Title: Puritan spirits in the abolitionist imagination / Kenyon Gradert.
Other titles: American beginnings, 1500–1900.
Description: Chicago : University of Chicago Press, 2020. | Series: American
    beginnings, 1500–1900 | Includes bibliographical references and index.
Identifiers: LCCN 2019049760 | ISBN 9780226694023 (cloth) | ISBN
    9780226694160 (ebook)
Subjects: LCSH: Antislavery movements—United States—History—19th
    century. | Puritans—Political activity—United States—History—19th
    century.
Classification: LCC E449 .G73 2020 | DDC 326/.80973—dc23
LC record available at https://lccn.loc.gov/2019049760

♾ This paper meets the requirements of ANSI/NISO Z39.48-1992
(Permanence of Paper).

To Mom and Dad
To Erin

CONTENTS

Introduction

A gala woke the ghost of Myles Standish. On December 22, 1845, the renowned captain of the Pilgrims' colonial militia was roused from his Duxbury grave by a Forefathers' Day celebration across the Kingston Bay in Plymouth, held in honor of his Pilgrim and Puritan brethren.[1] After an elegant dinner, the partygoers urged a word from their guest of honor, the venerable Edward Everett, US ambassador to the United Kingdom. The former minister, congressman, and governor obliged with expected praise for a "precious inheritance" passed down from the Pilgrims and Puritans: a "sacred fire of liberty" sparked by the Reformation's priesthood of all believers and guarded by the American republic.[2]

Such rhetoric contributed to a nationalist narrative of America's Pilgrim/Puritan origins that coalesced in the 1820s.[3] But by the 1840s this Puritan "fire of liberty" had grown unwieldy enough to worry Everett. Transcendentalists proclaimed that "truth lights her torch in the inner temple of every man's soul," while a growing movement of abolitionists applied this idea to the great sin of their era, declaring themselves "all on fire" against slavery even if meant the dissolution of the state.[4] Everett, the "Apostle of Union," attempted to quietly douse such incendiary talk by noting that the Pilgrims and Puritans were not "impracticable fanatics, endangering the state by doubtful allegiance," but instead represented "a fair share of the wealth and respectability of the [British] kingdom."[5] To drive his point home, he ended with a toast to "the harmonious actions of old Virginia and old Massachusetts." The night concluded with a "Pilgrim ball."[6]

This was too much for the fiery Captain Standish. He marched for Cambridge to protest with a poet.

"My name is Standish," the spectral captain declared as he materialized in the study of the young Brahmin James Russell Lowell. "I come from Plymouth, deadly bored / With toasts, and songs, and speeches," he vented, scoffing at the idea that "they understand us Pilgrims! they, / Smooth men with rosy faces." He grew angrier. "These loud ancestral boasts of yours, / How can they else than vex us? / Where were your dinner orators / When slavery grasped at Texas?"

The startled Lowell had scarcely stammered a halfhearted defense of "compromise" when Standish drew his broadsword, bellowing, "God confound the dastard word." As quickly as he came, the spirit vanished with a final hope that "this bleak wilderness" might reclaim "the glory of thy morrow."

Lowell scrambled to record his "vision," knowing that "neighbor Buckingham" was made of "Pilgrim-stuff that hates all sham, / And he will print my ditty." Indeed, Joseph T. Buckingham did publish Lowell's cheeky yet militant poem in his influential Whig journal, the *Boston Courier*. So did Eliakim Littell in his popular middlebrow weekly *Littell's Living Age* and William Lloyd Garrison in his radical abolitionist periodical the *Liberator*.[7] The variety of venues hints that Lowell was striking a chord with a range of readers. Was their precious Puritan inheritance—this "sacred fire of liberty"—indeed an antislavery torch in their own era?

Hundreds of abolitionists had cried "Yes!" since the movement's inception in the 1830s. When the antislavery preacher and printer Elijah Lovejoy was killed by a proslavery mob in 1838, the orator Wendell Phillips praised his armed resistance as heir to "the Puritans of Cromwell's day." In fact, America's most radical antislavery newspaper, the *Liberator*, invoked the Puritans over a thousand times in its weekly run from 1831 to 1865—every other issue, on average.[8] These writers used the Puritans not only to stoke an imaginative holy war against a major part of the American economy but also to support the public protest of female, working-class, and black Americans. Men from poor farm families like John Greenleaf Whittier and Parker Pillsbury found authority for their own protest in the Puritan past. Maria Weston Chapman, head of the Boston Female Anti-Slavery Society, authorized her controversial activism by casting herself as a neo-Puritan warrioress, and Lydia Maria Child even reimagined the Pilgrim myth as female antislavery militias fighting in Bleeding Kansas. Black writers like David Ruggles and William Wells Brown not only legitimized their own activism with the Puritan past but used it to elevate other black revolutionaries, praising the slave rebel Nat Turner and the Haitian revolutionary Touissaint Louverture as new Cromwells. Writers who experienced discrimination in a nation dominated by wealthy white men embraced this Puritan heritage as a platform for their own voices, using a legacy often figured as masculine and Saxon to claim their right to the kind of protest wielded by Brahmin peers like Lowell.

As the struggle with slavery grew more volatile in the decades before the Civil War, these Puritan spirits stoked increasingly militant visions of revolution. When the war with Mexico ended in 1848 with an ugly US victory, a vast expansion of slave territory, and a Congress still dominated by its architects, Lowell was so disgusted that he pined in the *Liberator* for "one hour of that undaunted stock, / that went with Vane and Sydney to the block." Lionizing Puritan regicides, he effectively called for an American equivalent of the English Civil War and new regicides to decapitate King Cotton.[9] Many felt that Lowell's wish was granted in 1856 and 1859 when the vigilante John Brown—himself an admirer of Cromwell—executed proslavery men with Standishesque broadswords in "Bleeding Kansas" and attacked the federal arsenal at Harper's Ferry in hopes of sparking a mass slave insurrection. Nearly all of the major writers who rose to Brown's defense— Lydia Maria Child, Ralph Waldo Emerson, Henry David Thoreau, Frederick Douglass, and many others—praised him as a Puritan reincarnate. Wendell Phillips deemed Brown "a regular Cromwellian, dug up from two centuries," defending his actions with a regicidal Puritan heritage. "Treason is our inheritance. The Puritans planted it in the very structure of the State," he concluded in his defense of the vigilante.[10] On the eve of the Civil War, then, a vision of militant Puritan spirits went so far as to sanction treasonous attacks on the federal government. The outbreak of war (and especially the Emancipation Proclamation that eventually graced it with antislavery purpose) transformed the status of the national government within this narrative. Abolitionists became patriots, and their imagined war became real. Daniel Aaron first noted the Miltonic tenor of of divine warfare prevalent among American intellectuals during the Civil War, but this was in fact the culmination of an imaginative project started thirty years prior.[11]

This was not merely self-affirming rhetoric among the antislavery likeminded but pervasive and aggressive enough to concern opponents. Many worried with Everett that this militant Puritanical righteousness would overturn American society altogether. Even outright opponents of abolitionism traced the movement's radicalism back to Puritanism. Senate Democrat Samuel S. Cox of Ohio declared that the Puritans' legacy had concentrated into the "hated focus of Abolitionism" and caused the chaos of the Civil War. "Puritanism is the reptile which has been boring into the mound, which is the Constitution, and this civil war comes in like the devouring sea!" he thundered, for "abolition is the offspring of Puritanism."[12] In an 1862 speech to the Mississippi legislature, Jefferson Davis himself declared

WORSHIP OF THE NORTH

Figure 1. Adalbert Volck, "Worship of the North," 1863

that "our enemies are a traditionless and a homeless race; from the time of Cromwell to the present moment they have been disturbers of the peace of the world. . . . They persecuted Catholics in England, and they hung Quakers and witches in America."[13] The Confederate sympathizer Adalbert Volck illustrated the notion with a political cartoon that crowded prominent antislavery figures around a diabolic altar built from stones reading "Socialism," "Atheism," and even "Free Love." Crowning its top was "Negro Worship," while its largest foundation stone boldly reads "PURITANISM."[14]

To Volck and many others, the abolitionist revival of Puritan radicalism threatened to upset all American mores—economic, religious, racial, even sexual. "Applying the old doctrines of Puritanism to our established order," Senator Cox argued, abolitionism "began, on moral grounds, to undermine the structure of our civil society" by continuing the tradition of "New England fanaticism [which] made compromise impossible." Nearly fifty years after the war, Henry Adams surveyed this "almost Cromwellian" atmosphere with wry precision: "Slavery drove the whole Puritan community back on its Puritanism," for it "scarcely needed a violent reaction like anti-slavery politics to sweep him back into Puritanism with a violence as great as that of a religious war."[15]

America's first major protest movement agitated for a second revolution with Puritan spirits that they found empowering, rebellious, even intoxicating, but "Puritan" today is likelier to be an insult for prudish sobriety, priggish conformity, or oppressive self-righteousness from an authoritarian majority, less regicide and embattled dissent than iron men in courthouses and pulpits littered with scarlet letters, banished antinomians, earless Quakers, hanged witches, and slaughtered Natives. Skeptical memories of the Puritans have come and gone in different shapes ever since the word was coined (an insult from the start), but this suspicion has acquired an ideological intensity ever since poststructuralist suspicion of metanarrative prompted a thorough interrogation of the Puritans' recurring role as a favored national origin story. Perry Miller's argument that the "meaning of America" could be found in the Puritan errand especially acquired a more sinister hue to a generation that came of age after Vietnam. Where Miller saw the errand as an anxious reaction to a dangerous cosmos, Sacvan Bercovitch saw a powerful "ritual of consensus" that in fact constricted doubts and dissent—a "hegemony unequaled elsewhere in the modern world."[16] The "New Americanists" push this skepticism further, arguing for nothing less than the Puritan origins of American empire, charging Winthrop with establishing the "theocratic precedent for the cold war state" that allowed it to "disavow catastrophic outcomes of its exercise—like the Pequot massacre, or slavery, or Hiroshima."[17]

Here is the latest episode in a long battle over our *memory* of the Puritans, our sense of how they still matter in our present, which should be distinguished from historiographical debates about who the Puritans actually were, despite their overlap. Abolitionists' revolutionary Puritan, much like Max Weber's proto-capitalist, H. L. Mencken's Jazz Age prude, Miller's Cold War exceptionalist, and New Americanists' atom bomb imperialist, generally says more about the moment in which it originated than about the Puritans themselves. In the most glaring contradiction for the present study, although Puritan theology and courts granted slaves certain rights and ordered emancipation for those who had been enslaved by "man-stealing," the Puritans of course owned slaves, and a growing number of studies have highlighted this gap between Puritan history and the common memory of New England as an antislavery region from the start.[18] For these reasons Gordon Wood concludes that claims about a "direct transmission" of an "actual Puritan inheritance"—whether for the Puritan origins of American revolution, capitalism, prudery, exceptionalism, or empire—often become "historically preposterous" the more we dig into the archive.[19]

And yet as Michael Kammen concluded in his magisterial study of

American memory, "what people believe to be true about their past is usually more important in determining their behavior and responses than truth itself," and this makes memory itself an influential part of the historical record, worthy of study in its own right. For this reason historians have a responsibility to demythologize nostalgia, but they also "need not be overly cynical about societies that 'invent' traditions. Sometimes that occurs in order to perpetuate power relationships or to foist a mystique of false consciousness; but sometimes it actually occurs for benign reasons."[20] This is especially welcome advice for our memories of Puritanism, where a polemical reaction to the Cold War roots of Puritan studies has made suspicion a dominant mood for the last thirty years. And that is precisely why the abolitionists' revolutionary memory of Puritanism matters: it pushes us beyond invented Puritan memories as either false consciousness or simply "benign" nostalgia and reveals an instance in which memory actively aided an ideological revolution. In turn, it offers a striking departure from our usual memories of Puritanism as a conservative force for capitalism, prudery, exceptionalism, and empire. In the latest instance, if the "Puritan origins thesis" has especially been attacked for its exceptionalist overtones, a tradition of thinkers from Walter Benjamin to Raymond Williams has argued that such origin stories are not always tools of jingoistic conservatives but may be arenas for contesting present values and reimagining future possibilities; in Benjamin's words, *Ursprung ist das Ziel*—if illusory roots, origin stories are useful *goals* for various ends, narrative targets.[21]

If origin stories need not be conservative, neither do the ideologies imagined through them. Yet most studies of the "Puritan origins of X" have presumed a definition of ideology as, at best, a static consensus and, at worst, false consciousness.[22] Teun van Dijk offers a more neutral definition of ideology as discourses that in fact draw their energy from *polarity* rather than consensus, from a contrast between the "positive properties of Us, the ingroup, and negative properties of Them, the outgroup."[23] In effect, an ideology is an imaginative battle line over conflicting values. Often its very urgency arises from the sense that We, a prophetic yet embattled minority, are on the ropes—a feeling that can bolster a revolutionary vanguard as much as a reactionary rearguard. This is precisely what abolitionists found so captivating about the Puritans, what they themselves wanted to be, a prophetic minority so enraptured with a moral-spiritual conviction that they could not compromise with a wicked status quo, even if it meant martyrdom and holy war. Wendell Phillips traced this sacred conviction from the English Revolution through the "holy war" of the American Revolution to "a holier and the last": the fight against slavery.[24] Lawrence Buell has noted how antebellum liberals often remembered the Puritans as a cautionary tale on the dangers of fanaticism and intolerance, but for restless souls who found their way to the antislavery movement, the Puritans' militant zeal acquired a new value in light of an increasingly belligerent slave power and a complicit North: where slavery was concerned, "tolerance" now looked like compromise with sin, while Puritan zealotry seemed "religion pure and undefiled" in a complacent world.[25]

Central to this imagination, then, was a Manichaean desire to challenge a slavery-sustaining status quo (in the North as much as the South) with millennial battle lines that cleaved the complex problem into the simpler, more exciting choice of good versus evil.[26] "Resistance to something was the law of New England nature," Henry Adams reflected, a tendency to view "the world chiefly as a thing to be reformed, filled with evil forces to be abolished," a "duty [that] implied not only resistance to evil, but hatred of it."[27] Adams's description was derisive, but for many antebellum intellectuals, this aggressive resistance signaled spiritual vitality in a languishing nation, a hatred *of sin*. For Emerson, abolition became a practical application of his belief that self-reliant "goodness must have some edge to it" if one hoped to change history, that Puritan "hatred must be preached" when love "pules and whines" in a depraved present.[28]

Historians often emphasize the pacifism of Garrisonian abolitionists, but even the most committed "nonresistants" (including Garrison himself) often walked an uneasy line between metaphoric and literal battle. As they rifled imaginative fire toward slavery with arms inherited from a sacred Puritan past, the line between attacking slavery with the pen and celebrating those like Brown who attacked it with bullets was not always firm. (Some writers like Thomas Wentworth Higginson did both for good measure.) Thus after thirty years of imaginative holy war, many embraced the real Civil War with a Miltonic zeal that could border on ferocity, as when Wendell Phillips gushed over Massachusetts soldiers with a "hand on the neck of a rebellious aristocracy . . . mean[ing] to strangle it."[29] No one was a more fervid student of Puritanism than Phillips, and the pugnacity he drew from this heritage helped enrapture vast crowds and launched him into the role of America's most renowned speaker even as it stoked his delight in war. In daring to draw a millennial battle line through the middle of a complacent status quo, the Puritan spirit in the abolitionist imagination offered the pleasures, pitfalls, and powers of a revolutionary holy war.

Before the Cold War, many critics recognized this pleasure and its revolutionary potential. William James called it "the moral equivalent of war" that "we now need to discover in the social realm . . . something heroic that will speak to men as universally as war does, and yet will be as compatible with their spiritual selves," and he too traced this spirit back to the Puritans and forward to "the Utopian dreams" of socialists and anarchists, impractical "saints" who were nevertheless "slow leavens of a better order" that "break the edge of the general reign of hardness."[30] Henry Adams wrote sardonically when he concluded that the New Englander "love[d] the pleasure of hating" sin, but he also wrote from personal experience as a former reformer consciously steeped in Puritan conscience.[31] George Santayana likewise chided the genteel residue of Calvinist conscience among Harvard dons who believed "it is beautiful that sin should exist to be punished," but he also noted that its transcendentalist reincarnation "embodied, in a radical form, the spirit of Protestantism as distinguished from its inherited doctrines; it was autonomous, undismayed, calmly revolutionary."[32] Despite Vernon Louis Parrington's distaste for colonial clerics, he opened his magnum opus with a meditation on the "dangerously revolutionary" core of Puritanism, and Van Wyck Brooks celebrated the abolitionists as "stiff-necked sectaries of Cromwell's army" in an unfinished "world-struggle of darkness and light."[33] Even Mencken, the Puritans' greatest foe in the twentieth century, begrudgingly granted that the abolitionist movement was perhaps the sole good instance of "Puritanism" as a "literary force" in America, still too moral for his Nietzschean tastes yet nearly Wagnerian in its sublimity. "Moral, devout, ecstatic," its "supernaturalization of politics" reached "astounding heights . . . not seen in the world since the Middle Ages," a "supreme discharge of moral electricity" that made "the American people forgot all about their pledges and pruderies."[34] In this respect the rebellious Puritan spirits in the abolitionist imagination are a memory that has only recently been forgotten.

The revolutionary pleasure that abolitionists found in the Puritans lay in their ability not only to sanction holy war in the present but to root that present in a sacred lineage and revive its still-living "spirit." If ideologies offer meaning by cleaving an ambiguous present into a battle between good and evil, they also do so by stitching adherents into the longer story of that battle, replete with heroic and villainous forebears. Without endorsing these stories, scholars can better understand their power if they concede that storytellers are not just doing bad history but are combing it for meaning in the present, an indispensable part of any political project. Sometimes this involves willful ignorance and flagrant cherry-picking, but more often it involves a subtler process of negotiating the past's failures and its potential so as to *use* history, in Nietzsche's words, critically as well as monumentally. All abolitionists agreed that the Puritans were flawed beings with a mixed legacy. Even in a commemorative speech Everett could admit, "I am not blind to the imperfections of the Pilgrims. I mourn especially that they did not recognize in others the rights which they asserted for themselves. I deplore their faults, though the faults of their age."[35] But this critique was tempered by other considerations—that moral standards evolve over time, that it is easy to judge past actors from a safe distance, that someone's good and ill often cannot be easily disentangled. All of these could be summed up as an effort to distinguish the actual past and its later potential, the doors it opened despite its flaws: Wendell Phillips instructed listeners to regard the Puritans "*in posse,* not *in esse,—*in the possibilities which were wrapped up in that day, 1620, not in what poor human bodies actually produced at the time"—what many referred to as the *spirit* of the Puritans. Today we might speak of this approach in Ricoeur's terms as a balance between historical hermeneutics of suspicion and of faith—"willingness to suspect, willingness to listen."[36]

Here was a distinctly pragmatic approach to history as something to be used in the present, one that could shift from critique to praise based on the needs of that present. That is, a problem was sometimes best attacked with historical debunking and other times with heroic myth. Lydia Maria Child, for instance, shifted from the former to the latter as the struggle with slavery grew more volatile: though she began her career with a scathing critique of Puritan history in *Hobomok* (1824), by the 1850s she reimagined the Pilgrim myth as a tale of heroic female antislavery militias in "The Kansas Emigrants," a story designed and timed to sway voters for an antislavery presidential candidate and a far more popular work than *Hobomok.* The fact that scholarship abounds on *Hobomok* and barely exists on "The Kansas Emigrants" (despite the latter's greater influence) aids my point: our present critical impulse toward suspicion favors these kinds of stories above more influential myths. Everett and Lowell hinted at these considerations in their reimagination of the Pilgrims even as they drove toward opposed political ends. "I doubt whether we have a right, living as we do in ease and luxury," Everett wondered, "to take for granted that this heavy burden could have been borne by more delicate frames and gentler tempers."[37] Lowell put similar qualifications into the mouth of his spectral Standish. "'Tis true, we drove the Indians out," he confessed, "and hung a score of Quakers; But, if on others' rights we trod, / Our own, at least, we guarded." Such statements make us uneasy today—as they should, for their inconsistencies can quickly be used to justify new horrors. But they also reveal a uniquely pragmatic approach to history as a mixed legacy always up for grabs in present politics.[38] Rather than cede its narrative potential to the likes of Everett, abolitionists wielded the Puritan past as what Nietzsche would call an "illusion in the service of life."[39]

This is thus not a study of "the Puritan origins of abolition" but of the resonance of the Puritan past within the abolitionist imagination.[40] To clarify this distinction, I shift terminology away from "origins" to what I call "genealogies," away from a symbolic logic unfolding through time to the ways in which writers reimagined lineages within their own moment. "History may also work backward," in the words of Robert Milder, as "legacies of thought, vestigial or outmoded in new intellectual times, come to reassert themselves figuratively as interpretive categories that respond to personal or communal crises."[41] While it has become common to speak of nations as a "daily referendum," in Ernst Renan's lasting description, fewer have explored what Renan felt the core of this referendum to be: a vote on a good story about the past. As imagined communities, nations continue to act upon imagined pasts, and *Puritan Spirits* recovers connected critics who used the Puritans to confront America with a choice between two futures.[42]

In sum, we have overlooked the Puritans' usefulness within a rebellious abolitionist imagination because we have presumed their influence to be a conservative one. *Puritan Spirits* demonstrates that their legacy need not be so and has in fact bolstered a progressive politics of memory. If careless history, this antislavery memory of revolutionary Puritanism was nonetheless influential as a usable past.[43] Even Gordon Wood concedes that "there is something in the experience of those seventeenth-century Puritans that apparently still has resonance," that "there is enough experience there in that remarkable body of Puritan literature to satisfy every conceivable meaning of America that subsequent generations will want to imagine."[44] Most importantly, while the Puritans' resonance today is usually a sinister sound, retrieving abolitionists' more revolutionary use of the Puritans unsettles our skepticism with spirits more alive than we supposed.

If this line of revolutionary holy war from Puritanism to abolitionism was a choice, it becomes all the more necessary to understand the individual and social factors that drove antislavery writers, readers, and opponents to imagine and act upon it. Negatively, this genealogy arose from discomfort with certain features of secularization and capitalism that joined in common complaint against American materialism. More positively, it was sparked by a desire for spiritual revival. Tellingly, Senator Cox's salvo against "Puritanism in politics" began with an attack on the "insatiate

cupidity" of "Yankee capitalists," and many New England intellectuals believed that he was entirely right. Most felt an awakening when they first
read Thomas Carlyle's lament in "Signs of the Times" (1829) and "History" (1830) that "this is not a religious age" but one that valued "only the
material, the immediately practical."[45] Emerson transplanted this critique
into American soil, while Whittier wondered if America's "Pilgrim spirits"
had been lost to "Mammon's lure or Party's wile."[46]

This impatience with a spiritless age aimed as much at the church and
antebellum religiosity as at the state and economy. Raised on heroic myths
of the Reformation and the Puritans that found their most influential expression in Bancroft's histories, many felt that American religion (despite
an ostensible "sea of faith" in the public at large) had slackened into a dull
affair of backwoods revival, bickering among the orthodox, liberal good
cheer, and Unitarian gentility, unheroic all.[47] Carlyle's popular *On Heroes,
Hero-Worship, and the Heroic in History* (1841) cast this present into sharp
contrast with a historical panorama of heroes who combined spiritual vision with powerful will, elevating Martin Luther, Oliver Cromwell, and
the Puritans as the greatest heroes of history. Inspired by this vision, many
anticipated the Nietzschean critique that morality without will became
little more than sanctimony, agreeing with Ann Douglas that a stern and
"masculine" church had softened into irrelevance.[48] "Religion in the old
virile sense of the word has disappeared," Henry James Sr. complained, "replaced by a feeble Unitarian sentimentality."[49] Even Harriet Beecher Stowe
grew impatient with modern sentimentality when she reflected on a declining Puritan heritage. "The doctrine that a minister is to maintain some
ethereal, unearthly station," she wrote in a study of the Puritan clergy,
"is a sickly species of sentimentalism, the growth of modern refinement,
and altogether too moonshiny to have been comprehended by our stouthearted and very practical fathers," who "had nothing sentimental about
them."[50] If most of these writers were self-professed liberals happy to be
beyond Puritan theology, intolerance, and provincialism, this progress also
engendered new uncertainties, the foremost being the sense that religion
was now as spineless as it was civilized, far from the heritage which Carlyle
painted in steel and cannon fire: "Puritanism has got weapons and sinews;
it has firearms, war-navies; it has cunning in its ten fingers, strength in its
right arm; it can steer ships, fell forests, remove mountains;—it is one of
the strongest things under this sun at present!"[51]

These frustrations and desires converged in passionate opposition to
slavery as an enemy worthy of new religious battle, abolitionism an outlet
for desires that preceded and exceeded the cause as it offered the chance

to revive the kind of religious experience felt to have faded in a materialist present. Critics of a spiritless age and a dead church found no better example of their complaint than when American churches failed to unite in clear opposition to slavery, the latest and greatest symptom of a long decay. Abolitionists in turn denounced America's proudly Protestant churches as "papal" in their silence toward a despotic slave economy, legitimizing their anticlericism and come-outerism with a Puritan pedigree.[52] Whether in Lowell's sword of Standish, Brown's Cromwellian Touissant, or Child's Pilgrim-Amazonians in Kansas, abolition was imagined as a cause akin to the great Protestant movements of the past, worth dying and fighting for as Puritan roots lent abolitionism the imaginative power of a new religion.[53]

In turn, critics like Cox declared abolitionists to be Puritans in their propensity for mixing religion and politics. "To sum up the general aspect of this Puritanism," he wrote, "instead of making the church the tomb of dissentions [sic], it made the church the theatre of strife, and carried into the State the same pretension and bigotry."[54] Like Cromwell's fanatical soldiers, abolitionists threatened to destroy the nation in their polarizing obsession with spiritual purity. Puritan spirits lent imaginative fire to the abolitionist cause, but this broader discourse also reflected the uncertainties of secularization in the antebellum era as the border between sacred and secular were shifting in a nation where church and state had only separated relatively recently. Abolitionists responded to Cox that apolitical and spiritless religion was no religion at all, that—as the entire history of Protestantism made clear—religion was at its most vital when protesting a dead church and despotic state, that they would leave institutional religion altogether if need be. Cox in turn wasn't sure whether abolitionists' Puritanism was better described as fanatical or godless, possessed of too much or too little religion; it supernaturalized politics yet "winds up in that perfect infidelity and scepticism which Parker preached and Emerson sung."[55] Scholars of abolition still differ on the degree to which the antislavery movement was a secularizing or religious force, but the debate is better understood beyond this either/or as instead a mark of secularization in Charles Taylor's sense, a transformed rather than a shrunken religiosity, a new kind of framework for the sacred and secular.[56]

This book traces the Puritan spirits in the abolitionist imagination as they unsettled various facets of antebellum American culture. Chapters 1 and 2 examine how the Puritans came to signify a "virile" and "manly" religiosity reclaimed by abolitionist men and, more controversially, women. The first chapter notes how three of abolitionism's most prominent orators—Ralph Waldo Emerson, Wendell Phillips, and Theodore Parker—

reimagined antebellum masculinity as spiritual heroism, connecting their public role as antislavery orators to Puritan antecedents through a shared spiritual militancy that culminated in their public support for John Brown, virile and "Cromwellian." Chapter 2 moves from the lone "manly" orator to the communal female organizing that both reinforced and broadened this image, in particular a group of writers centered in the Boston Female Anti-Slavery Society, from its aggressive leader Maria Weston Chapman to influential literary disciples like Julia Ward Howe and Lydia Maria Child. It argues that these antislavery women both met a female audience's desire for the kind of "manly" and righteous Puritans performed by male orators and claimed this same "masculine" Puritan militancy for their own burgeoning activism.[57]

I then turn from gender to a more explicit examination of aesthetics through a study of abolitionist periodicals and poetry. Chapter 3 situates editor-journalist William Lloyd Garrison and his paper the *Liberator* within the antebellum "print explosion" and its shift from Protestant scarcity to Victorian abundance; it tracks how Garrison responded to this landscape cannily by positioning his paper as heir to a revolutionary Puritan print culture marked by an iconoclastic style and prophetic role that captivated readers. Chapter 4 notes the special place of poetry in this project. Through a study of leading antislavery verse by Charlotte Forten, John Greenleaf Whittier, and James Russell Lowell, I argue that these poets explicitly modeled their vocation after Milton and, much like Garrison and the journalists of the *Liberator*, situated their work within a prophetic Puritan lineage. Here too the results captivated readers, but Lowell in particular opens a window onto the risks of this project as he came to regret his "violent imagination" after the Civil War claimed three of his nephews.

The final two chapters conclude on religion and race as the two facets of culture most unsettled by abolitionists' neo-Puritanism. Chapter 5 explores how the Garrisonian critique of the church challenged the Puritans' most direct institutional heirs, the "Presbygationalist" clergy, and how Henry Ward Beecher and Harriet Beecher Stowe continued their father's effort to protect and update the Puritan errand by imagining "la belle Puritaine," a lovelier Puritanism that could guide the nation on slavery. This vision of Puritanism was often intertwined with a sense of Anglo kinship that clarifies a central concern for the book: despite its ability to gather interracial alliances, abolitionists' reimagination of Puritanism was often a white affair that carried a tension between the universal potential of the Puritans' legacies and their entanglement in a white racial imagination. Theodore Parker, for instance, was radical in his leadership of the interracial Boston Vigilance

Committee yet sometimes Saxonist in his estimation of black Americans, much as Stowe imagined an Anglo-Puritan foundation for America that would paternalistically guard black and Native rights. Thus my focus on white New Englanders is a purposeful choice. It seeks to answer why any white writers chose to involve themselves in the volatile issue of slavery at all when they had no immediate interest in doing so—when activism was likely to steal time from their literary endeavors and risk their livelihoods.[58] In many instances, the motives included not just a disinterested concern for the slave but also a desire to play the part of a Puritan prophet, to revive a fading heritage of tough religiosity, to become a protagonist in a narrative of America that began at Plymouth. As early as 1836, the abolitionist Elizur Wright could admit that "legislation against liberty, thanks to the sturdy rectitude of our Puritan fathers is, if possible, a more 'delicated subject' than Slavery itself" for his white audience.[59] And yet framing issues in this way helped goad white Americans toward the antislavery fold. This strange mix of progressivism and chauvinism also deserves study.

My final chapter thus asks what, if anything, this Puritan heritage meant to black writers, who were usually dedicated Protestants (and often ministers) though rarely blood descendants of the Puritans and entirely uninterested in submitting to Anglo-Protestant paternalism. In a review of not only major figures like David Ruggles, Maria Stewart, Henry Highland Garnet, Martin Delany, and Frederick Douglass but also lesser-known and unknown journalists from black periodicals, I was surprised to discover the frequency with which the Pilgrims and Puritans appeared and the diverse ends to which they were applied, sometimes cited as a reason to join with Garrisonians, other times as a precedent for black nationalism and emigration out of America. This led to my concluding argument that Protestant-Puritan heritage did mean something to black Americans beyond rhetorical garnish for swaying a white audience (though it was also very much that). As a whole, black writers not only stitched themselves into Protestant genealogies and availed themselves of its universalist potential, but also reimagined these genealogies for more resolutely black purposes, tracing the Puritans back to the Egyptian and Ethiopian roots of Judaism and forward to revolutionary black activism of figures like Louverture and Nat Turner, and ultimately the colored regiments of the Civil War, all imagined as the providential culmination of a story that was both African and American.

This chapter reaffirms the utility of the Puritans in the abolitionist imagination but also reveals the emergence of another genealogical imagination intertwined with yet distinct from it: a black vision of a multiracial republic. If white abolitionists imagined the modern world emerging from unwieldy Puritan roots, black writers imagined a diverse counterculture within and beyond it.[60] After the outbreak of the Civil War, the *Christian Recorder*, official paper of the African Methodist Episcopal Church, urged black readers to view the conflict as a holy war in which America's Puritan heritage and black resistance joined in arms to extinguish slavery. "A feud of nearly two hundred and fifty years' standing is being settled to-day," warned a Massachusetts war chaplain in one of several similar *Recorder* articles, when "at Jamestown a load of negro slaves was landed, at Plymouth a band of Christian pilgrims."[61] When Lincoln made the controversial decision to arm black troops in his Emancipation Proclamation, blacks enlisted at once, eager to strike for liberty. Many imagined themselves as taking up the sword of Standish, Touissaint, Turner, and Brown in the bloody beginning of a more perfect Union.

I conclude on Melville's tragic vision of the Civil War and his mixed feelings toward the abolitionists in order to offer my own evaluation of their Puritanical drive toward holy war, the most controversial facet of their legacy. Most recently Harry Stout and Andrew Delbanco echo Melville's critique of abolitionist self-righteousness. Manisha Sinha, John Stauffer, and Eric Foner meanwhile defend abolitionist prophecy as a revolutionary force that "redefined the politically 'possible,'" echoing Aileen Kraditor's conclusion that the problem was not "moral absolutism" but "absolutely antagonistic moral systems."[62] In this respect, abolitionist battle lines forced the nation to confront what Edmund Morgan called the "American paradox," its founding contradiction between the Declaration of Independence and the white supremacy safeguarding its slave economy.[63] Was the abolitionist propensity for Puritanical holy war then ultimately tragic or revolutionary? I conclude yea *and* nay, for the debate rests on a false opposition. All revolutions combine progress and tragedy as what Raymond Williams called a "working through of a deep and tragic disorder."[64] This is not to diminish either element but to highlight their entanglement. "One of the two you must enact—either the will of God, or of the devil," Theodore Parker concluded: "*Aut Deus aut Diabolus*. There is no other alternative, 'Choose you which you will serve.'"[65] With the sword of Standish he drew a line in the sand. But he would not live to see the bloody conflict that obeyed his command.

ONE

Great Grim Earnest Men!

What an invincible heroism, will possess the breasts of those who fight *pro aris et focis*, for their religion. . . . This will give spirit to the lifeless.

—Zabdiel Adams, *"The grounds of confidence and success in war, a sermon preached . . . to a detached company of militia," 1775*

On October 18, 1859, a team of marines commanded by Robert E. Lee battered open the doors to the Federal Arsenal at Harper's Ferry, Virginia. Inside they found the small band of men that had seized the arsenal two days prior, hoping to maim slavery by sparking a mass insurrection throughout the South. Their leader, the steel-eyed tanner named John Brown, had gained notoriety for the "Pottawatomie Massacre" in Bleeding Kansas when he executed proslavery settlers with broadswords in the name of God. A marine returned the favor, dealing Brown a blow of his saber. When the old man "fell senseless on his side," he was arrested and charged with treason.[1]

If Americans could countenance James Russell Lowell playing the part of antislavery Puritan in his poems, the pikes and rifles through which Brown expressed his Calvinist faith were entirely too literal and thus fanatical. But as Brown awaited his trial and eventual execution with a martyr's composure, a cadre of leading writers and orators leaped into speeches aiming to sanctify his reputation. The transcendentalist Theodore Parker was among the "Secret Six" who secretly funded Brown's raid, and as Parker lay dying in Rome he declared that Brown's "sainthood is crowned with martyrdom." After considering but ultimately declining Brown's invitation to participate in the raid, Frederick Douglass fled for Scotland to escape incrimination yet defended Brown from abroad as "a noble, heroic, and Christian martyr."

Concord's prickly prophet Henry David Thoreau deemed Brown "an angel of light," while Wendell Phillips pronounced him simply "a saint." The typically withdrawn Ralph Waldo Emerson went a step further, declaring to a full crowd at Boston's Tremont Temple that Brown was not a madman but a new Christ who would make "the gallows glorious like the cross."[2] Participating in Brown's raid vicariously, these men worked to transfigure treason into holy war and shaped the last months of 1859 into one of the most revolutionary moments in American literary history.[3]

Their vocabulary hinted at their motives. Brown was "simple" and "manly," an "individual" of "action" rather than talk—above all, a "hero." Importantly, Brown's heroism was undertaken neither for power nor for wealth but from "faith" in a higher "principle," an "ideal." David Reynolds argues that these men embraced Brown because he spoke to their increasingly frustrated desires to "supplant their culture's materialism, conformity, and shady politics with spiritual-minded individualism." Federal compromises on slavery in the 1850s especially radicalized a latent propensity for "anarchistic individualism" and "pushed them toward a sympathy with anarchistic violence."[4] A curious final word of praise suggests that these inclinations were not entirely "anarchistic" but grew from deeper historical and even national desires: "Puritan." Nearly everyone who rose to Brown's defense reached for the term. Douglass lauded Brown as "the brave old Puritan" just as Emerson celebrated his "perfect Puritan faith." Parker blended the Pilgrims with the New Model Army, "glad [Brown] came from that Mayflower company" which "trusted in God, and kept their powder dry."[5] Phillips memorably deemed Brown "a regular Cromwellian, dug up from two centuries," while Thoreau (with characteristic belligerence) noted that Brown "was one of that class of whom we hear a great deal, but, for the most part, see nothing at all,—the Puritans."[6]

In lauding Brown as the only visible Puritan in a culture that claimed to value them, these orators were partially being savvy rhetoricians, revising the terms of a shared national narrative in order to invert the most common critique of the abolitionist movement, that it risked destroying a fragile Union with its fanatical mixture of religion and politics. By linking radical abolitionists like Brown to a venerated nonconformist heritage, they forced their audience to consider that antiabolitionist calls for national stability might be less a principled desire for the republic's survival and more the modern equivalent of depraved Stuarts suppressing religious conscience, their "Unionism" a series of morally degrading compromises with sin. In turn, abolitionists' supposedly dangerous mix of religion and politics became *true* religion practicing its faith, their "fanaticism" the simple application of beliefs that Americans professed. Just as Lowell drew Standish's sword at "that dastard word" *compromise*, Phillips argued that John Brown's "fanaticism" and "treason" were in fact the true "lesson of Puritanism." Anyone who claimed to value their Puritan heritage, he maintained, "must imbibe fanaticism," for "treason is our inheritance. The Puritans planted it in the very structure of the State."[7]

Fueling this rhetorical strategy was the desire to revive the kind of religious experience imagined to have faded since Puritanism: iconoclastic yet monumental, individualistic yet national, emotional yet masculine, spiritual yet martial—in a word, *heroic* religion. The fight against slavery emerged by the 1850s as the legitimate heir to this tradition experientially as much as historically, the most viable place to revive the Puritans' heroic spirituality. For these speakers, the role of antislavery *orator* in particular and the growing market for lectures emerged as the best means for achieving this heroism in the present. Emerson, Parker, and Phillips in particular achieved national fame as speakers in part by assuming the role of prophet speaking truth to power. America's most renowned reform orators seized upon the antislavery cause as an outlet for dissatisfactions and desires that preceded and exceeded the cause. If abolition appeared as a revolutionary duty within these desires, the Puritans likewise emerged as a radical heritage in the basic sense of the word: a source of revolution rather than of fine-tuned political reform. But *radical* here can also be taken in its etymological sense as a return to roots. Even in their most anarchic moments, forward-looking individualists like Emerson were "radicalized" by digging into their nation's historical soils and sorting through its roots, tearing up those that were dessicated and tapping into what remained vital for breaking through the encrusted complacencies of the present.[8]

Heroic Religion

Ironically, the first to name this desire was Thomas Carlyle, a man who by the Civil War would alienate himself from American disciples with contrarian defenses of slavery.[9] David Reynolds notes how Carlyle's laudatory portraits of Oliver Cromwell in the 1840s fueled transcendentalist praise of John Brown as a "dug up Cromwellian."[10] Beyond reevaluating Cromwell, Carlyle especially influenced American abolitionism by enrapturing these disciples with a new vision of religious experience and its role in modern society. Charting this influence in turn helps to explain why figures like Emerson and Parker resisted allying themselves with abolitionism until the mid-1840s and why they embraced the movement with such fervor by the 1850s.

Carlyle's work had been received enthusiastically in the United States since early essays like "Signs of the Times" (1829) established his persistent complaint that the present was "not an Heroical, Devotional, Philosophical, or Moral Age, but, above all others, the Mechanical Age." In contrast with the mechanical present, Carlyle lauded the Protestant Reformation, the English Civil War, and even the French Revolution (despite his distaste for its faithlessness) as successive struggles for "an Idea; a Dynamic, not a Mechanic force," each linked by a "mystic and ideal aim."[11] Rather than nostalgia, Carlyle linked these events so as to urge their revival.

When it appeared in America in 1836, *Sartor Resartus* proved especially popular for dramatizing what it might feel like to experience this kind of revival at the individual level. *Sartor* sucked readers into its Sturm und Drang conversion narrative of an intellectual who loses his faith amid an "atheistic century" and regains it by "retailoring" its core reality for the needs of the present.[12] The result was a portrait of modern religious experience that was far more intense, affective, iconoclastic—indeed heroic—than antebellum American readers had ever encountered. "Thus have we a warfare," Teufelsdröckh declares upon reclaiming his faith, "when such God-given mandate first prophetically stirs within him, and the Clay must now be vanquished or vanquish . . . and there fronting the Tempter do grimmest battle with him."[13] Here was an entirely different imaginative landscape from the Boston equanimity in which Phillips, Emerson, and Parker had been trained. For many members of this generation, Carlyle was appealing in part as "a Calvinist without the Calvinism," rejecting its theology while reviving its affective intensity and heroic qualities. (William James would later sketch a similar feeling of heroism that could result from the conversion experience. "What is attained is often an altogether new level of spiritual vitality, a relatively heroic level, in which impossible things have become possible, and new energies and endurances are shown. . . . 'Sanctification' is the technical name of this result," he noted, drawing on Calvinist language.)

In *On Heroes, Hero-Worship, and the Heroic in History* (1841), Carlyle expanded these Protestant genealogies and conversion experiences into a more comprehensive historiography and ideology. The book was ostensibly a study of heroism, what Carlyle defined as a battle with "sham" culture motivated by sincere faith in a higher spiritual reality. But *On Heroes* was also a broader theory of modernity centered on the Reformation, "the grand root from which our whole subsequent European History branches out." In Carlyle's estimation, Luther's rebellion against "spiritual sovereignties" was "Act One" in the great drama of Western history, while "English Puritanism, revolt against earthly sovereignties, was the second act" and "the enormous French Revolution itself was the third act, whereby all sovereignties earthly and spiritual were, as might seem, abolished." Marveling at the democratic forces unleashed by these events, Carlyle heroicized those individuals who shaped that energy into a new order—Cromwell above all.[14] Thus Carlyle did not merely rehabilitate Cromwell's reputation but challenged the broader social and ideological order that had condemned Cromwell in the first place.

For young American readers like Emerson and Parker, this critique clarified their dissatisfactions with the present and fed their desire for a more heroic form of religiosity by offering them a revolutionary lineage that they could inherit through "retailoring." These desires in turn influenced Emerson's and Parker's slow but eventually fervent embrace of abolitionism. Most explanations of this hesitancy emphasize Emerson's argument in "New England Reformers" (1844) that modern reformers suffered from spiritual myopia by substituting a cause for the broader and more difficult work of transforming one's self. Robert Milder describes Emerson's argument as one for "Reform" rather than "reform," similar to the Calvinist prioritization of grace above works.[15] The distinction is important but not impermeable. Even while Calvinists prioritize grace, they insist on its close and at times ambiguous relationship with good works. Similarly, if Carlyle prioritized the inward revelation and individual transformation (Reform/Justification) of heroes like Luther and Cromwell, he also highlighted the revolutionary social transformations catalyzed by their heroism (reform/sanctification) as necessary components *of* that heroism; or, inspired heroes were inspired *to do something*, to unfold history just as God's elect were elected to enact sacred history. Rather than a strict boundary between Reform and reform, salvation acquired its meaning in large part by drafting individuals into a millennial mission to reform the world. Here Carlyle anticipated one of Charles Taylor's core arguments in *A Secular Age*: modern reform and revolution originated in the Reformation's impulse toward what Taylor similarly calls "capital-r Reform," the "drive to make over the whole society to higher standards" derived from the Protestant faith in the priesthood of all believers. Echoing Carlyle in uncanny ways, Taylor declares that "this drive to Reform was the matrix out of which the modern European idea of Revolution emerges."[16] For Emerson as much as for Carlyle, the Reformation inaugurated a modern world in which Reform and reform were entangled facets of providential history.

Even in "New England Reformers" Emerson expressed a Carlylean admiration for modern reformers as a continuation of the Reformation's nonconformist and activist legacies. "The *fertile* forms of antinomianism among the elder puritans," he reflected (emphasis mine), "seemed to have their match" in antebellum reformers.[17] Emerson even imagined a Carlylean lineage in which modern reformers and transcendentalists were in fact spiritual kin who shared an antinomian impulse traceable to the legacies of the Reformation and Puritanism.[18] In "The Transcendentalist," a lecture delivered two years before "New England Reformers," Emerson traced a similar antinomian impulse running from the Reformation to transcendentalism as much as to modern reform. "Falling on superstitious times, [it] made prophets and apostles; on popish times, made protestants," he noted, "on prelatical times, made Puritans and Quakers; and falling on Unitarian and commercial times, makes the peculiar shades of Idealism which we know."[19] This sense of reformers' and transcendentalists' shared Protestant lineage persisted throughout Emerson's career. In the 1861 lecture "Boston," for instance, he again sketched a rebellious genealogy of "heresiarchs" running from the city's Puritan foundations to Garrisonian abolitionists, united by "the moving principle itself, the *primum mobile,* a living mind afflicting the mass and always agitating the conservative class with some odious novelty."

This entanglement of Reform and reform long predated "The Transcendentalist," being present as early as Emerson's 1835 lectures on Protestant heroes like Luther and Milton. Emerson lauded both as paragons of Reform and draped them in militaristic metaphors that anticipated Carlylean heroism; Luther "gave way to an irresistible conviction that he was summoned by God to set up a standard of Reform, and to do battle with the infernal hosts," while Milton "opens the war and strikes the first blow." Though he maintained that both men enacted "a spiritual revolution by spiritual arms alone," Emerson also admired how their Reformation spilled into reform and even violent revolutions that brought about social progress. He lamented, for instance, Luther's denunciation of the German Peasants' War because this proto-democratic movement, in his eyes, grew directly from Luther's own spiritual heroism. Similarly, though Emerson believed Milton superior to his Puritan allies in Cromwell's army, he felt that the poet's inspiration was kin to theirs, thriving in "the stern, almost fanatic, society of the Puritans." He celebrated the New Model Army and the Peasant Warriors alike as proto-democratic movements inspired by the heroic faith of Protestant prophets.[20] Summing up his view of the Reformation's revolutionary legacy, Emerson concluded that "all religious movements in history and perhaps all political revolutions . . . are only new examples of the deep emotion that can agitate a community of unthinking men, when a truth familiar in words, that 'God is within us,' is made for the time a conviction."[21]

All of this first came to bear on abolitionism in Emerson's 1838 lecture "Heroism," one of his first attempts to decide who continued the Reformation's heroic legacies in the present. If abolitionists were not promising candidates initially, Emerson began to change his mind with the death of Elijah Lovejoy, a Presbyterian preacher murdered by Missourians in 1837 for publishing abolitionist tracts. Antislavery presses elevated Lovejoy as a martyr for a holy cause even though they remained uncomfortable with the fact that he had died fighting back against his assailants with a rifle. For Emerson, by contrast, this resistance was a mark of spiritual heroism, a willingness to fight for one's faith. Emerson warned his audience that they must not "omit the arming of the man" nor "go dancing in the weeds of peace" when a holy principle was under attack. As he had implied for Luther and Milton, Emerson arrived by way of Lovejoy at a more explicit definition of true heroism, what he described as "the military attitude of the soul . . . the state of the soul at war."[22]

Other major abolitionists similarly defended Lovejoy's right to righteous violence as a part of New England's heritage of revolutionary religion. When news of Lovejoy's death reached Boston, the Reverend William Ellery Channing garnered permission from nervous city officials to convene a public meeting at Faneuil Hall. Just two years prior, the firebrand abolitionist editor and organizer William Lloyd Garrison had narrowly escaped lynching by a Boston mob, and officials feared more agitation. In the audience that evening was a twenty-six-year-old Wendell Phillips, known only as the son of Boston's first mayor, likely destined for the law. But since his recent marriage to Ann Terry Greene, Phillips had been radicalized. Greene was a devoted member of the Boston Female Anti-Slavery Society, a remarkable multiracial group of women who had organized the 1835 meeting that nearly got Garrison lynched. (If moral heroism was often gendered masculine, these women faced down the same mob when they moved the meeting to a new location.) Phillips dated his conversion to abolitionism from the day he had witnessed the Boston lynch mob, and his dedication had deepened since his engagement to Greene.

When Phillips attended the Faneuil Hall gathering on Lovejoy, he had no plans to speak. But then Massachusetts Attorney General James Austin opened the meeting by belittling the respected Channing and Lovejoy alike. Both, Austin suggested, had forgotten their place as ministers in their hasty mixture of religion and politics. Further, Austin declared that Lovejoy's assailants were rather like Boston's revolutionary patriots, an "orderly" mob defending their rights. Infuriated by both suggestions, Phillips shouldered his way to the stage for an unplanned rejoinder. "The earth should have yawned and swallowed [Austin] up," he declared to a surprised audience, for uttering such statements on "soil consecrated by the prayers of Puritans and the blood of patriots." *Lovejoy* was in fact the rightful heir of Boston's heroic patriots, while his murderers were a lawless mob in fear of free speech. On the topic of political religion Phillips grew even more aggressive, enlisting Puritan regicides to sanctify his interpretation of Boston's revolutionary history. If Austin believed that politics didn't belong in the pulpit, "shades of Hugh Peters and John Cotton, save us from such pulpits!" Phillips retorted, invoking the chaplain of Cromwell's army, executed for regicide, and the New England minister.[23] That is, Boston's heroic achievements—American democracy itself—sprang from a revolutionary strain of political religion, and abolitionists like Lovejoy continued this legacy.[24]

In this respect Emerson and Phillips were closer than either would have likely admitted. "While I admired his eloquence, I had not the faintest wish to meet the man. He had only a platform," Emerson later reflected, while Phillips occasionally charged the ethereal Emerson with floating away from any kind of platform whatsoever.[25] They differed in emphasis over Reform versus reform, but the difference was one of degree. In reality, Phillips found himself drawn into the antislavery cause by a desire to revive the heroic legacies of his Puritan heritage, just as Emerson's initial skepticism of the abolitionist movement and his later zeal both stemmed from a Carlylean desire to revive heroic religious experience. For both, Lovejoy's death catalyzed a decade-long process of triangulating the abolitionist movement's place in history that would reach its apex in the 1850s as the abolitionist cause began to look prophetic and providential, confronting a growing slave power with courage that increasingly fit Emerson's definition of "the state of the soul at war." For Emerson and Phillips alike, Lovejoy and John Brown bookended a period in which both came to feel that the fight against slavery was far more than a plan to reform the nation's economy: it was a spiritual revolution that would salvage the heroic soul of democracy.

Heroic Democracy

Phillips' Faneuil Hall speech hinted at a widening fissure between Carlyle and his American readers in the decades before the Civil War: namely, democracy. Carlyle distrusted it while his American readers fought to believe in its promises even at the nation's lowest. In *On Heroes*, Carlyle deemed the democratic forces unleashed by the Reformation and Puritanism to be "anarchic," symptoms of a crumbling social order and anticipations of heroes who would channel these forces into a superior "genuine sovereignty and order." For Carlyle, the development of modern democracy was apocalyptic rather than millennial, painful birth-pangs preceding new messiahs. In his critique of industrialism in *Past and Present* (1843), for instance, Carlyle lauded American transcendentalists' growing enthusiasm for reform as "old godlike Calvinism . . . pip[ing] again in the winds . . . heralding new spirit-worlds, and better Dynasties than the Dollar," but unlike these American reformers, he prophesied that these new spirit-worlds would find their fulfillment in a new aristocratic hero class, "Captains of Industry" forming a "Chivalry of Labour" that would channel the powers of industrial capitalism toward a holier social order as Cromwell had done with Puritanism.[26]

American historian George Bancroft, by contrast, captured the view of peers like Emerson, Parker, and Phillips when he celebrated "the Place of Puritanism in History" not as anarchic energy to be shaped by new aristocrats but as "Religion struggling in, with, and for the People," an unabashedly and aggressively democratic religion.[27] Here was the core of many writers' vision of American history. As Phillips emphasized in his Fanueil Hall Speech—and as other writers evoked constantly—Puritans and Patriots were chapters in a shared spiritual history that ran from Christ and his apostles through the Reformation and would culminate in the antislavery cause. In an Independence Day celebration with the Massachusetts Anti-Slavery Society, Parker outlined "four great movements in the progressive development of mankind; whereof each makes an Epoch in the history of the human race": Christ's birth, Luther's Ninety-Five Theses, the Pilgrims' landing at Plymouth, and the American Revolution, each a culmination and further blossoming of the former. In the American Revolution "Plymouth was becoming national, Protestantism going into politics. . . . The Declaration of Independence was the American profession of faith in political Christianity."[28] These four chapters remained constant in most American writers' sense of history, as did the central plot of religion's democratic development via heroic "epochs" and revolutions that clashed with an entrenched status quo.[29] If Emerson, Phillips, and Parker remained as eager as Carlyle for a more spiritual and heroic age, they diverged in seeking more democratic forms of heroism than Carlyle's aristocrats.

An immediate source for this kind of heroism was family history and local memories of what scholars now called "lived religion." Phillips often returned to his family genealogy as a precedent for his work as abolitionist dissenter. After his graduation from Harvard, Irving Bartlett notes, he began to obsessively research the Phillipses, most interested in "establishing his roots in seventeenth century New England" via the Reverend George Phillips, family patriarch in colonial New England and a Puritan minister whose passage to America had been underwritten by John Winthrop himself.[30] Despite Winthrop's patronage, Phillips discovered that his reverend ancestor had asserted a colonist's right to an Anabaptist book and defended colonial Catholics in defiance of the governor—"one of the first protests here against a State-Church & an ecclesiastical tyranny," Phillips proudly noted.[31] The reverend's rebellious streak toward colonial authorities rang true to Phillips's own experience among his family as he became more involved with Garrisonian abolitionism and obeyed its "come-outer" call to leave churches that wouldn't denounce slavery. For Phillips as for many ordinary believers, the call was a painful endeavor wrapped in family tensions and a much-loved ancestral church, Boston's "Old South" (which he would push to preserve later in life). When his elder brother George, named after the ancestral patriarch, began attending a church that had condemned Lovejoy, Wendell urged his mother to remind his brother that he bore "the honored name of George" and was "bound to think if he can conscientiously give such a man his support."[32]

Even Emerson, despite his protests against the "sepulchres of the fathers," lauded spiritual heroism in his family tree. Ironically, his greatest model for this kind of "manly" spirituality was his quixotic aunt Mary Moody Emerson and her peculiar mix of radicalism and conservatism, smitten by German Romanticism yet proud of her Puritan past. She "was not a Calvinist, but wished everybody else to be one," Emerson reflected, concluding that the "influences of ancestral religion" conveyed through her "hoarded family traditions" was a far better education than Harvard—"I doubt if the interior and spiritual history of New England," he wrote in 1837, "could be truelier told than through the exhibition of family history such as this."[33] As with his vision of Luther, Milton, and Lovejoy, he praised the "military attitude" of her soul, admiring how she "repudiated the weakness of women in favor of masculine heroism" and delighting in her aggressive style and her tales of Puritan ancestors like his great-grandfather Samuel Moody, who smote congregants with aggressive sermons and "dragged them forth & sent them home" when they loafed at the pub.[34] Mary Moody, Emerson concluded, "held on with both hands to the faith of the past generation . . . and poetised this beloved Calvinism." In turn, she demonstrated how Emerson too might "purify the old faith . . . and import all its fire into the new age."[35] In Phyllis Cole's brilliant telling, Mary

Moody helped Emerson achieve a Carlylean "recasting of older and more spirit filled ways of faith."[36] Similarly, when Emerson's step-grandfather and Concord's longtime preacher Dr. Ezra Ripley passed away in 1841, he honored the influential community leader as "one of the rear-guard of the great camp and army of the Puritans."[37] If Emerson inclined toward Mary Moody's individualist and pietist "Reform" over Ripley's communal "reform," he admitted that the latter had its heroic qualities too, the "last banner" in "a mighty epoch," the "planting & the liberating of America" begun by the Puritans. As the entanglement of Reform and reform grew more evident to Emerson (after all, Mary Moody and Dr. Ripley were both devout abolitionists themselves), he wondered what would take the place of Ripley's Puritan army and concluded, "What is this abolition . . . but the continuation of Puritanism."[38] "Great, grim, earnest men," he addressed them: "my affection hovers respectfully about your retiring footprints"—an attitude that matched his growing esteem for the abolitionist movement.

Emerson expanded these private journal musings into a broader vision of American democracy in a series of lectures on New England in 1843–44 that, as Bosco and Myerson note, was significant as an early effort to remake himself as a lecturer and discover "new congregations of men" in the nation at large.[39] Though diplomatic with an audience of non–New Englanders, Emerson was forthright in his belief that America's best future would grow from New England's Puritan past. His audience would not have known it, but Emerson drew these conclusions directly from his journal reflections on Ripley and Mary Moody, often incorporated verbatim. Emerson began the series not with the common origin story of the Pilgrims' landing at Plymouth Rock but, more controversially, with the English Civil War as the strongest expression of the same impulse that drove "the idealists of England, the most religious in a religious era," to settle North America and pass on their fiery faith "like a religion in the blood." Here Emerson hinted at his familial sources while reusing his journal reflections on Mary Moody: New England's "interior and spiritual history" was best told "through the exhibition of town-, of village-, of family-history," and its Puritan faith could still be found "in individuals imbuing all their genius and derived to them from hoarded family traditions, from so many godly lives and godly deaths of sainted kindred." Emerson quoted amply from Puritan texts like Francis Higginson's *New England's Plantation* (1630) and Concord's founder Peter Bulkeley (and, of course, Milton), but his central vision came directly from Mary Moody: "I picture New England to myself as a mother, sitting amidst her thousand churches, at once religious and skeptical—a most religious infidel. She holds on with both hands to the faith of the past generation . . . extolled and poetised in this beloved Calvinism." In applying this vision to the American present, Emerson repeated his belief (drawn from Ripley) that the "great grim, earnest men" who planted and liberated America would have recognized abolitionism as "the continuation of Puritanism."[40]

If this progressive path from Puritans to Patriots to abolitionists was a foundational part of these speakers' faith in American democracy, it was not without its challenges. Emerson, Phillips, and especially Parker strained to harmonize their hope for a more heroic and spiritual democracy with the real state of the nation, which into the 1840s seemed to confirm the common critique that republics leveled a populace into mediocrity and conformity.[41] Three months after Emerson's final New England lecture, President John Tyler made a bold bid for reelection when he presented the US Senate with secret negotiations for the annexation of the Republic of Texas. As a vast expansion of American slave territory, Tyler's proposal formed a central point of contention in the 1844 presidential election and, after annexation passed in 1845, sparked the outbreak of war with Mexico.

While abolitionists opposed annexation and war as an illegal and immoral scheme from a growing "Slave Power," Emerson, Phillips, and Parker viewed its success as further evidence that New England's heroic heritage required revival in the antislavery cause. In an 1844 address, "Emancipation in the British West Indies," Emerson made his tentative public entrance into the cause with a revealing hesitancy. "What is most original about Emerson's antislavery writings," Lawrence Buell notes, "is not their views of slavery or abolition as such but how they sift through . . . the proper relation of the work of the 'scholar' to the work of the activist."[42] If Emerson glimpsed spiritual heroism in Elijah Lovejoy's martyrdom in 1838, the 1844 speech revisited abolition's status as a whole, opening with the lament that "the great-hearted Puritans have left no posterity." If quietly, Emerson implied to an audience of abolitionists that they were promising heirs to this tradition.[43] When Emerson accepted an offer to speak at a Fourth of July celebration sponsored by the Massachusetts Anti-Slavery Society two years later, he again lamented that New Englanders were "snivelling nobodies" who denied the "good blood in their veins" in their support for the war. In contrast, he celebrated "the growth of the abolition party, the true successors of that austere Church, which made nature and history sacred to us all." As heir to the heroic Puritans, abolitionism promised to toughen Americans who had softened into a "Parisian manner of living," for "what can better supply that outward church they want, than this fervent, self-denying school?"[44] Here too Emerson was careful to sublimate abolitionist efforts into the higher workings of Reform—"I am glad, not for what it has done," he disclaimed, "but that the party exists. Not what they do, but what they see, seems to me sublime"—but the change was unmistakable: he could now admit publicly that abolitionists had weakened the boundary between reform and Reform in his mind, that the antislavery cause might be the legitimate heir to the "army of the Puritans."[45]

Wendell Phillips found a new hero in one of the abolitionist movement's rising stars, Frederick Douglass. A month after President Taylor signed Congress's annexation bill, Phillips endorsed Douglass's risky decision to publish his *Narrative* by grafting it into the same Puritan-Patriot lineage he had lauded at Faneuil Hall. "They say the fathers, in 1776, signed the Declaration of Independence with the halter about their necks," he wrote, and "you, too, publish your declaration of freedom with danger compassing you around." Phillips confessed his shame that New England could not protect Douglass except through "the fearless efforts of those who, trampling the laws and Constitution of the country under their feet, are determined that they will 'hide the outcast,'" but he looked forward to the day that these rebels "shall stereotype these free, illegal pulses into statutes; and New England, cutting loose from a blood-stained Union, shall glory in being the house of refuge for the oppressed . . . consecrating anew the soil of the Pilgrims as an asylum for the oppressed."[46]

For Theodore Parker especially, the Mexican War strengthened his feelings that he was a spiritual outsider facing a retrograde status quo. Parker, a brilliant scholar who came from a farming family, had long nursed hopes for respectability among New England's learned establishment but was thwarted when his heterodox 1841 sermon "The Transient and the Permanent in Christianity" prompted Unitarian preachers to close rank and deny him pulpit exchanges. By the time Parker accepted a call to lead Boston's independent 28th Congregational Society in February 1845, he had come to accept the role of prophet. and to his surprise, he discovered a national audience for the role. He played the part with growing verve. In "A Sermon of War" (1846) he declared defiantly that America's Congress, its press, and especially its churches were "little better than dead" in failing to oppose the war. As the grandson of Captain John Parker, revered Patriot commander at the Battle of Lexington, Parker reveled in accounts of heroic battles as much as the next American, but like Emerson he contrasted mere military daring—"that strutting glory which is dyed in blood"—with the higher spiritual heroism of "they who win great truths from God, and send them to a people's heart." Reviving his early enthusiasm for Carlyle, he contrasted the current "iniquitous" war with Mexico with "self-protecting war[s] for freedom of mind, heart, and soul" like the English, American, and French Revolutions.[47] As he continued to protest the unfolding war, Parker invoked New England history to urge Americans toward spiritual rather than military heroism, and he faced mobs with his own heroic performances. "I call on the men of Boston, on the men of the old Bay State," he declared to a hostile crowd at an 1847 antiwar meeting in Fanueil Hall (much like Phillips nearly a decade earlier), "to act worthy of their fathers." When he indicted "the famous men who deceive the nation," he met with "cries of 'Throw him over; kill him, kill him!' and a flourish of bayonet." In response, Parker declared, "*Kill him!* I shall walk home unarmed and unattended, and not a man of you will hurt one hair of my head." (He did.)[48]

When the war concluded with American victory in May 1848, Parker seemed even more dispirited about the state of American democracy, disgusted that not "a single man in all New England lost his seat in any office because he favoured the war" and full of prophetic fury toward "Whig demagogues and demagogues of the democrats; men that flatter the ignorance, the folly, or the sin of the people, that they might satisfy their own base purposes."[49] As Paul Teed notes, Parker momentarily rallied by founding the *Massachusetts Quarterly Review*, a "striking combination of history, memory and antislavery politics" that promoted a progressive vision of New England heritage which Parker hoped might strengthen support for "Conscience" Whigs like Senator Sumner. In the *Review*'s first issue, Parker sniped at Massachusetts representative Robert C. Winthrop, descendant of the Massachusetts Bay founder and an advocate of the Mexican War, asking if there was "no tinge from the heart of the Pilgrim . . . in that puritanic blood of theirs."[50] Teed concludes that "against a traditional sectional memory that cast the Puritans as petrified monuments of traditional virtue," Parker rejected "the shibboleths of New England filiopietism" and instead promoted the Puritans' more revolutionary legacies.[51] The truth is that Parker had been drifting toward the role of revolutionary and iconoclast through much of the 1840s, pushed by a growing dissatisfaction with the American social order. The war was only the latest and most aggressive symptom of a deeper social sickness that he had intimated since his ostracization in Boston: much of America, from its Congress to its churches, was complacent, unheroic, spiritually "little better than dead." While Parker lauded Conscience Whigs like Sumner and Palfrey as heirs to New England's spiritual heroism, he lamented that they were exceptions to a broader depravity. "Now and then there rises up an honest man, with a great Christian heart," he wrote in the *MQR*, but "such honesty is a rare honesty. . . . The son of the Puritan, bred up in austere ways, is sent to Congress to stand up for Truth and Right, but he turns out a 'doughface,' and betrays the Duty he went to serve. Yet he does not lose his place, for every doughfaced representative has a doughfaced constituency to back him."[52]

If the complacent 1840s failed to produce democratic heroes, the 1850s created something nearly as good: an enemy.

Aut Deus aut Diabolus

Rising in the Senate chamber on March 7, 1850, the revered Massachusetts senator Daniel Webster gambled and lost his reputation on what he felt was an effort to unite moderates around the preservation of the Union in Senator Henry Clay's proposed compromise. In his "Seventh of March" speech, which would soon become infamous among Northern writers, Webster defended Clay's latest attempt to balance the nation's free and slave states and threw his weight behind its most controversial element, a strengthened Fugitive Slave Act which would require Northern states to actively assist slaveowners in returning runaways inside their borders. Webster argued that this provision was a simple acknowledgment of slaveowners' constitutional property rights and, more important, a necessity for national unity.

Abolitionists were furious, and even moderates felt that their sovereignty had been challenged, their states opened to mercenary slavehunters. The shock was all the stronger because of Webster's high reputation in New England. A man who had risen from humble beginnings into the Senate's "Great Triumvirate" alongside Clay and Calhoun, Webster had long been lauded as one of America's most eloquent leaders. Webster's reputation had a distinctly regional cast for New Englanders, who celebrated his humble origins in New Hampshire. In his widely lauded "Plymouth Oration" on Forefathers' Day 1820, Webster himself lionized these origins and applied them to antislavery ends, concluding that "it is not fit that the land of the Pilgrims should bear the shame longer." Webster had since stepped back from his early antislavery stance for the sake of national unity, and his "Seventh of March" speech became vilified as moral treason to New England and God. Horace Mann hissed that "he has walked for years among the gods, to descend from the empyrean heights and mingle . . . in a masquerade full of harlots and leeches."[53] Webster's betrayal and the Fugitive Slave Act did more to radicalize Northern intellectuals than perhaps any single event before the Civil War, and they set the stage for a decade of radicalization that would culminate in Emerson's, Parker's, and Phillips's praise for John Brown as Webster's antithetical Puritan hero.

Webster sparked fury even in the cool Emerson. "'Liberty! liberty!' Pho! Let Mr. Webster for decency's sake shut his lips once and forever on this word," he scratched into his journal: "the word *liberty* in the mouth of Mr. Webster sounds like the word *love* in the mouth of a courtezan."[54] More importantly, the Fugitive Slave Act clinched Emerson's public conversion to the abolitionist cause. When a group of Concordians asked him to speak on the issue, he delivered one of his most impassioned addresses, opening with a blunt demand for disobedience to the new federal law: "The law is suicidal, and cannot be obeyed." He did take comfort in the fact that the present crisis "ended a great deal of nonsense we had been accustomed to hear on the 22nd December" (Forefathers' Day) and clarified a battle line over America's Puritan past and the future of democracy.[55] Emerson turned to Cromwell in an unabashed call for spiritual—perhaps even literal—war: "You must be citadels and warriors, yourselves the Declaration of Independence, the charter, the battle, and the victory. Cromwell said, 'we can only resist the superior training of the king's soldiers, by having godly men.'"[56] Mary Moody despised the act as much as her nephew did and wrote to him shortly after its passage, again invoking their ancestry as a call to arms. "I like a conscience war as did our kindred," she avowed.[57] Emerson finally agreed. On the issue of slavery, the distinction between Reform and reform had collapsed; a new holy war was needed.

In his own maiden Senate speech just three days after Webster's, New York senator William Seward sharpened the conflict with an argument that anticipated Brown's revolt. Against Webster's insistence on constitutional property rights, Seward proclaimed that "there is a higher law than the Constitution," bestowed not by man but by "the Creator of the universe."[58] Theodore Parker had long insisted that there was a higher law beyond humanity's historically conditioned religions and governments, and he had come to accept his role as an iconoclast prophet who harped on this unwelcome truth. By the late 1840s he found a growing audience for his performance as heroic Puritan heir, and he seized upon Webster and an invading Slave Power as worthy enemies. On the 25th he returned to Faneuil Hall for an "Anti-Webster Meeting," wielding the sword of Standish to cleave Webster's compromise into the simpler choice of right or wrong, liberty or slavery, higher or human law. "One of the two you must enact—either the will of God, or of the devil," Parker told his audience, "*Aut Deus aut Diabolus*. There is no other alternative, 'Choose you which you will serve.'"[59] In imaginations raised on Milton and Carlyle, the tragic aspect of Webster's fall from grace quickly hardened into holy war as writers made an intuitive discovery: nothing fulfilled their hunger for heroic religious experience and a spiritual revival for American democracy quite like battle lines and clear enemies, elevated beyond political complexities into the realm of the millennial, the divine and diabolic.

Informing this desire for spiritual heroics, Parker's "either God or the devil" was propelled by a dialectic vision of Providence in which progress was inevitable yet revolutionary. If Christ, the Reformation, the English Civil War, and the American Revolution were the major chapters in the American narrative of modernity, its recurring theme was the clash of some latest unfolding of democracy with a recalcitrant status quo. Like most other abolitionists, Parker believed that slavery was destined to end because it defied the progressive tendencies built into the laws of history ("It cannot be saved . . . until you repeal the will of God") but that violent revolution might be required to end it. To him, Webster's betrayal suggested that America might be approaching such a moment in the present. Having confronted his audience with the choice between God and the devil, Parker concluded his anti-Webster speech with a stanza from James Russell Lowell's antislavery poem "The Present Crisis" (1848), immensely popular in part for its Carlylean ability to convey the feeling that Americans were just as capable of heroism today as in the past if they simply refused to bargain with evil: "The soul is still oracular; amid the market's din, / List the ominous stern whisper from the Delphic cave within— / 'They enslave their children's children, who make compromise with sin.'" Like Parker, Lowell dramatized the urgency of this present crisis by confronting his readers with a moral battle line ("Once to every man and nation comes the moment to decide, / In the strife of Truth with Falsehood, for the good or evil side"—a hymn still sung in Unitarian churches today).Like Parker he grafted this choice onto a heroic spiritual lineage, concluding with the exhortation that "we ourselves must Pilgrims be, / Launch our Mayflower, and steer boldly through the desperate winter sea." The desire for spiritual heroism was aided as much by battle lines in the past as by those in the present.

At the New England Anti-Slavery Convention in Boston two months later, Parker more carefully outlined the shape of the diabolic "Slave Power" that had provoked the current crisis. The Fugitive Slave Act, he began, clarified a sixty-year-old battle between two ideas: "the American idea" that "all men are created equal" versus the "idea of slavery" that "one man has a right to hold another man in thraldom," as "irreconcilably hostile" toward one another as "the worship of the real God and the worship of the imaginary devil."[60] Fighting for the latter was a "Slave Power" alliance of "demagogues of the parties . . . [and] of the churches," the "Toryism of America" (those who preferred the "property of mankind to man himself"), and "the spirit of trade." Opposing them was the "American idea" itself, destined to triumph as the progressive element in the present, as well as "the spirit of the majority of men in the North, when they are not blind-folded and muzzled by the demagogues of State and Church."[61]

Parker's disclaimer hinted at his growing self-image as a prophetic gad-fly for a chosen yet complacent nation, and although he drew this voca-tion from a heroic Puritan past, his sense of prophecy was different from the traditional jeremiad. With his transcendental vision of history as the unfolding story of humanity's spiritual development, Parker imagined his prophecy not simply as the act of recalling a stubborn people to their cov-enant but as revealing a *new* truth that most of a nation could not yet see, once more blurring the distinction between Reform and reform. It antici-pated William James's estimation of modern "saints" as "a genuinely cre-ative social force" in fighting for visions that were ahead of their times, whether in Cromwellian soldiers' battle for the "kingdom of heaven" or "the Utopian dreams" of twentieth-century socialists (whom James linked in a spiritual genealogy). "Like the single drops which sparkle in the sun as they are flung far ahead of the advancing edge of a wave-crest or of a flood," he noted (with a telling ambiguity between "wave" and "flood"), "they show the way and are forerunners. The world is not yet with them, so they often seem in the midst of the world's affairs to be preposterous. Yet they are impregnators of the world, vivifiers and animaters of potentialities of goodness which but for them would lie forever dormant." Parker would have most certainly approved of such a description (not the least for the idea of being a spiritual "world-impregnator," with his frequent calls for "manly" spiritual heroism).

Wendell Phillips revealed how this new understanding of history could influence even abolitionists who considered themselves orthodox Chris-tians. Throughout his life, Phillips identified as a Congregationalist loyal to what he called the "old faith" of New England, but he tended an idealist and romantic spark that, like Emerson's abolitionism, heated with rising tensions around slavery and urged him into closer company with transcen-dentalists than he would have likely admitted. As early as 1839, he urged Garrisonians to sustain an individualist rather than a mobbish enthusiasm, "the old Greek definition—the God within us," and the antinomian poten-tial of this "God within" grew more pronounced in the decades to come.[62] In an address to the Massachusetts Anti-Slavery Society on "Public Opinion" (1852), Phillips aimed to encourage abolitionists who, like him and Parker, were frustrated that much of the nation remained complacent toward slav-ery. A minority voice, he reminded his audience, could nonetheless be a major power through persistent protest; he unfolded his argument with organic metaphors and a vision of history reminiscent of Emerson's antinomian genealogies and the "primum mobile" that powered them. "The living sap of to-day outgrows the dead rind of yesterday," Phillips declared, for "only by unintermitted agitation can a people be kept sufficiently awake." Such was the lesson of the Reformation, that "the church has to be regenerated, in each age." For Phillips as for Parker, this mission had reached a crisis point and clarified battle lines in the wake of Webster's perfidy. (Phillips quoted directly from his Milton, lamenting that "no man, since the age of Luther, has ever held in his hand, so palpably, the destinies and character of a mighty people" as Webster, whose betrayal was the "fall of another Lucifer . . . into that 'lower deep of the lowest deep.'") In the midst of this crisis, abolitionists must stand ready, like their Puritan forefathers, "with their musket-lock on the one side and a drawn sword on the other."[63]

For the same occasion the following year, Phillips waxed even more fiercely Miltonic in "The Philosophy of the Abolition Movement," among the most comprehensive and impassioned manifestos of American abolitionism. After a thorough historical review that cataloged the movement's elect and reprobate, Phillips crowned his list of the damned by fuming that Washington, DC, "always brings to my mind that other Capitol, which in Milton's great epic 'rose like an exhalation' 'from the burning marl.'" (He went so far as to parallel specific senators with Miltonic demons.) The failure of America's churches on this front was especially "momentous among descendants of the Puritans," Phillips declared. By contrast, come-outer abolitionists best honored this separatist heritage. "Some tried long, like Luther, to be Protestants, and yet not come out of Catholicism," he noted, "but their eyes were soon opened." As a final testament to his radicalization, Phillips enlisted Cromwell's army to attack those who still believed that slavery could be ended through Constitutional means. This belief, he scoffed, was like England's belief during the Restoration that "the memory of the scaffold . . . would be guaranty enough for [Charles II's] good behavior." Here was essentially a call for neo-Cromwellian soldiers to maintain their arms against a corrupt power. Much like his ancestor George, Phillips rejected the very basis of American political authority through a vision of Puritanism's ongoing mission to draw battle lines during moral crises.[64]

Within a year of Phillips's call for holy war, President Franklin Pierce and Senator Stephen A. Douglas opened the door to real war with the Kansas-Nebraska Act of 1854, leaving the status of slavery in these new territories up to a vote by settlers. Antislavery emigrants flocked to seize these territories from the Slave Power, while "border ruffians" from Missouri responded with a campaign of intimidation that soon broke out into violence, sparking a civil war in miniature that came to be known as "Bleeding Kansas." Many antislavery settlers had come from New England or regions settled by New Englanders (including northern Ohioans like John "Osawatomie" Brown), a regional trend which strengthened Theodore Parker's belief that the current crisis between "God or devil" could be traced to irreconcilable differences in America's founding colonies. In an 1854 sermon, "The Nebraska Question," Parker traced the conflict to an older antithesis between New England's religious foundations and Southern colonies' origins as primarily economic ventures. As a poignant symbol of the difference, Parker contrasted the *Mayflower's* landing at Plymouth in 1620 with the first ship of enslaved African slaves brought to Anglo North America, which docked at Jamestown in 1619, the origins of a battle between American conservatism and "the instinct for progressive development" that, if not perfectly mapped onto North versus South, nonetheless developed more progressively in New England as the Puritans continued the Reformation's "great warfare for the right of man's nature to transcend all the accidents of his history."[65] As his first example, Parker pointed to the fact that New England had offered asylum to exiled Puritan regicides after "the dreadful axe of Puritanic Oliver Cromwell shore off the divine right of kings." Parker also attributed slavery's relatively mild and shrinking form in early New England to the fact that the colony's religious origins fostered "a good deal of conscience" as "the Puritan still looked up to a higher law." If the Northern and Southern colonies found a tentative unity in the later protest against King George, old fissures between Puritan New England and the mercantile South had erupted anew in Bleeding Kansas. More importantly, the violence in Kansas portended that the struggle between God and devil might be resolved only through national bloodshed of the sort that had occurred in the English, American, and even Haitian Revolutions. If slavery had survived the divine right of kings in America, Parker posed a prospect that would have unnerved white Americans: "Must the axe of a more terrible Cromwell shear that also away? Shall it be a black Cromwell? History points to St Domingo."[66]

Bleeding Kansas propelled Phillips as much as Parker toward defenses of Puritan "fanaticism" that not only anticipated John Brown but paved the way for his eager embrace of the Civil War as a battle with Miltonic rebels. At a Forefathers' Day celebration held in Plymouth in 1855, Phillips performed his most radical resurrection of the Puritans yet.[67] He had managed to squeeze onto the celebration's dinner list, and after a toast honoring the Pilgrims' gift of "prosperity and peace," he arose once more for an unplanned rejoinder, aggravated by this delusional sense of concord amid the turbulence of Bleeding Kansas. Phillips told his audience that if they truly wished to honor their forebears, they must regard them "*in posse,* not *in esse,*—in the possibilities which were wrapped up in that day, 1620, not in what poor human bodies actually produced at the time." This hermeneutic was essentially Emerson and Carlyle's vision of history as not a hobby for antiquarians but a source of new possibilities in the present. And the Pilgrims' legacy for the present, Phillips asserted, was nothing short of revolutionary. "Do you suppose that, if Elder Brewster could come up from his grave to-day, he would be contented with the Congregational Church?" he posed (himself a Congregationalist). "No, Sir; he would add to his creed . . . the thousand Sharpe's Rifles, addressed 'Kansas,' and labelled 'Books," a reference to disguised arms that had been shipped to the antislavery resistance in Kansas. Just as Emerson described providential history with romantic nature metaphors, Phillips transformed Plymouth Rock into a quaking stone that "has cropped out a great many times" in America's inspired individuals—now again in Kansas as much as in Elijah Lovejoy's rifle.[68]

The speech's conclusion emphasized how much Phillips had embraced a transcendental historiography. He left his audience with a folk story acquired in his genealogical research. The Phillipses came from Andover, he began. There, a story goes, a man shot at an owl, and the gun's wad, landing in hay, set a barn ablaze. Residents gathered around the fire, lamenting the destruction. Then a quiet man appeared and asked, quite simply, "Did he hit the owl?" Perhaps to his own surprise, Phillips's conclusion was met with "tumultuous applause" as he commanded his audience to always ask the same, no matter the material damage: "'Did he hit that owl?' Is liberty safe? Is man sacred? They say, Sir, I am a fanatic, and so I am. But, Sir, none of us have yet risen high enough. Afar off, I see Carver and Bradford, and I mean to get up to them." Phillips's desire to "rise high enough" was essentially transcendental, and he even imagined the Pilgrim William Brewster arising from the grave to exchange pulpits "at the Music Hall" with Parker or Emerson. In four years, this "barnburner" vision would soon sweep all three into support for Brown's counter-state militancy and a millennial zeal for America's bloodiest war.[69]

Charters of Humanity, Writ in Blood

Theodore Parker was in Rome fighting to survive consumption when he received news of Brown's attack on Harper's Ferry. It confirmed his growing belief that America's battle between God and devil would come to real warfare, and he accepted the prospect as the price of Providence. "All the great charters of humanity have been writ in blood," he wrote to a friend—"I once hoped that of American Democracy would be engrossed in less costly ink; but it is plain, now, that our pilgrimage must lead through a Red Sea, wherein many a Pharaoh will go under and perish."[70] Six months later he himself died, spared the war that would claim more lives than all of America's prior conflicts combined.

Emerson and Phillips shared the stage at Music Hall to deliver eulogies for their friend, by now also sharing an ideological platform. Emerson could praise Parker the radical abolitionist while Phillips could honor the heretical transcendentalist, both against early inclinations and both from a common vision of their religious heritage. Parker was the best of New England stock, a Yankee yeoman and a spiritual militant, "his merit, like Luther," Emerson reflected, "to speak tart truth."[71] Phillips chose another Reformation warrior, imagining Parker "at Zwingle's [Zwingli's] side, on the battlefield, pierced with a score of fantastic spears."[72]

America's fiercest spiritual warrior died just as the nation began to unravel. A week after Parker's death, the Republican National Convention in Chicago nominated Abraham Lincoln as its candidate for president. Like other Garrisonian abolitionists, Phillips was skeptical. Remembering the course of the presidency in the 1840s and 1850s while reviewing Lincoln's mixed comments on slavery, he held little hope that the candidate would aid the cause in any substantial way. Phillips went so far as to declare him the "Slave Hound of Illinois" in a June article for William Lloyd Garrison's radical periodical the *Liberator*. But he began to change his mind as he witnessed black Americans and progressive whites unite around Lincoln with genuine antislavery zeal. At a Boston rally for the Republican candidate the month before the election, city streets were "thronged by spectators as never before, illuminations and fireworks being seen in every direction, and the popular enthusiasm reaching a high point . . . ten thousand strong by accurate count," according to one *Liberator* reporter. If skeptical of Lincoln himself, Phillips, like the departed Parker, would have thrilled to see New Englanders march with banners reading "Free labor and free men all over God's heritage"; "The Pilgrims did not found an Empire for Slavery"; and "Plymouth Rock the corner-stone of a Free Republic." As a testament to the progressive potential of this spirit, a company of two hundred black men called the "West Boston Wide Awakes" marched alongside whites under another banner: "God Never Made a Tyrant or a Slave."[73] The day after Lincoln won the election, Phillips went before an expectant crowd in Tremont Temple for one of the "Fraternity Lectures" established in honor of Parker. "Ladies and gentlemen," he began, "if the telegraph speaks truth, for the first time in our history the *slave* has chosen a President of the United States." The temple filled with cheers.

The exultant mood only seemed to grow with secession and the outbreak of war the next March. For even the most pacifist and disunionist of Garrisonians, the war prompted a groundswell of zeal, transforming antislavery sentiment from a project of fringe dissenters into a matter of patriotism. Phillips wasted little time celebrating the conflict as a new holy war. In a speech to Parker's congregation just one week after Fort Sumter, he seemed giddy as he celebrated Massachusetts soldiers with a "hand on the neck of a rebellious aristocracy . . . mean[ing] to strangle it," again worthy of their ancestors as they "carried Plymouth Rock to Washington." If the American Revolution was "a holy war, that for Independence," he proclaimed this new conflict "a holier and the last,—that for liberty." Some months later he again paralleled America's civil war to England's. "This is no epoch for nations to blush at. England might blush in 1620," he said, "when James forbade them to think; but not in 1649, when an outraged people cut off his son's head."[74] Perhaps Phillips even imagined Cromwell and Brown arising to decapitate Jefferson Davis and Robert E. Lee.

After Fort Sumter, many free blacks rushed to enlist for service but were turned away due to a 1792 federal law that banned their bearing arms in the military (despite, as abolitionists and blacks frequently noted, their former service in the American Revolution). Disappointed, a group of black Bostonians urged Lincoln to change the law, and the administration began to countenance the prospect by the summer of 1862, when military necessity demanded it. In November the first official black regiment was organized, the First South Carolina Volunteers, led by Thomas Wentworth Higginson, a renegade Unitarian preacher who, much like Parker, had gained his first taste of spiritual heroics in 1854 when he led a group of men in storming Boston's Federal Courthouse in hopes of rescuing the fugitive slave Anthony Burns. For Wendell Phillips as much as Higginson it seemed self-evident that a holy war against slavery ought especially to be waged by blacks themselves. Phillips went so far as to praise the Carlylean spiritual heroics of Touissant Louverture, leader of the Haitian Revolution, which Americans had long pictured as a bloodbath of black savagery. "Toussaint . . . had a vein of religious fanaticism, like most great leaders—like Mohammed, like Napoleon, like Cromwell, like John Brown," Phillips declared (listing Carlyle's heroes, plus Brown). As elsewhere, Phillips meant puritanical "fanaticism" as praise.[75]

Phillips's black Cromwell complicates the current scholarly consensus that even the most progressive of white abolitionists fell short in their attitudes on race, prey to a lurking Saxonism or Puritan pride that hindered their ability to imagine a multiracial republic. Equally interesting is how some progressives managed to reach revolutionary ideas like black Cromwells at all, by way of as much as in spite of entrenched Saxonist and Puritan presumptions. Lawrence Buell rightly notes that Emerson's thoughts on slavery often seem "more concerned with national purification than with national diversification," which makes it difficult to determine how much "the liberationist thrust of Emerson's antislavery thought was compromised by Anglocentrism." But if applied too heavy-handedly, this twenty-first-century moral distinction between liberation and Anglocentrism can cloud an interesting historical process at work in Phillips's black Cromwell and abolitionists' usable Puritan past at large: if unconscious representatives of their era's Anglocentric presumptions about the link between race and nationhood (e.g., the Saxon roots of American democracy), they also drew from the liberationist elements *within* that culture and (sometimes unwittingly) directed them toward less Anglocentric and more revolutionary ends.[76] It is thus misleading—or at least incomplete—to conclude that Emerson's "dream of black emancipation had a disconcerting way of metamorphosing into a dream of white emancipation."[77] More accurately, Emerson stumbled in the direction of still hazy notions of black citizenry within the mental environment of his own cultural presumptions and biases. If indeed capable of disconcerting remarks on race that ought not to be shrugged off ("the captivity of a thousand negroes is nothing to me," he reflected of the Fugitive Slave Act, compared to "the absence of moral feeling in the whiteman"), Emerson was equally able to reject white-saviorism by way of his own faith in self-reliance, reflecting as early as 1844 that "the negro has saved himself, and the white man very patronisingly says, I have saved you."[78] Even in his first public antislavery address on British emancipation (from the same year), Emerson concluded that

in part it is the earning of the blacks. They won the pity and respect which they have received, by their powers and native endowments. I think this a circumstance of the highest import . . . The arrival in the world of such men as Toussaint, and the Haytian heroes, or of the leaders of their race in Barbadoes and Jamaica, outweighs in good omen all the English and American humanity. The anti-slavery of the whole world is dust in the balance before this,—is a poor squeamishness and nervousness: the might and the right are here: here is the antislave: here is man: and if you have man, black or white is an insignificance . . . that is the great anthem which we call history.[79]

Emerson indeed relied on nineteenth-century beliefs in certain "native endowments" among the African and Anglo-Saxon races, but he just as often entertained the possibility that Carlylean heroism was not only possible for both but in fact the more important factor in determining their final place in history.

This belief persisted throughout the war, especially with the advent of a new "great charter of humanity" in 1863 when Lincoln's Emancipation Proclamation granted the war an explicitly antislavery purpose and—just as controversially—authorized the arming of black troops.[80] Massachusetts's antislavery governor John A. Andrew (who had organized defense funds for John Brown's trial) was the first to take initiative, hoping to lead the nation by bringing together the Massachusetts Fifty-Fourth Colored Regiment. Andrew convinced the merchant-philanthropist George Luther Stearns (one of John Brown's "Secret Six") to organize recruitment efforts; Stearns then drafted an all-star team of black recruiting agents that included Martin Delany, Henry Highland Garnet, William Wells Brown, Charles Lenox Remond, and Frederick Douglass, who was especially proud to see his sons Charles and Lewis be among the first to enlist. Governor Andrew expressed openness to a black officer's leading the regiment but felt that this would alienate support for an already controversial venture; instead he urged the position upon twenty-five-year-old Robert Gould Shaw, the handsome son of wealthy Boston abolitionists and transcendentalists, deeming it a historic duty that "will go far to elevate or depress the estimation in which the character of the colored Americans will be held throughout the world."[81] When the Fifty-Fourth made a daring frontal assault on Fort Wagner in July, many lauded their efforts as ample vindication of black courage. Among the dead, the young Colonel Shaw was unceremoniously buried with his troops in a shallow mass grave. The Northern press attributed this act to Confederate General Johnson Hagood's reported remark "Had he been in command of white troops, I should have given him an honorable burial." Hagood denied making the statement and insisted that the burial was a matter of expediency rather than insult.[82] Whether this was fact or fiction, abolitionists reclaimed the mass burial as a fitting symbol of the Union's dedication to equality and democracy.

In response, Emerson composed "Voluntaries," a poetic tribute to the heroic self-redemption of the colored troops as much as Shaw's leadership. The poem in fact opened neither with the colonel nor with the typical accolades for fallen leaders, but with a captive slave testifying to his race's potential amidst American failures. "Low and mournful be the strain, / Haughty thought be far from me," he begins (lines 1–2), setting "Tones of penitence and pain" (3) rather than accolade. He highlights the failure of "Great men in the Senate . . . Checked by the owners' fierce disdain, / Lured by 'Union' as the bribe" (23, 29–30), paving the way for the present war's divine judgment as Destiny declares ominously, "Pang for pang your seed shall pay, / Hide in false peace your coward head, / I bring round the harvest day" (32–34). Emerson then turns from America's craven leadership to the moral complacency of American society writ large, asking, "In an age of fops and toys, . . . / Who shall nerve heroic boys / To hazard all in Freedom's fight?" (55–58). A haphazard reading of the poem presumes Shaw to be the answer, but Emerson in fact wields a purposeful ambiguity in which Shaw and his black troops blend democratically into a shared heroism as much as a common grave, equal warriors for God's "Eternal Rights" (107). Emerson brings back the angel named Freedom who in "Boston Hymn" leads the Pilgrims to the New World, but here "all winged expands, / Nor perches in a narrow place," for if "Long she loved the Northman well / . . . She will not refuse to dwell / With the offspring of the Sun," the African race who

> has avenues to God
> Hid from men of Northern brain,
> Far beholding, without cloud,
> What these with slowest steps attain,
> If once the generous chief arrive
> To lead him willing to be led,
> For freedom he will strike and strive,
> And drain his heart till he be dead. (31–54)[83]

An excess of pronouns makes it unclear where the "Northmen" start and the "Offspring of the Sun" stop, who is taking the "slowest steps," who is "the generous chief," who is the *him* "willing to be led." Upon a first hearing, the average white New Englander would likely have presumed that Emerson was honoring Shaw (and Anglo New England at large) as the moral leadership that would redeem America from its long spiritual torpor—which Emerson most likely intended and in part believed. But the poem's pool of pronouns—so wide as to be purposeful—leaves interpretive room for individual black soldiers to lead slow Northern brains down God's avenues. This is no interpretive stretch but rather the precise message Emerson had already conveyed in his 1844 address when he concluded, "Here is the antislave: here is man: and if you have man, black or white is an insignificance." It is a striking yet altogether logical conclusion to Emerson's career-long search for spiritual heroism in past and present, a fitting culmination to his interpretation of the war as "a great revolution, still enacting the sentiment of the Puritans, and the dreams of young people 30 years ago."[84]

If Emerson, Phillips, and Parker indeed worked within nineteenth-century assumptions that closely linked theories of nationhood with race, they also drew from the universalist potential of Protestantism that had always grated uneasily against theories of race in granting the possibility—indeed the necessity—of God's grace taking root in individuals of all races. Rather than plotting figures like Emerson on a spectrum running from Saxonist racism to universalist human rights, the two tendencies are better understood as an entangled tension within the history of Protestantism, inherited by white abolitionists as they felt their way toward modern theories of state and nationhood. That is, the heroic-hungry imagination of Parker, Emerson, and Phillips was not simply an unconscious representative of certain cultural presumptions but a half-conscious search for new possibilities within residual and dominant antebellum paradigms. If their holy war was shaped by Saxonism, New England chauvinism, and (by today's standards) retrograde conceptions of race, gender, and religion, it was nonetheless radical in its willingness to entertain the possibility of black Cromwells and violent revolution.

This vision unsettled boundaries of race and religion as it cast about for a more perfect democracy, empowering those who felt impotent within a materialistic culture while revitalizing liberal faith. But playing the part of prophet also raised the question that Lincoln's Second Inaugural would pose in the midst of war: how does one negotiate between antithetical prophets, both "deadly in earnest" yet irreconcilable? Emerson, Parker, and Phillips found themselves less ironically than Henry Adams swept back into a Puritan heritage that might cleanse America of its original sin—but only through a holy war that nearly undid the nation in the process.

TWO

Deborahs and Jaels

Engage in this holy War. Arise with Deborah, a Mother in Israel; go forth against the Enemy. . . . In the holy Army of Martyrs who overcame by the Blood of the Lamb, we have some heroic Examples of Courage and Firmness of Mind even among Women.

—Joseph Sewall, *"The Holy Spirit Convincing the World of Sin" (1741)*

"As for our four fearful years of slaughter, of course, you won't deny that there the ladies were the great motive power," chides a flirtatious Confederate war veteran to a women's rights reformer in Henry James's *The Bostonians*. "The Abolitionists brought it on, and were not the Abolitionists principally females?"[1] Counterpoised to his charm is James's portrait of frigid women reformers descended from "Abolitionist stock" and New England's "Puritan code, the ungenial climate, the absence of chivalry. Spare, dry, hard, without a curve, an inflexion or a grace," all are heiresses to a tradition of holy warriors who would be bored in a world rid of evil.[2] "Of all things in the world contention was the most sweet to her," James gibes at his protagonist, and "she was glad to have been born before [evil] had been swept away, while it was still there to face, to give one a task and a reward. When the great reforms should be consummated, when the day of justice should have dawned, would not life perhaps be rather poor and pale?"[3] James is only slightly kinder toward "an old Abolitionist" who puffs her conscience with martial grandeur. "I am only myself, I only rise to the occasion, when I see prejudice, when I see bigotry, when I see injustice, when I see conservatism, massed before me like an army," she proclaims, for "I must have unfriendly elements."[4]

If James lampooned female reformers rather cruelly, he captured not only their leading role in the antislavery cause as the "army of abolition-ism" but also something of the martial Puritan spirit that male allies and enemies likewise perceived in their challenge to the boundaries of feminine propriety and good bourgeois taste as they led the cause with Cromwellian intensity.[5] In his controversial yet influential pamphlet on how slavery en-couraged "the abrogation of the Seventh Commandment" (1835) through serial rape, the black writer David Ruggles tapped into this imaginative framework by fusing Victorian sensibilities regarding femininity with a heroic spiritual legacy available to ordinary women as much as to men. "Slavery owes its continuance in the United States chiefly to the women," he began with a blunt accusation of untapped feminine power, for "had American females come forward in all the mightiness of their legitimate and resistless influence," it would have ended at once. Ruggles provoked disgust by focusing on the endemic rape within slavery as a brutal assault on spiritual and sexual purity alike. "Purity is the exception" in slavery, he noted, because it incentivized rape as an economic advantage for own-ers, systematically annulled the sacred sphere of marriage and family, and corrupted the church. Ruggles urged women to "regenerate the temple of Jehovah" with "evangelical weapons" and reclaim what James 1:27 (a fa-vorite abolitionist verse) called "pure religion and undefiled." "What can a small number of women do? WHAT CANNOT THEY DO?" he wrote, pointing to the example of biblical women whose faith "triumphed, where the luke-warmness, pusillanimity, and irresolution of men had failed."[6]

As his ultimate example Ruggles cited the biblical story of Deborah and Jael, respectively the female Israelite judge who prophesied that the general Barak would achieve victory through a woman, and the woman who fulfilled this prophecy by hammering a tent peg through the head of the Canaanite general Sisera. Ruggles argued that American women could similarly aid "the Lord against the mighty, and like Deborah encourage and fortify Barak, until another Jael shall arise and nail the Sisera of do-mestic slavery fast to the ground" while singing "the song of the inspired prophetess—'So let all thine enemies perish, O lord!'" As new warrior-prophetesses, American women "must form an impenetrable phalanx" against God's enemy "and must take up arms which they can successfully wield, with matronly purity, dignity, and authority." To clinch his call for a purifying holy war, Ruggles signed off with his trademark antislavery pseu-donym, "Puritan."[7] Writing to an audience of Northern women and Tap-panite evangelicals—many of whom possessed moderate sensibilities on gender roles and deep roots in "Presbygationalist" churches—Ruggles not only appealed to their identity as Republican-Victorian mothers and wives but urged them toward public antislavery activism by appealing to their identity as Christian warrioresses and descendants of Puritan foremothers, just as capable of prophecy and spiritual warfare as were men.

Abolitionists' opponents in turn felt that women's activism necessarily abdicated "matronly purity" in neglecting the domestic sphere, that the call for a nation of "Deborahs and Jaels" to wage Puritan warfare would in fact destroy God-ordained gender norms and with it the basis of American society. In his satirical cartoon *Worship of the North*, Confederate sympathizer Adalbert Volck included "FREE LOVE" as one of the heretical bricks that composed the satanic abolitionist altar to "NEGRO-WORSHIP," all built atop a foundation that read "PURITANISM." Though no advocates of free love, leading antislavery women writers like Maria Weston Chapman, Lydia Maria Child, and Julia Ward Howe did claim the same legacy of Puritan spiritual heroism lauded by Ruggles and wielded by men like Parker and Phillips in order to sanction their own impulses toward spiritual warfare beyond the domestic sphere. Reimagining the "manly" Puritans as a lineage equally open to women, these writers empowered their own voices by assuming an equally heroic role within providential history. If the cult of true womanhood, in Barbara Welter's lasting definition, was defined by piety, purity, submissiveness, and domesticity, antislavery women like Chapman, Howe, and Child provoked a tension in which true piety and purity might in fact demand activism that rejected submission and went beyond the domestic sphere.[8] If the abolitionist revival of Puritan holy war offered men like Phillips and Emerson a sense of spiritual renewal in a time of religious impotence, it offered far more to women who struggled against more immediate and practical forms of disempowerment.

The BFAS and General Chapman's Women of New England

In his portrait of female reformers, James may have drawn inspiration from the haughty Maria Weston Chapman, deemed the "Lady Macbeth" of wealthy Garrisonians known as the Boston Clique (alongside her talented Weston sisters). An educated, well-married, and beautiful Brahmin, Chapman defied class expectations when she cast her lot as a leader of activists, who already in the nineteenth century faced the caricature of the homely and angry woman. "So unlike was she in *external appearance* to the group of anti-slavery women-workers, that it seemed impossible she could be one with them," the Boston *Woman's Journal* stated.[9] Harriet Martineau reflected that Chapman "exuded the Brahmin presence," while fellow reformer Lydia Maria Child deemed her "one of the most remarkable women of the age."

She seemed to especially annoy men, even allies like Whittier, who deemed her Garrison's "evil genius." The more conservative New York abolitionist Lewis Tappan described her less favorably: "self-assured, aristocratic, arrogant," she was "a talented woman with the disposition of a fiend."[10]

The aristocrat was particularly proud of her Puritan pedigree. Privately and publicly, the Weston sisters "rejoiced in their Puritan ancestry," Clare Taylor notes, and Maria in particular "stressed this point continuously, even tactlessly."[11] Chapman's elitist bearings more than once caused tensions with women of lesser station and black allies; William Lloyd Garrison's wife Helen and Frederick Douglass felt themselves the targets of her condescension more than once. Chapman wielded her Puritan pedigree as an escutcheon in more than one sense, both as an aristocratic herald of her right to leadership and as an imaginative buckler for the combative style she employed in her many written works—which often took aim at male complacency as much as the Slave Power. Early on, Chapman sparred with Boston's "gentlemen of standing" as a leading voice within the the Boston Female Anti-Slavery Society, founded in 1833 as the first women's society devoted to a Garrisonian platform of immediate abolition. The BFAS soon garnered the disapproval of men who felt that they had crossed the line from an acceptable female benevolence society by speaking publicly and aggressively on a political matter as volatile as slavery.[12]

The issue came to a head in October 1835 when the BFAS played a leading role in the events that culminated in William Lloyd Garrison's infamous near lynching. For their annual meeting, the BFAS hoped to host the renowned British abolitionist George Thompson, but growing antiabolitionist animus in the city convinced them that Thompson should wait until feelings cooled. The August prior, prominent Boston businessmen and politicians had organized an immense meeting at Fanueil Hall to formally denounce Garrison and the abolitionist movement as *"dangerous men . . . plotting the destruction of our Government,"* and they had even less patience two months later when women rekindled the issue.[13] Though Thompson stayed away and Garrison agreed to speak in his stead, word spread that he was indeed in Boston via a handbill posted in city hall and passed around town. It advertised a $100 pot "raised by a number of patriotic citizens to reward the individual who shall first lay violent hands on . . . that infamous foreign scoundrel THOMPSON" so that he might "be brought to the tar kettle before dark. Friends of the Union, be vigilant."[14]

When members of the BFAS gathered for their meeting at the *Liberator's* office on the corner of Washington and Cornhill, a crowd of such "Friends of the Union" awaited them. The women nonetheless proceeded with their meeting but grew unnerved as the crowd became rowdy and swelled into the thousands, many of them the same gentlemen as at the August meeting. The mob then began trying to break into the building. Boston's mayor, Theodore Lyman, intervened despite his opposition to abolition and his presence at the August meeting. Slipping inside, he demanded that the women leave for their own safety. Chapman retorted that Lyman's "personal friends are the instigators of this mob" (which he denied) and took a martyr's dramatic stand, declaring, "If this is the last bulwark of freedom, we may as well die here as anywhere." (The mayor later joked, "I smiled, and replied, 'At any rate they could not die there.'")[15] The BFAS voted to reconvene at Chapman's house. Garrison attempted to escape from the building's rear but was captured and marched toward Boston Common amid talk of a lynching; though not the foreign scoundrel Thompson, Garrison was an excellent second choice. By the time they reached State Street, Mayor Lyman once more intervened, taking Garrison into city custody. The women meanwhile marched phalanxlike through the mob toward Chapman's home, "greeted with taunts, hisses and cheers of mobocratic triumph, from 'gentlemen of property and standing from all parts of the city.'"[16]

Much like Lowell in his resurrection of Captain Standish, Chapman soon struck back by reclaiming a martial Pilgrim heritage in the next issue of Joseph Buckingham's *Courier*, read widely among Boston's gentlemen of property. She shamed these men as fallen "sons of the pilgrim fathers" in provoking a "spirit of outrageous violence on the daughters of the noble male band who shared their conflict with public opinion." Chapman insisted that the BFAS were truer daughters of the Pilgrims through their "identical" struggle for a "holy cause" in the face of a hostile public, and she drew out the female elements of this heritage in opposition to modern Boston gentlemen. "We have wondered how those devout and honorable women obtained strength to rend the bonds that knit them to their far fatherland. We do not wonder now," Chapman reflected, for "we read their chronicles with an anointed eye. We find it written there, that gentlemen of influence and standing forbade their assembling to worship God according to the dictates of consciences, enlightened by reason and scripture. There is no newly discovered continent for us, even if we could think it right to quit *this* sphere of duty. We must bide the brunt." In the face of mob censorship, Chapman felt her Pilgrim foremothers come to life through a shared spirit of opposition against powerful men. Declaring that "our sons shall not blush for those who bore them," Chapman concluded her attack with a Miltonic poem of her own, urging Boston's clergy to live up to this heritage. "Speak! each devoted preacher for the right! / No servile doctrines, such as power approves, / *They* to the poor and broken-hearted taught; / With truths that tyrants dread, and conscience loves, / They winged and barbed the arrows of their thoughts. / *Sin in high places* was the mark *they* sought."[17]

Chapman delighted in the language of spiritual warfare, as much for the purpose of rousing her fellow female troops as for attacking gentlemen of standing. With the advent of the new year, Chapman oversaw a comprehensive analysis of the mob in the annual report of the BFAS, which she titled *Right and Wrong in Boston*, gathering together antiabolitionist newspapers accounts in order to craft the BFAS's official interpretation of the event and employ it as propaganda for the inspiration of her fellow warriors. Writing about what the mob portended for the future of women's role in the abolitionist cause, Chapman found herself swept up in the role of a Cromwellian general directing troops in a carefully planned holy war. The women of the BFAS—all the women of the North—must organize for "the demolition of this bastile [*sic*], with a disposition to co-operate in the arrangement and direction of their force . . . or some will spring a mine under the cornerstone, while others are wasting arrow-flights against the battlements, and others striving to enkindle a general conflagration." Chapman's troops, like Cromwell's, must fuel this work with individual conviction, "must come *personally*, or they will be deceived by the distant war-shout of the enemy. The demon of oppression raises the cry of blood-thirsty fanatic," she wrote, as if pointing to a retrenched satanic castle where "immediately must we raise our scaling ladders, immediately must we begin to remove this temple built to Moloch and to Mammon." Here too Chapman sanctioned her martial rhetoric by tracing it back to a female Puritan-Patriot origin story, invoking "the women of every New England hamlet who shrunk not from sacrificing the first born, when the question was of freedom or slavery." Chapman went beyond maternal sacrifice to female warfare as she related a story of colonial Puritan soldiers who declared that they could fight unto death if not for their worries about the women back home; Chapman claimed a place for women on these battlefields through an imagined Puritan wife who retorts, "Never heed *us*. We can bring you bread and water, and serve out ammunition and fill the places of the fallen." In contrast with these brave "mothers of New England," Chapman lamented their descendants, "sadly degenerate" and little different from the English women who "showered abuse and obloquy upon their 'fanatical and weakly deluded' sisters, who helped to found the Massachusetts Colony."[18] Even more than in her *Courier* salvo, Chapman traced the BFAS's genealogy back to a revolutionary vision of its Pilgrim and Puritan women, both groups eager to fight for a sacred cause in a manner traditionally restricted to men.

Chapman's vision of Spartan "mothers of New England" bearing sons for holy war yet themselves eager to join the frontlines betrayed a tension that plagued abolitionist women as a whole: how might one reconcile antebellum conceptions of femininity, centered on the power of Christian-republican motherhood in the private sphere, with the desire to participate in the same spiritual heroics as men like Parker and Phillips, agitating more publicly and aggressively as they felt the occasion demanded? In a way that increasingly disturbed women from more orthodox religious backgrounds, the liberal Unitarian Chapman and her fellow Garrisonians addressed the tension in a Carlylean manner by recasting antebellum femininity as "clothes" now in need of retailoring to revive the heroic spiritual impulse underneath. "Woman they assure us was not meant for moral conflict. They term it 'leaving our proper sphere, the domestic fire-side,' to feel and act like immortal souls," Chapman concluded in her review of the Boston mob, "but we cannot, if we would, believe that this garment of womanhood wherewith our souls are invested, debars us from the privileges or absolves us from the duties of a spiritual existence."[19]

Chapman further implied that many of the women of the BFAS had already traded in much of the current fashion in the "garment of womanhood" for the apostle Paul's full armor of God. "We have all passed through the state of mind we now deprecate. We once verily believed we were in the way of duty, when we carefully eschewed every enlarged and comprehensive purpose, as masculine, and unsuited to our sex," Chapman reflected, but "our eyes being opened to our error, we cannot be expected again to close them to the value of the Christian character as it may and ought to be exemplified in woman." Just as Emerson, Phillips, and Parker struggled to reject physical violence even as they seemed to delight in language of spiritual war, Chapman exhibited a similar tension in her call for women warriors. On physical violence, "we reject the idea, not as unfeminine, but unchristian; for there is as much to admire in a Semiramis, a Boadicea, a Margaret of Anjou, as in an Alexander, a Charles, or a Napoleon," Chapman noted, ranking history's heroic women warriors with its men. Yet true Christianity nonetheless demanded a similar warfare, if in spirit rather than flesh. "Human nature," Chapman asserted, "is made for moral conflict. Scripture calls the Christian life a warfare; and in declaring that the weapons are not carnal, it fulfils one of its main purposes—to annul all distinctions but those of the soul. The shield of faith, the sword of the spirit, and the helmet of salvation, are a panoply alike for all whose spirits feel their need."[20]

Of all the outward distinctions that clouded the simpler and truer spiritual distinction between good and evil, Chapman especially took aim at gender and at the clergy who used it as a means of spiritual subordination. If Emerson could declare, "Here is the antislave: here is man: and if you have man, black or white is an insignificance," Chapman challenged his masculine presumptions by unfolding his argument a step further: if you have a soul, male or female is an insignificance. Theodore Parker's battle line between *aut Deus aut Diabolus* cleaved women as sharply as men into the more important category of elect and reprobate. Somewhat paradoxically, this act of declaring gender irrelevant through spiritual leveling in fact enabled thrilling possibilities for explicitly female instances of spiritual heroism, precisely what made the antislavery cause exciting for many women.[21] Sarah Neall, a Philadelphia Quaker, lamented the dullness of Pennsylvania activism compared to "the fiery spirit that lives and thrives . . . up there among the wild hills of Puritan New England, [where] has begun the struggle between the free spirit of the People and the tyranny of ecclesiastical organizations."[22]

For other women this rhetoric was more unsettling than exciting as it grew into fiercer attacks on the church. In the next year's address to the BFAS, Chapman found herself disappointed with the Northern clergy's failure to heed her call the year prior to snipe at "sin in high places," more plainly in their hesitancy to grant the BFAS speaking venues and advertisement of its meetings—even, Chapman noted, among Boston's liberal Unitarians, who claimed to be invested in a fight for free religious inquiry. In response, the BFAS's annual report was subtitled "A Sketch of the Obstacles Thrown in the Way of Emancipation by Certain Clerical Abolitionists and Advocates for the Subjection of Woman." Swiping at the clergy, Chapman opened by addressing "the Women of New England" as "the true descendants of the pilgrims [who] cannot fail to cherish in their inmost souls, the principles of Christian Freedom." Once more she drew on dramatic martial language, declaring that "the clergy are battalions drawn up against freedom," a battle "which will end only with a reformation hardly less startling or less needed than that of Luther."[23] But as David Ruggles implied in his pamphlet and as historians of female abolitionism like Debra Gold Hansen and Julie Roy Jeffrey have noted, a majority of the North's antislavery women remained devout members of more orthodox Congregationalist, Presbyterian, or Baptist churches, traditions that also held a claim to New

England's Puritan heritage, and with more precise institutional and theological continuities than the hazier "principles of Christian freedom" by which Chapman claimed the Pilgrims' mantle. Further, many such women were founding members of the BFAS and felt a growing distance from Chapman on this front. Hansen concludes that the BFAS "elicited a variety of interpretations of women's roles and responsibilities, with upper-class women advocating economic, political, and spiritual equality and women of the middle class defending domesticity and motherhood," while Jeffrey emphasizes the role of anticlericism over class in fracturing the BFAS.

The two forces overlapped as many upper-class antislavery women came from Unitarian or transcendentalist backgrounds that tended to emphasize the antinomian, aggressive, and revolutionary forms of continuity with the Protestant past over ecclesiastical or theological continuity.[24] By 1840 the conflict ruptured into a split as a group of women led by Mary Parker withdrew from the BFAS and founded the Massachusetts Female Emancipation Society. Traditional histories of abolitionism have often emphasized the split over anticlericism and women's rights at the American Anti-Slavery Society's annual meeting in May 1840, where more conservative members left the group in protest to form the American and Foreign Anti-Slavery Society, or the World Anti-Slavery Convention the next month in London, where female delegates like Elizabeth Cady Stanton and Lucretia Mott were refused a seating at official proceedings at the request of Arthur Tappan, in turn prompting Garrison and other allies to sit out in protest; though indeed momentous, these events were not simply a feud between Garrison and the Tappan brothers but the result of older tensions that had long been simmering among antislavery women themselves.

A central source of this tension was not solely class and anticlericism but a struggle over what imaginative shape the abolitionist cause should take: would it be a reform movement that worked within existing forms of culture, including antebellum womanhood and the church, or would it be a more revolutionary force that offered women a chance to retailor these trappings as they tapped into a more aggressive and heroic spiritual legacy? Like Emerson and Parker in their rebellious turn to abolition as a protest against the placidity of Unitarian religious experience, the remaining Chapmanite contingency of Northern antislavery women—smaller yet fiercer and more eager to make their voices known through literature— would exert an oversized influence in shaping the imaginative landscape of the antislavery cause in the decades to come, especially through its two most successful allies: Lydia Maria Child and Julia Ward Howe.

The Liberty Bell's Battle Hymns

Beyond BFAS speeches, reports, and letters to editors, Chapman combined her canny organizing and her martial imagination in other collaborative literary ventures, including compiling and editing an antislavery hymnal, *Songs of the Free* (1836), that riposted after the Boston mob with fierce battle hymns. Many have noted the neo-Calvinist militancy of Julia Ward Howe's "Battle Hymn of the Republic" with its deity trampling out the grapes of wrath, but few have recognized that it grew from a thirty-year tradition of women-led Garrisonian hymns that at times make the "Battle Hymn" sound restrained. "The Lord will come! The earth shall quake," Chapman's opening hymn trumpets, "The Lord will come! A dreadful form, / With wreath of flame and robe of storm: / Master and slave alike shall find / An equal judge of human kind."[25] Chapman herself cried, "Equip me for the war, / and teach my hands to fight," as she noted that the hymnal's purpose was to aid "the spiritual warfare in which they are engaged."[26] To honor the Garrisonian commitment to pacifism and nonresistance while nonetheless stoking imaginative holy war, Chapman's hymns returned constantly to the prospect of martyrdom as a way to engage in warrior fashion yet nonviolently with earthly powers, fitting the mission into a lineage of persecuted nonconformists with roots in the early church. "The Son of God goes forth to war," one hymn by Reginald Heber proclaims: "who follows in his train ? / A glorious band, the chosen few . . . they met the tyrant's brandished steel, / The lion's gory mane . . . a noble army, men and boys, the matron, and the maid." Straining spiritual weapons against tyranny, abolitionist women imagined themselves alongside men in a superior army by wielding a warlike force toward moral rather than physical ends.[27] As Marcus Wood notes, "British Nonconformist hymnology (Watts and Wesley pre-eminent) and the tradition of British seventeenth-century radical dissent" was a primary influence on this tradition, revealing a more concrete genealogy from seventeenth-century British nonconformism to the "Battle Hymn of the Republic."[28]

Beyond her battle hymns, Chapman especially expressed her knack for marshaling militant imaginations in *The Liberty Bell*, an annual "gift book" anthology which she organized and edited from 1839 until 1858. As Ralph Thompson first noted, from 1820 through the Civil War the gift book was a well-established fundraising tradition often spearheaded by women, but Chapman directed this polite medium toward nonconformist ends.[29] Every year the *Bell* was a central presence at the National Anti-Slavery Bazaar, an important and vast fundraising event organized by the BFAS which drew visitors from across the North and gathered contributions from female antislavery societies throughout the nation. Chapman spearheaded the bazaar with the same aristocratic intensity as the BFAS, priding herself on its good taste in wares as much as its imaginative intensity. A *Liberator* advertisement for the 1848 Bazaar mentioned, among other goods, "silk-crocheted and beaded ladies' bags and purses," "glove and ribbon boxes, Jewel cases, &c," "paisley and Edinburgh shawls," "silk and satin aprons, plain and richly embroidered," and "an immense cheese, from the Ladies Garrisonian Anti-Slavery Society of Austinburgh, Ohio . . . at the Refreshment table."[30] Each contribution offered ordinary women a way to participate in a sacred cause within the bounds of feminine propriety, but the *Liberty Bell* also tempted bazaargoers like a crate of gunpowder lurking among the immense cheeses and ribbon boxes, filled with literary contributions that gravitated toward Chapman's Puritan taste for spiritual rapture, martyrdom, and holy war.

As editor, Chapman achieved a striking balance between a unified style and a variety of voices. The *Liberty Bell* was especially strong in publishing unknown women, most of them poets. Aspiring writers like Susan C. Cabot, Harriet Winslow (later Sewall), Mary Eliza Robbins, Henrietta Sargent, Maria Lowell (née White), Louisa Jane Hall, Georgiana Fanny Ross, Emma Michell, and many more could see their works printed alongside those of respected literary Brahmins like William Wetmore Story, Henry Wadsworth Longfellow, John Quincy and Charles Francis Adams, John Pierpont, and Edmund Quincy; national antislavery voices like Emerson, Garrison, Parker, Phillips, and Lowell; and international greats like Harriet Martineau, Alexis de Tocqueville, Frederika Bremer, George Thompson— even the polyglot English mayor of Hong Kong John Bowring and the Italian revolutionary Giuseppe Mazzini. The *Bell*'s transatlantic component was strong, featuring frequent Irish writers, translations of German works (several done by the above women), and a particular attraction to French antislavery writers like Victor Schœlcher, Jean-Jacques Ampère, François Arago, Ernest Legouvé, and the father-daughter duo Emile and Marie Souvestre, among others (most printed in the original French). In the 1856 *Bell*, Chapman published a letter she had received from the Russian novelist Ivan Turgenev just as he came onto the world stage for his *Hunter's Album* (1852), which has been compared to *Uncle Tom's Cabin* in its effect on swaying public opinion against Russian serfdom. In the letter, one of his first appearances in the States, Turgenev praised Garrison, "thoroughly persuaded that all success obtained in America in the cause of the coloured race will be eminently serviceable to my poor countrymen in Russia."[31] Chapman generally included an excess of household Anglo-American names for the sake of sales, but she devoted an admirable amount of space to ordinary women, international voices, Garrisonians from poorer backgrounds (Charles C. Burleigh, John A. Collins, Abby Kelley Foster, and Parker Pillsbury), and fringe radicals like Adin Ballou and Nathaniel P. Rogers, eccentric even by Garrisonian standards.[32]

As in her battle hymns, Chapman organized this remarkable exchange of voices around a spiritual propensity for the intensities of rapture, chosenness, holy war, martyrdom, divine judgment, and purifying fires that erupted from commitment to a sacred cause. Chapman inaugurated the first *Liberty Bell* by casting the titular bell as a summon for "mother" and "sire" to "rouse our country's utmost bound," followed by Lydia Maria Child's praise for abolitionists as "Ye glorious band! Ye chosen few! / On whome God's Spirit came." Chapman's younger sister Caroline wrote a lengthy poetic chronicle of the world's ancient enmity toward such spirit-filled prophets, prefaced with a paraphrase from the Gospel of John: "If the world hate you, ye know that it hated me before it hated you."[33]

Chapman raised abolitionists from hated prophets to valiant holy warriors through frequent contributions that poeticized spiritual warfare. William Howitt quoted *Samson Agonistes*'s rendition of the Hebrew warrior's final feat of strength against the wicked to lend similar strength to the antislavery cause, where "but once is given the battle's glorious field / Where we may prove our birth / Is godlike, and for God lift spear and shield / . . . and fight the holy fight / Which Christ himself began, / And hero-saints have waged for the right." Abby Kelly echoed Chapman when she answered "What Is Real Anti-Slavery Work?" as "warfare," quite simply, "direct[ing] our blows . . . for the annihilation of Slavery" while awaiting the day that a demonic Slave Power "forthwith sends one of his bruised victims to us, to beg of us the means by which we are prosecuting this holy warfare of the spirit against himself."[34]

A step higher than martyrdom and holy war alike was an eagerness to place abolitionists at the right hand of a wrathful God as he leveled a tyrannical economy by dispensing judgment on the Slave Power. In galloping anapaest, Pierpont imagined "the trumpets of angels . . . pealing around" when "the murdered slave / Comes forth from his grave, / And smiles at the flash of th' / Avenger's glaive, / And the world shall accord / In the righteous award / To both tyrant and slave, in that day of the Lord." In the first *Bell*, Garrison returned American readers to a Calvinist Jehovah appropriate to abolitionist war if increasingly unpopular in the sunnier climes of antebellum optimism at large; "Scatter thy foes as chaff is driven before the whirlwind!" he gushed—"O, sublime is the conflict."[35]

Such an aesthetic can be labeled "Puritan" if for no other reason than the fact that the *Bell*'s contributors themselves frequently traced their imaginative holy war to a Pilgrim-Puritan heritage. When James Russell Lowell asked readers, "If ye in pride your true birthright have spurned . . . how in Truth's name have ye earned / The holy right to fight for liberty?," others often raised Plymouth Rock as the cornerstone of this birthright, as when Eliza Follen dedicated a martial marching song "to the Pilgrim's spirit true" or when Pierpont opened the 1841 *Bell* by placing readers in the midst of the Pilgrims as they disembarked at Plymouth Rock, proclaiming, "Here stand we . . . Thy freemen, Lord! and not of man the slaves!" Chapman similarly praised "sea-worn pilgrims . . . Who sought the God of Freedom" as she hoped that Boston, "city of the pilgrim fathers," would continue their faith "by making all men free!" Chapman's sister-in-law Ann Greene Chapman claimed the Puritans' armor of God even as she distanced herself from their real battles, singing, "I war not as my fathers did, though I bear their arms; / but the spirit that supported them in battle's fierce alarms— / their lofty spirit shall be mine." A few pages later in the same issue, Chapman's sister Anne sketched a similar parallel in a poem titled "The Come-Outers of the Sixteenth and Nineteenth Centuries," imagining a young woman abolitionist who finds the courage to leave her proslavery church by recounting the experience of a sixteenth-century woman leaving the Catholic Church to follow Luther.[36]

Even non-Americans recognized these puritanical tendencies, as when the English John Bowring wrote "To the American Abolitionists" to recount how "OUR fathers and your fathers bore / The spirit-stirring strife of yore, / Our shores flung on your / welcoming shore, / The patriot-pilgrims' sail:—/ And ye are worthy of the name, / And the bright ancestry ye claim; / The same the sires—the sons the same— / Hail! brothers! hail!" In a letter to Chapman, the Swedish feminist writer Frederika Bremer asked,

> Is not the genius of America called upon to be on earth the missionary of God, to proclaim the freedom of man in the name of the Redeemer? Look at her origin and history! *Spiritual Freedom!*—was the watchword of those one hundred Puritans who fled to the desert and planted there the tree of liberty. . . . *Political Freedom!*—was the banner under which America rose to its national self-control and greatness. *Human Freedom!* spiritual and political freedom *for every soul redeemed by God,* is the great truth still left for America to pronounce and to make real in her realm.

Wendell Phillips imagined the narrative more ironically. "Puritan!" he reflected, "how the wits of Charles II. rinsed their mouths with rich wine after uttering the disgusting name! little thinking that Liberty would soon crown the despised party as her noblest apostles. To 'crop-eared knaves' of 1649, Governments now are proud to trace their pedigree."[37]

If Chapman counterbalanced this variety of European and American, male and female voices with a New England–centric mission, she also revealed how such a focus could overlook the most important actors in the antislavery cause: black people themselves. The most glaring gap in the *Bell's* diverse roster was its dearth of black writers, who contributed fewer than ten total pieces in its nearly thirty-year run (by Richard Allen, William Wells Brown, Frederick Douglass, Charles Lenox Remond, John Telemachus Hilton, and the Afro-Cuban poet Plácido). Such a gap reveals the same tension seen in Parker's and Phillips's different senses of the relationship that white abolitionists and their prized Pilgrim heritage had with the black Americans they purported to aid. Even more than the farm-born Parker, the aristocratic Chapman came to abolitionism as much through Saxonist presumptions about the Anglo roots of liberty and chauvinistic desires to play Puritan hero to blacks-in-distress as through a democratic commitment to equality and black citizenry. Phillips realized better than Parker and others that his dedication to New England's Puritan heritage needed to be reimagined toward less ethnocentric ends, but Chapman rarely paused her antislavery organizing long enough to consider if her Puritan heroics, despite an admirable degree of progressivism and cosmopolitanism, might reproduce certain ethnocentric presumptions about American nationalism that the fight against slavery—equally a fight *for* black citizenry—in fact aimed to overcome. (Chapman's omission also hinted at future tensions within the women's rights movement between black men and white women as the latter grew frustrated when the struggle for black enfranchisement seemed to steal momentum from the fight for female suffrage.)

Chapman's similar outlook runs through the *Bell* as its zeal for Puritan prophetesses often excluded more empathic or complex encounters with what it meant to be black in antebellum America. Though written by a white Englishwoman, a single poem nearly makes up for these omissions and is perhaps the *Bell's* most lasting and valuable contribution to literary history: Elizabeth Barrett Browning's "The Runaway Slave at Pilgrim's Point," first published in the 1848 *Bell* and one of Browning's first appearances in America. From its opening lines, the poem creates a vicious energy by lashing out at Pilgrim filiopiety through the eyes of a fugitive slave who collapses at Plymouth Rock in flight from slavehunters, having murdered and buried her child, the product of rape by her master, "on the mark, beside the shore, / Of the first white pilgrim's bended knee; / Where exile changed to ancestor, / And God was thanked for liberty." In place of urging readers to honor a liberty-loving Pilgrim ancestry à la Chapman, Browning attacks readers with cutting irony by emphasizing the fugitive's separation from this legacy of "*white* pilgrims," once exiles like her but since monumentalized into "ancestors," petrified totems for filiopious descendants who hunt the exiles of their own era and sing praises in the passive voice: "God is thanked for liberty." As "pilgrim-souls" arise "proud and slow / From the land of the spirits, pale as dew," the fugitive kneels in what we assume is prayer. Although she can "feel your souls around me hum" much as abolitionists like Chapman often did, the fugitive swerves unexpectedly into a black woman's curse rather than a white woman's praise, "lifting my black face, my black hand, / Here in your names, to curse this land." She begins the poem's bitter refrain, "I am black, I am black," wondering why God made her so only to "cast his work away / Under the feet of His white creatures, / With a look of scorn, that the dusky features / Might be trodden again to clay."

The fugitive recounts the events that brought her to Pilgrim's Point: her separation from a lover and subsequent rape by her master, God's silence in the face of both, and finally the birth of a child "far too white—too white for me. / As white as the ladies who scorned to pray / Beside me at church." As the fugitive "could not bear / To look in his face, it was so white," Browning relates how she smothers it in ghastly detail until "fine white angels" come to free "the white child's spirit" from its white body. She is reconciled to her child only when she buries it, where "all changed to black earth,—nothing white,— / A dark child in the dark." On the shore of Plymouth, she then realizes that "the Pilgrims' ghosts have slid away," for "my face is black, but it glares with a scorn / Which they dare not meet by day." In their stead come seven of "their hunter-sons" in pursuit of the suicidal fugitive. "I am not mad,—I am black!" she declares, while "ye are born of the Washington race!" She casts herself off the cliff. The Pilgrims' sons leave with nothing but her "broken heart's disdain."[38] Far more successfully than most contributors to the *Liberty Bell*, Browning sharpened the traditional jeremiad by filtering it through the fugitive's refrain "I am black, I am black," stripped of its sanctimony to confront *Bell* readers with its harshest failures. If Theodore Parker innovated on the jeremiad by using it to deliver new rather than old truths, Browning transformed it by dramatizing its clash with an exile so far beyond its communal bonds as to prompt infanticide and suicide as a lasting curse. Above all, the poem is a brooding challenge to the presumptions of the *Liberty Bell*'s heroic white readers.

Though far less challenging than Browning's jeremiad, Julia Ward Howe's strident "Battle Hymn of the Republic" remains perhaps the most sublime descendant of Chapman's imagination in its role as the eventual anthem of the Union war effort. By the outbreak of the Civil War, Chapman and her allies had established a tradition of puritanical battle hymns and an arena of feminine dissent that created artistic possibilities for an unhappily married woman to reimagine her Calvinist heritage and participate vicariously in John Brown's war. As Elaine Showalter relates, though Howe had rejected her mother's "strictest rule of New England Puritanism" for Unitarianism, she found herself returning to its militant and millennial intensities during a lifelong struggle with failed literary ambitions and a patriarchal marriage.[39] When Howe's father passed away in 1839, she found that Calvinism "now came home to me with terrible force, and a season of depression and melancholy followed." She took to writing devout poetic elegies, distributing religious tracts, and instituting a spartan orthodox regimen in the household.[40] Howe eventually found emancipation from depression through Unitarian faith and romantic literature. Yet trouble returned with marriage and a decade of struggle with a patriarchal husband who had little patience for a wife's literary ambitions. Until the war, Howe produced only two minor collections of poetry, revealing a tumultuous inner life.

When war broke out, Howe watched powerlessly, eager to participate but too old to lend direct aid. As she absorbed the scenes of war—battlefields littered with campfires and lamps, rows of gun-barrel steel, the blare of trumpets—her imagination reached back to the Calvinist language of her youth. The "Battle Hymn" was born in 1861 outside of Washington, DC, when Howe and her husband toured a Union camp and heard the troops' rendition of "John Brown's Body," a ditty celebrating the abolitionist vigilante to the tune of a black spiritual. Howe had herself praised Brown as "Puritan of the Puritans, forceful, concentrated, and self-contained," and after it was suggested that she set her own words to the tune, she awoke in a fit of inspiration the next morning and found that the Puritanical lines "were arranging themselves in my brain" as if beyond her will.[41] She scrambled to record the revelation and submitted the lines to James T. Fields at the *Atlantic*, who bought, titled, and printed them on the February issue's front page.

The hymn was, as Showalter writes, "the turning point in her life," as well as her own experience of being "swept back into Puritanism."[42] Its millennial vision of a wrathful God speaking a "gospel writ in steel" through historical conflict presents a livelier and more militant version of Lowell's "The Present Crisis" (which Howe would have certainly read). While critics like Shoewalter have situated the song within Howe's struggle against patriarchy, the hymn can be read more broadly as the culmination of an imaginative tradition inaugurated by Chapman, the last and greatest in a line of abolitionist women who reclaimed the Puritans' legacy in the antislavery cause as an avenue to the practical empowerment and spiritual heroism of their own battle hymns. One might imagine Howe's "Battle Hymn" as the collective voice of these women, singing its way through the Union army as they participated in male heroics and sharpened the war with the arc of sacred history.[43]

Lydia Maria Child's Puritan Education

While "The Runaway Slave at Pilgrim's Point" and the "Battle Hymn" remain the most captivating and sublime descendants of the BFAS, Lydia Maria Child was the group's most consistently successful and politically influential reform writer. Born on Boston's cultural as much as geographic outskirts, Child nevertheless had New England roots that stretched as far back as those of most Brahmins (to the arrival of Richard Francis in 1636 Massachusetts), but her family remained of humbler stock.[44] Child had a modest upbringing under an industrious mother and a baker father who remained emotionally distant and staunchly Calvinist long after their reverend drifted toward Unitarianism. While Chapman and other antislavery writers could admire a usable Puritan "spirit" from a Unitarian distance, Child first struggled to escape what she called the "fierce theology" of an actual Calvinist upbringing, ("devil worship," she later reflected, "strictly and truly").[45] After her brother Convers left for Harvard in 1811 (eventually to become a Unitarian pastor and early member of the Transcendental Club), Child often felt trapped as she contended with a girl's limited educational opportunities and a father who viewed her growing love of books with concern. She soon began to associate Calvinism with patriarchy and would struggle throughout her career with the feeling that—as she lamented to her hero Charles Sumner—she had "the heart of a man imprisoned within a woman's destiny."[46]

As with other members of the BFAS, this feeling of entrapment especially entailed a desire for spiritual heroism in a culture that gendered it masculine. Ironically, though Child would begin her career in rebellion against Calvinism, she would return to the Puritans' feminine and militant legacies as she reckoned with an increasingly belligerent Slave Power and aimed to fuse her literary and activist callings. As her biographer Carolyn Karcher has noted, the Civil War prompted Child's "Puritan education," but the process in fact preceded the war by decades, prompted by the BFAS and aggravated by rising violence.[47] Like Chapman and Howe, Child felt herself swept back into Puritanism as the struggle acquired the imaginative fervency of spiritual warfare.

Child first attacked Calvinist patriarchy and racism in her breakout literary success, *Hobomok* (1824), the story of a Puritan girl rebelling against her bigoted father and brethren by wedding the Native American Hobomok and bearing him a son, nearly as scandalous for nineteenth-century readers as for seventeenth-century Puritans. Child partly acknowledged the reservations of her readers by resurrecting a white fiancé to whom Hobomok nobly concedes the marriage, but Mary ultimately "returns to the Puritan community on her own terms, unscathed by her violation of its taboos," in Karcher's astute reading—an accurate description of Child's own relationship with American culture in the decades to come.[48] Child began her own lifelong struggle with marriage when she wed David Lee Child in 1828. Though both were aspiring writers eager to create a relationship founded on equality, David's lack of ardor, inferior literary talents, and frequent moves to escape a trail of debt increasingly strained the relationship. As she tapped into a hot market with domestic guides like *The Frugal Housewife* (1829) and *The Mother's Book*, Child tried to embrace the ideals of republican domesticity for herself even as she found them unfulfilling. When the newlyweds moved to Boston in 1828, Child found an alternate source of fulfillment in the growing abolitionist movement that had begun to coalesce around William Lloyd Garrison and (three years later) the *Liberator*.

Child thus joined the cause, like most, for reasons that exceeded the ethical demands of abolition. "Absorbed in poetry and painting,—soaring aloft, on Pysche-wings, into the etherial regions of mysticism," Child felt that Garrison "got hold of the strings of my conscience, and pulled me into Reforms," where "all things became new" and a "stimulus [seized] my whole being."[49] She felt like a broom brought to life, she said, as the abolitionist cause transformed her from a domestic tool into a "living, energetic being."[50] Child increasingly described her artistic "mysticism" and her antislavery activism as competitors, though her words also reveal how her entrance into abolitionism was itself an intensely imaginative and affective affair. Her sense of being transformed from a broom into a living being likely grew in part from the exciting group of antislavery Brahmin women like Louisa Loring and Henrietta Sargent who adopted the rising literary star into their elegant Boston society. For someone of Child's humble background, their mix of wealth, intellect, and progressivism certainly made an impression, as did their most energetic leader, Maria Weston Chapman. Child especially adored Chapman's razor witticisms and her "dazzling complexion . . . golden hair . . . swift eyes of clear steel-blue," and she would channel Chapman's steely militancy toward more successful literary ends into the 1850s.[51]

Encouraged by Garrison and her new friends, Child began to hone her own opinions on slavery with a vast research project that grew into her first great success in reform literature, *Appeal in Favor of That Class of Americans Called Africans* (1833), a "full-scale analysis of the slavery question" that combined "facts and arguments from an unprecedented array of sources" into "the first American book to call for immediate emancipation, an end to all forms of racial discrimination, and the integration of African Americans as equal citizens," in Karcher's telling.[52] In arguing for full black equality, Child went further than even Chapman would have likely found agreeable, praising Touissaint Louverture's revolution in the same terms as she had used to laud King Phillip's war against the Puritans, and (in the same breath) defending the right to interracial marriage as tantamount to the freedom of religion for which the Puritans had founded New England.[53] The *Appeal* strained Child's relationship with family and old friends, ultimately costing her the brief fame she had enjoyed in respectable literary circles. One month prior, the venerable *North American Review* had praised Child as "just the woman we want for the mothers and daughters of the present generation."[54] But Child's "heart of a man" had already begun to strain against a culture that would limit her authority to that of an orthodox woman speaking to mothers and daughters. Child wanted to speak to the nation, to the world, to men. If measured solely by the individuals it converted to the cause—Wendell Phillips, William Ellery Channing, Thomas Wentworth Higginson, Senator Charles Sumner, and more—the *Appeal* punched far above a Victorian woman's weight and transformed Child into one of the abolitionist movement's leading voices.[55]

This new and exciting role was cut short in 1837 when Child felt compelled to accompany her husband in his latest move to South Natick and later Northampton, a sleepy village and orthodox outpost in western Massachusetts that contrasted starkly with her life in Boston. Child's loneliness would be a decisive factor in militarizing her imagination as it prompted her to cleave to antislavery activism even more fiercely as a lifeline out of small-town provincialism. "The people in this village are dead while they live—about slavery and everything else," she lamented, for "their priest is a mere feeder on husks."[56] Carlyle's *Sartor Resartus* thus appeared in her life with providential timing. As a friend of Emerson, her brother Convers had been one of Carlyle's first American readers in 1836, and he soon passed one of the eight initial pamphlet copies of *Sartor* along to his literary sister, surely knowing how much it would mean to her in the midst of village life. The book enraptured Child so much that she wrote to Carlyle out of gratitude. "I placed it nightly under my pillow," she told him, "that with the morning light I might refresh myself from its pages." She especially noted its "pure, strengthening breeze . . . when I was alone in a remote country town, struggling with worldly discouragements, craving sympathy and spiritual food."[57] Just as Leon Jackson has noted Carlyle's special allure for doubting Calvinists, before *Sartor* gave Child a vision of spiritual heroism and revolutionary history, it gave her a final lifeline out of her parents' fierce theology.[58]

But like Carlyle himself, Child's rejection of Calvinism never found a satisfying emotional home in Unitarian equanimity after she had experienced its Boston society up close, and she grew increasingly impatient with its resistance to abolition and transcendentalism, sometimes gendering it as feminine cowardice. When she hoped to convert the Chapmans' pastor, William Ellery Channing, to abolitionism, Child found the brilliant man overrefined into inaction. "What a pity that a mind like his should be bound round with Lilliputian cords by his wife and daughter," she wrote to Louisa Loring, eager to "batter away the glazings of his prejudice, false refinement, and beautiful *theories*, into which the breath of life was never infused by being boldly brought into *action*." Men like Emerson and Phillips similarly admired John Brown for expressing his faith in action ("Puritanism," Phillips declared in his defense of Brown, "is *action*"), but the notion was more poignant for Child, who found the inaction of good men twice as damnable for their access to a broader arena of possibilities.[59] After reading Carlyle in Northampton and pining for her rebellious antislavery sisters in Boston, Child sometimes even went so far as to find more worth in Calvinism than Unitarianism and, like Emerson, traced modern abolition and transcendentalism to its sterner, hotter legacy. "Of all varieties of the human school, I have the least liking and the least respect for the Nortonian," she wrote to Louisa, where even "Calvinistic bigotry, odious as it is, gains by the comparison; for at the root there is somewhat of an honest, though superstitious, belief; it is not *mere* 'decencies forever.'"[60] Transcendentalists and abolitionists alike revived these legacies, for "no controversy, since the Reformation," she declared to Louisa, "has done so much to emancipate men's minds from every species of thraldom."[61]

Here as elsewhere, Child and her transcendentalist allies were unfair in belittling Unitarianism as "decencies forever," a polemical foil for their own desire to be neo-Puritanical warriors. If Channing's antislavery work studiously avoided the pyrotechnics of Garrisonian prophecy and perhaps put too much faith in the progressive possibilities of genteel debate, it was nonetheless a serious, sincere, and significant effort from one of America's leading clerics. William R. Hutchinson and especially Daniel Walker Howe first noted that the Unitarians themselves "greatly admired their Puritan forbears, despite a strong distaste for their theology," especially "their social morality: their 'deep tone of seriousness,' their 'disinterestedness.'" This ardent Unitarian conscience, Howe concludes, was itself a serious attempt to sustain "Puritanism without Calvinism."[62] Still, Child found (as Howe himself admits) that the Unitarian clergy's genteel faith in their own leadership and their desire for orderly peace put them increasingly out of step not only with the more aggressive facets of their Puritan heritage but with the radical tenor of the times.

While Child cast transcendentalism and abolition as heirs of the Reformation against "decencies forever," both movements aggravated her tug-of-war between "mysticism" and "conscience" for much of the 1840s. Child left Northampton and began an informal separation from David in 1841, when she moved to New York City to edit the *National Anti-Slavery Standard*. Garrisonians complained when she began to steer the paper toward more political ends. While wrangling with radicals, Child also pursued nonreform writing, most prominently in her well-received *Letters from New York*. There was also the practical matter that with every new charge into abolition, Child limited the venues willing to publish her nonreform writing. "Anti Slavery has put me at a disadvantage always, with regard to a choice of publishers," she vented to Henrietta Sargent.[63] Pulled between art and activism, "I feel that they are opposite—nay discordant," she reflected, where "my affections and imagination cling to one with a love that will not be divorced; my reason and conscience keep fast hold of the other, and will not be loosened. Here is the battle of free-will and necessity with a vengeance! What shall I do? The temptation is to quit reforms; but that is of the devil."[64] Transcendentalism and literature satisfied Child's aesthetic, affective, and imaginative life, but its mystic delights pulled her away from the duties of reform, similar to Emerson's distinction between Reform and reform.[65] But as for Emerson, this conflict melted into collaboration into the 1850s as the antislavery struggle itself became a fecund imaginative project in its battle with the devil.

More than anything else, the rising violence inaugurated by Bleeding

Kansas brought Child back into a full commitment to antislavery activism by way of rather than in spite of her literary aspirations. When her beloved Senator Charles Sumner was beaten by Preston Brooks in 1856 for his remarks on the conflict, Child resolved to wield her literary powers heroically; she was more exasperated than ever that some prominent Garrisonians continued to obsess over ideological purity in a time when decisive action was demanded. When Chapman denounced Senator Sumner and Harriet Beecher Stowe as "ephemera," Child bit back: "I should like to be performing as glorious a mission, as *either* of those ephemera." The eruption of violence convinced her not only that changing times called for political and perhaps literal weapons as much as moral ones, but also that antislavery literature could satisfy her imagination and conscience simultaneously.

The resulting mix was *The Kansas Emigrants,* a novella best described as half feminist Western and half Puritan errand into the wilderness, a striking departure from her critiques of Puritanism in *Hobomok* and ultimately one of Child's most far-reaching works (yet also one of the most understudied).[66] Serialized in the *New York Tribune,* Child's installations drew from news reports about Bleeding Kansas and purposely reached their climax just before the crucial presidential election of 1856, in which she hoped to see her work unite Garrisonians and moderates behind John C. Frémont. The story centers upon two sets of Massachusetts newlyweds, John and Kate Bradford and William and Alice Bruce (names evoking John Winthrop and William Bradford) who join the Kansas struggle out of fealty to their Puritan ancestry. "The story of our forefathers was all familiar to me; and I always reverenced the Puritans," William tells his wife, "but the grandeur of their character never loomed up before my mental vision as it does now. With all their faults, they were a noble set of men and women."[67] As he looks upon a moral New England landscape dotted with churches and schools, he feels an urgency to plant the same civilization in Kansas: "All of this we owe to those heroic pilgrims, who left comfortable homes in England and came to a howling wilderness to establish a principle of freedom; and what they have done for Massachusetts, John Bradford and his companions may do for Kansas. It is a glorious privilege to help in laying the foundation of states on a basis of justice and freedom." He confesses, "To speak the plain truth, dear Alice, I have something of the old Puritan feeling, that God calls me to this work."[68]

Alice fears that she lacks the Puritan mettle necessary for such an errand; William teases her—"You seemed greatly to admire that young Puritan bride, who cheerfully left home and friends behind"—but promises not to take his fragile bride to the frontier, for "such a delicate flower as you are needs to be sheltered from the blast and the storm."[69] With this opening frame, Child appeals to women of moderate and radical sensibilities alike, betting that feminist readers will be peeved by William's "delicate flower" talk while more moderate readers may share Alice's inhibitions; Child's desire for Puritan heroism purposely appeals to both groups and establishes her plot as a woman's jeremiad reversed: a daughter of the Puritans finds the will to reclaim her foremothers' heroism for spiritual battle in a moral wilderness.

Though initially hesitant, the women begin to steal the show as they meet rising violence with divine courage. When "John Bradford and his band of pilgrims" arrive in the Free State stronghold of Lawrence, a clean and enlightened town that stands apart from run-down proslavery villages, their first act (like the Puritans they admire) is to set up a printing press for an abolitionist newspaper in the West, the *Herald of Freedom*.[70] As proslavery ruffians increase their intimidation, Free State women rise to the challenge with "masculine" and even explicitly militant heroism. When ruffians sack the Bradford house, Kate throws herself upon her husband and dares the assailants to kill her first. "How manfully you stood by me!" John afterward praises his wife. "How womanfully, you mean," Kate replies with feminine modesty. John stands by his language, for "it required more courage to refrain from seizing my rifle, than it would have done to discharge its contents among those rascals."[71]

Once more Child split the ideological middle between pacifism and armed resistance as much as between feminine demure and masculine heroism; antislavery women could be both women and new Puritan heroes. With whispers of an attack on Lawrence, Kate smuggles arms through enemy lines, hiding ammunition under her skirt while rightly reasoning that the men won't suspect well-behaved Yankee women. Soldiers are inspired by her to begin drilling themselves, proclaiming that "the old spirit of Lexington and Concord is here! They had better not trifle with the Puritan blood much longer!"[72] The women follow suit when the struggle reaches a breaking point and ruffians drag a woman into the woods, "where she was subjected to their brutal outrages." Upon discovering the crime, Kate becomes "stern almost to fierceness" and begins practicing with a pistol. Other women follow her lead and agree to act under her command, even undertaking their own militia drills. In Kate, Child created the literal female warrior that she desired herself to be, participating vicariously in the Kansas conflict.

The story climaxes with New England's failure to intervene and the infamous 1856 "Sack of Lawrence," which had recently left the town in ashes. Kate holds out hope that Massachusetts will live up to its Puritan mission as "her old love of New England increased a hundred-fold; for all her hopes centred *there*. The Pilgrims that came over in the May Flower, the men and women of '76, had always been the heroes of her imagination; and the crisis, in which she now found *herself* living and acting, rendered *their* crown of glory more luminous in her memory."[73] But when New England quietly refrains from sending aid, she sobs in despair, "Oh, Massachusetts! How I have *loved* thee!"[74] Abandoned to the mercy of Quantrill's goons, the settlers defend themselves, and Kate once more leads the way, now the star of a riotous western conclusion as she hides arms and aids the sick while wielding her pistol. To the end, she refrains from violence for courageous moral witness. Pistol in hand as she watches ruffians set fire to her home, Kate feels a strong temptation to take revenge, but she instead rebukes her assailants with a prophetic declaration. "You *think* you have silenced the Herald of Freedom, because you have demolished the printing press; but you are mistaken. That trumpet will sound across the prairies yet," she proclaims before riding off. "What a hell of a woman!" a drunken ruffian laughs.

In contrast to this heroism, the narrator repeats a plaintive refrain: "What cared New England that *her* six stars were looking down upon the scene, in shameful 'Union' with that blood-red flag?"[75] Child rechannels the Puritan spirit away from New England and into women's heroism as the settlers continue their ancestors' unfinished errand.[76]

The Kansas Emigrants failed to secure Frémont's election, but it did reach the widest and most receptive audience of any of Child's works to date, and three years later she repeated its potent mix of imagination and conscience plus "masculine" heroism and "feminine" moderation with even greater success in a defense of Bleeding Kansas's most infamous hero. After John Brown's failed attack on Harper's Ferry, Child found herself more than ever pulled between pacifism and battle. She lamented Brown's strategy as "sadly mistaken" but praised its purpose and again found her imagination electrified by its millennial hues, what she deemed "the 'Concord *Fight*' of an impending revolution."[77] Lauding Brown as "that honest old Puritan" who "believed, more earnestly than most of us do, that . . . it was serving God to fight in a righteous cause," she took up her pen not only to aid that cause but to participate vicariously in it.[78] As Brown sat imprisoned in Virginia, Child wrote to him with an expression of sympathy and solidarity. To ensure that Brown would receive the letter, she also included a tactful letter to Virginia governor Henry Wise, requesting permission to write and perhaps visit the prisoner. Child intended both to be private. They would become her most public work as Child attempted a more literal enactment of the kind of Puritan female heroism she enshrined in *The Kansas Emigrants*—at once feminine and heroic, peaceful and moral yet willing to fight.

Child's letter to Governor Wise balanced persuasion with conviction. She opened by grounding her motives in traditional gender values, invoking her "impulse of sympathy for the brave and suffering man," for Brown "needs a mother or sister to dress his wounds."[79] But Child quickly shifted to a plain profession of convictions. "I have been for years an uncompromising abolitionist, and I should scorn to deny it or apologize for it," she states, and though she regretted Brown's violence, "if I believed our religion justified men in fighting for freedom"—as many of her abolitionist allies increasingly did—"I should consider the enslaved everywhere as best entitled to that right." Child concluded on a more diplomatic note, promising to keep such opinions to herself if allowed to visit.

Wise replied with what he supposed was a clever rebuke to feminine naiveté. "Why should you not be so allowed, Madam?" he opened politely. He was "bound to protect" Child's citizen rights, should she visit—though he couldn't guarantee similar kindly treatment from other citizens, he warned. In a sharp pivot, Wise was as honest in his own convictions as Child had been. "We have no sympathy with your sentiments of sympathy with Brown, and are surprised that you were 'taken by surprise when news came of Captain Brown's recent attempt.' His attempt was a natural consequence of your sympathy," he said, mocking her sentimental tropes of sympathy as a cover for Brown's barbarity. As a final insult, Wise sent the private correspondence to the press, confident that the public would applaud his retort.[80]

When Child discovered both her letter and Wise's reply in the *New York Tribune*, the gloves were off. She crafted a multistage response that would transform a private expression of sympathy into a biting public rebuke and her most influential piece of writing. First, Child cunningly ignored Wise and instead wrote a piece called "Explanatory Letter to the Editor," noting that she never intended publicity but simply desired "to go and nurse that brave and generous old man, . . . to slip away quietly, without having the affair made public." Child also submitted her original letter to Brown in order to shift the debate back onto her own terms, where she pledged herself an "an earnest friend of Kansas"—writing herself into her own *The Kansas Emigrants* story, which had appeared in the *Tribune* a few years prior—and again balanced pacifism with heroism. "Believing in peace principles, I cannot sympathize with the method," she maintained, but "I admire your courage, moral and physical." She concluded once more with sympathy for this heroism, which she now aimed to extend throughout America via a vivid imagination of Brown's martyrdom. "Thousands of hearts are throbbing with sympathy as warm as mine," she affirmed. "I think of you night and day, bleeding in prison, surrounded by hostile faces, sustained only by trust in God and your own strong heart. I long to nurse you—to speak to you sisterly words of sympathy and consolation." In this manner Child turned on its head Wise's attempt to depict a chivalric statesman and a naive woman. In aiming to publicly humiliate a maternal and moral woman, Wise now looked like an ungentlemanly fiend, while Brown, framed by the conventions of womanly sympathy, looked less like a violent fanatic and more like a fallen Puritan hero from Child's Kansas story. Child in turn positioned herself as a catalyst and conduit for national sympathies toward such heroism.[81]

Child let her letter circulate for a week before landing a more aggressive takedown of Wise himself, again bundling a variety of tactics for widest appeal.[82] She amplified her arguments some weeks later when the wife of a Virginia senator attacked her in the press. In response, Child lauded "all the women of New England" for habits of philanthropy and fair wages that shamed Southern womanhood. ("After we have helped the mothers," she concluded bitingly, "*we do not sell the babies*.")[83] When the woman called for a boycott of her writing, Child successfully synthesized her dueling desires for literature and reform, imagination and conscience, rapture and war. "Literary popularity was never a paramount object with me," she remarked casually though disingenuously. In her concluding paragraph, she listed her "honorable company" among fellow antislavery holy warriors:

> Dr. Channing's writings, mild and candid as they are, breathe what you would call arrant treason. William C. Bryant, in his capacity of editor, is openly on our side. The inspired muse of Whittier has incessantly sounded the trumpet for moral warfare with your iniquitous institution . . . answered, more or less loudly, by Pierpont, Lowell, and Longfellow. Emerson, the Plato of America, leaves the scholastic seclusion he loves so well, and, disliking noise with all his poetic soul, bravely takes his stand among the trumpeters. . . . The genius of Mrs. Stowe carried the outworks of your institution at one dash, and left the citadel open to besiegers, who are pouring in amain. In the church, on the ultra-liberal side, it is assailed by the powerful battering-ram of Theodore Parker's eloquence. On the extreme orthodox side is set a huge fire, kindled by the burning words of Dr. Cheever. Between them is Henry Ward Beecher, sending a shower of keen arrows into your intrench-

ments; and with him ride a troop of sharp-shooters from all sects. . . . The fact is, the whole civilized world proclaims Slavery an outlaw, and the best intellect of the age is active in hunting it down.[84]

If these writers were replaced with Garrisonian activists, such a passage could have come from the Cromwellian imagination of Chapman herself. Papers across the nation reprinted Child's exchange with Wise and Mason, and an astounding number of Northern readers expressed their sympathy. Garrison and the American Anti-Slavery Society compiled and reissued the exchange as a five-cent tract that achieved a phenomenal circulation of three hundred thousand copies, Child's most successful work yet. As Child was receiving a flood of letters at once supportive and critical, she aimed to answer at least twenty a week.[85] The tract was even sent overseas in hopes of enlisting writers and revolutionaries like Harriet Martineau and Victor Hugo, Kossuth and Mazzini. Like Alice of *The Kansas Emigrants*, Child had performed her own Puritan revival of spiritual heroism. If she partly assumed the expected role of a motherly nurse extending her sympathy to the "honest old Puritan" while condemning his violence, such was an expression of her deeper impulses toward moral pugnacity and her desire to launch a "man's heart" out of "woman's destiny."

Through the Red Sea

As for many others, Child's thirty-year-long desire for Miltonic holy war was exacerbated by the outbreak of the Civil War. "I don't know how we could account for half the things that happen in the world," she wrote as the war ground on, "without calling in the aid of 'the dear old Devil,' as Emerson calls him."[86] But the war also gave her a pragmatic reason for venting this imagination: if violence akin to John Brown's was now inevitable on a national scale, she could use her literary energies to aim the conflict toward the same heroic and moral ends as she had done in *The Kansas Emigrants* and her letters to Brown. When President Lincoln refrained from declaring emancipation for the sake of the Border States' neutrality, Child wrote a letter to Lincoln himself, daringly challenging the president to hallow the war through emancipation. "It may seem a violation of propriety for a woman to address the Chief Magistrate of the nation," she began—in part facetiously, for Child and her readers felt that she had seized the nation's ear since *The Kansas Emigrants*—nearly threatening Lincoln as she lobbed quotes from the prophet Obadiah, warning him that "God is not mocked."[87] In a tone that at times lapsed from boldness into condescen-

sion, she asked, "Are you not aware that moral enthusiasm is the mighti-
est of all forces?" An emancipation proclamation would invigorate the
Union war effort with moral purpose and weed out its internal enemies,
an "Ithuriel's spear to disguised forms of selfishness and treason" that
"touched the toads and started up devils."[88] Child invoked Milton's devil-
revealing spear (a favored Garrisonian image) to prod Lincoln beyond political realism toward the higher calling of a righteous war, to "look upward
instead of downward." She urged the president to take up the spiritual warfare in which she and Chapman had been engaged for decades. "Lay your
right arm on the buckler of the Almighty, and march fearlessly forward to
universal freedom," she urged, "guided by Him who has said: 'First righteousness; and then peace.'"[89]

In addition to insisting on a proclamation of emancipation, Child
urged the president to sanctify the war by arming black troops, who she felt
were entitled more than anyone to the kind of militant revolution that she
had countenanced in John Brown and participated in imaginatively herself. If Chapman's Puritan militancy grew from an aristocratic demeanor
and Saxonist inclinations that strained her interactions with black activists,
Child aimed her militancy at artificial racial barriers as much as at gender.[90]
As early as 1841 Child had dramatized spiritual heroism's ability to break
down racial categories in a piece for the *Liberty Bell*, "The Black Saxons," the
story of a slaveowner who hears echoes of his own enslaved Saxon ancestry
when blacks debate whether or not to kill their masters, asking, "Was not
the spirit that gleamed forth" among his slaves "as brave as theirs?"[91] With
the outbreak of war, Child similarly found herself "groan[ing] out, O Lord!
O Lord! How we *do* need a Cromwell!," whether black or white, to maim
the sin of white supremacy as much as slavery.[92]

She found her desires fulfilled and her Puritanical imagination again
provoked by the martyrdom of Robert Gould Shaw and the black troops
of the Massachusetts Fifty-Fourth. Taking to the newspapers to lionize their
courage, she argued that Shaw's mass burial with his black troops was no
insult to any "pure and heroic soul" lifted "by principles . . . above the
possibility of feeling degraded by suffering with, and dying with, and being buried with God's despised and persecuted poor." Like a more heroic
version of Arthur Dimmesdale's vision of the Scarlet Letter in the sky, Child
even saw Shaw's initial floating in the air, "a narrow line of intensely brilliant sunlight, precisely in the form of an S." Though she admitted that
reading in this Puritanical way was silly, she reflected that "we are all more
or less inclined to be superstitious" when "the soul, in its utter helpless-
ness, looks tremblingly beyond this dark vale of shadows, and implores

some light from Heaven." Before the S disappeared into the clouds, Child felt lifted from "deep despondency," as if she had "caught a glimpse of the immortal glory into which he had entered" to rejoin other members of the noble Shaw family who "fought the moral battle against slavery with quiet but steadfast heroism for many years." She imagined Shaw reunited in eternal glory with the departed black soldiers of the Fifty-Fourth, now equals with their earthly leader.[93]

Child maintained her call for a holy war against prejudice after the end of the war, when even many antislavery activists found themselves battle-weary. With the work of reconstruction ahead, she aimed to empower freed slaves with their own heroic history through *The Freedmen's Book*, a series of her own biographical sketches of prominent African Americans interspersed with poetry and prose from black writers like Frances Harper, Charlotte Forten, George Moses Horton, and more. Child promised to direct all excess profits to the Freedmen's Aid Association and dedicated the book to the heroic Robert Smalls, a slave who freed his family by stealing a Confederate steamship. Despite her pacifism, Child devoted her lengthiest and most vivid sketch to "the pure and great soul of that martyred hero" Toussaint Louverture (fifty pages compared to most others sketches' ten). Like Wendell Phillips, she praised Touissant as a Carlylean hero in Puritanical hues, declaring through Whittier that "men shall learn to speak of thee / As one of earth's great spirits," emphasizing his "religious turn of mind" as a core part of his courage and his place in providential history. "God raised him up to do a great work, which he faithfully performed," Child concluded, and like Brown, Shaw, and the Fifty-Fourth, "his spirit is still 'marching on.'"[94]

Child sensed these black and white spirits marching in an unfinished war for reconstruction, especially as the Johnson administration grew conciliatory toward former Confederates and hostile toward Republicans. For nearly her last time, she went to the press with "Through the Red Sea into the Wilderness," typologically titled and strategically published just as Congress reconvened, in hopes of urging congressmen towards radical reconstruction by recounting the nation's heroic yet incomplete achievements. Child opened the piece by celebrating how much had already been achieved; the very fact that *The Freedmen's Book* had found an eager publisher with "the best press in the country," Ticknor & Fields, struck her as a poignant example. She marveled that a denigrated race was now seen "in every form of art and literature"—in new paintings and photographs, in the ubiquitous "John Brown's Body," in Massachusetts sculptor John Rogers's most famous works like *The Wounded Scout* (1864) depicting "a stalwart negro guiding a wounded soldier," a poignant vision for recon-struction. "There is indeed something marvelous in the moral electricity which flashes through all classes when the hour of great reformations is approaching. It is doubtless evolved by spiritual laws" akin to "the natu-ral laws which produce thunder and lightning when the atmosphere needs purification," she reflected, using the present-participle "is approaching" to emphasis this reformation's ongoing work and anticipating Eric Foner's view of Reconstruction as "America's unfinished revolution."[95] In an ex-plicit instance of Puritanical typology, she cast the war and reconstruction as an ongoing exodus: now that the nation had passed through the Red Sea of war, she wrote, "here we are in the Wilderness, with multitudes ready to bow down and worship the golden calf of trade, and a doubtful sort of Moses, who seems to occupy himself more earnestly with striving to save the drowning host of Pharaoh than he does with leading Israel into the promised land."[96] With the aggressive tone that had increasingly marked her political writing, Child challenged the Republican-controlled Congress to stand firm against Johnson in the same "solid phalanx" that antislavery women like Chapman and the BFAS had pioneered as Deborahs and Jaels for over thirty years: "Heaven preserve them from the old chronic disease of Congress—weakness of the spine!"[97]

As Child reflected on the nation's transformations since her entrance into abolitionism nearly four decades prior, she celebrated her prophetess sisters in the BFAS as heroic trailblazers in their spiritual warfare yet dis-tanced their work from the actual bloodshed of the Civil War. "The electric-ity of anti-slavery was attracted toward heroic natures, and its touch made them more heroic," she stated, echoing Emerson's language of spiritual heroism while lifting up the BFAS's courage in the face of the 1835 Boston Mob as her primary example.[98] In retrospect, the violence of that mob now seemed prophetic. "We early Abolitionists, you know, dreamed of great miracles to be wrought by moral influence," she reflected, admitting that "we were mistaken in that." Yet if they had failed to end slavery peacefully, antislavery women had successfully steeled the public to end it violently, for when "the sword came, would Northern sentiment have been in any readiness to meet the grand emergency had it not been for truths previ-ously scattered broadcast through the land by the warnings, exhortations, and rebukes of the early Abolitionists? I trow not."[99] Child never consid-ered whether her fellow Deborah and Jaels' attraction to spiritual heroics and the rhetoric of holy war had actually helped to provoke armed conflict rather than simply scattering idealist seeds to be reaped with the arrival of a separate war that they found unfortunate if necessary. For Chapman,

Howe, Child, BFAS members, and writers for the *Liberty Bell*, the short step from spiritual to real war was in fact much of the excitement for an emergent feminist consciousness eager to participate in both. But metaphors of holy war depended on real wars for their energy, and while such vision could inspire antislavery women with a fervency of cause, it strained against their commitment to nonviolence.

After William Lloyd Garrison died in May 1879, Child concluded her Puritan education with her last published work, a eulogy in the *Atlantic* for the reformer whose work had made her feel like a broom transformed into a living being. As with many eulogies for mentors, she spoke implicitly about herself as much as about him: "His character, had, undoubtedly, a strong stamp of Puritanism, partly in his organization, and partly the result of being reared in an atmosphere of Calvinism, . . . always stern and uncompromising in the rebuke of wrong."[100] In the midst of her celebration of life, Child said nothing of the current Exoduster crisis, a tragic inversion of her more hopeful vision of exodus as desperate freedpeople fled to Kansas to escape new forms of quasi-enslavement that had arisen with Reconstruction's collapse. The Promised Land seemed more distant than before, and it remained for a new generation of souls to resume the march. A year and a half later Child passed away, her own good fight fought.

THREE

A Paper Puritan of Puritans

The Lord began to work for his Church, not with sword and target to subdue
His exalted adversary, but with printing, writing and reading. . . . Either the pope
must abolish knowledge and printing or printing at length will root him out.

—John Foxe, *Book of Martyrs, 1563*

As Christmas 1865 approached the first year of peace since the start of the
Civil War, William Lloyd Garrison inked the type for the final issue of the
Liberator, awed that he had lived to see the revolution in public opinion
and the end of the sin that his paper had fought weekly for the last thirty-
five years. Yet Garrison had begun this mission in 1831 with the certitude
of a prophet. Expressing his gratitude to Boston's black community for the
support that sustained the *Liberator* in its first year, he spoke in a manner
that was confident, grandiose, even pompous, many would say. He foresaw
a "path which I am destined to tread," one that would lead him unharmed
through foes "prophesying, and expecting, the downfall of the paper." He
did not "despair of a change in public sentiment" even in 1831, when the
entire nation seemed set against the cause, for he had his own prophetic
vision: he was "ready to give up his life for them and become a martyr to
a great cause" because they were all living in an "age of great events" when
"our enemies are growing less confident, and begin to 'hide their dimin-
ished heads.'"[1] The quote, one of Garrison's favorites, came from *Paradise
Lost* as Satan rued "warring in Heaven against Heaven's matchless King."
It was an apt image for his prophetic sense of "great events" in the making
akin to a new English Revolution.[2] In 1865 he felt that the war had confirmed his Puritanical prophecies.

Many contemporaries agreed that the *Liberator* had crafted a potent Puritanical rhetoric in the decades leading to the war, for better or for worse. Garrison was especially pleased, for instance, to print a letter to the editor from one "B" in the *Liberator*'s final issue. "We want a paper that shall be Puritan of the Puritans," B wrote, "and such a paper I esteem the Liberator to have been. Puritanism in the best sense is moral, not ecclesiastical; and herein it is to be transmitted and perpetuated." B was only repeating what the *Liberator* itself had said with astounding frequency over its continuous 1,828-issue run from 1831 to 1865. The Puritans appeared in every other issue, on average (it took nearly a thousand nonabolitionist newspapers to reach the same frequency), more frequently as tensions rose around slavery, and usually positing the same radical genealogies as Lowell, Emerson, Child, or Chapman.[3] In 1856 a journalist praised the New England guerrillas bleeding in Kansas as "worthy sons of Puritan sires," while in 1864 Unitarian clergyman Amory Dwight Mayo sketched a more explicit genealogy of "religious opposition to despotism" similar to Emerson's heresiarchs. "The priestly and civil absolutism of the sixteenth century called it 'fanaticism,'" he wrote, while "the church and crown nicknamed it 'Puritanism,' and persecuted it till it turned and cut off the head of Charles the First, and secured religion's liberty. The slave aristocracy stigmatized 'Abolitionism,' and let loose upon it every infernal agency in its power." Mayo concluded that the "best in Northern society" grew from "this 'fanaticism,' 'Puritanism,' 'Abolitionism.'"[4]

Garrison's platform of immediatism (attacking slavery less as a political problem than as a sin requiring immediate moral conversion) may be one reason the *Liberator*'s writers went back to the Puritan past so often. Another was his skillful use of what friends and foes deemed "harsh language," imagined by many as a revival of the Reformation's iconoclastic legacies. But even more specifically, these journalists invoked the Puritans because they believed that the *Liberator* was reviving their sacred use of print. Hundreds of writers joined B in praising the *Liberator* as "Puritanism in the best sense," lionizing not just "manly" orators and female organizing as its modern heirs but especially a dissenting press. Wendell Phillips resurrected the Puritans at Faneuil Hall to defend Elijah Lovejoy's work as an antislavery printer, for instance, while Child used one of the country's first truly national newspapers to serialize a neo-Pilgrim western that culminated in the destruction of an abolitionist press. Both traced their moral awakening on slavery not to a preacher, philosopher, or politician, but to a printer and his paper, Garrison arising as their Gutenberg, Luther, and Milton in one.[5] Garrison welcomed and bolstered these frequent comparisons as he and his allies situated the abolitionist press squarely within a revolutionary Protestant print heritage. Many joined Garrison in praising the "descendants of the Pilgrim Fathers" and the "earnest seekers" who "go much further than did Luther," Calvin, and even Milton in defending "that great palladium of human rights, the press."[6]

Cassius M. Clay furnished a representative example when he contested the Mexican War with an "empire of liberty" sprung from Protestantism and print. "When I consider the Reformation and the invention of the press," he declared, and "a continent open for the infusion of those elementary principles of liberty which were dwarfed in European soil, I have conceived that the hand of destiny was there! When I saw the immigration of the Pilgrims from the chalky shores of England . . . I have ventured to think that the will of Deity was there!"[7] Here too was a usable past rather than good history; of course Catholics utilized print as well, while the Puritan colonies had hindered freedom of speech for Quakers and dissenters like Roger Williams and Anne Hutchinson. If abolitionists admitted (and lamented) such history, they generally approached such episodes as exceptions that proved the broader arc of providence: after a more enlightened, democratic, "purer" religion had been salvaged from papal and monarchical tyranny by print-savvy Protestant and Puritan reformers, it especially blossomed in the fertile soils of the New World with the Pilgrim-Puritan colonies and the American Revolution. When Reverend Mayo lauded the Puritan roots of "all that was best in Northern society," he especially meant a tradition of Protestant print culture, and one that was increasingly under attack for its critiques of slavery. After the pope and two English kings, the Slave Power was the final despot waiting to be toppled by print-slinging Protestants.

As with shifting antebellum gender norms, the revolutionary Puritan hue subscribed to and bolstered by the abolitionist press arose in response to an increasingly secular and capitalist public sphere, especially embodied in a print culture that had grown explosively from the local and regional to the national, from tracts, sermons, and select devotional texts to a mass media landscape dominated by penny presses and affordable weeklies churned out with the help of new technologies like cheap paper, stereotype plates, the steam press, and railways.[8] David Hall argues for a shift from Protestant scarcity to Victorian abundance, from a print culture with relatively few books and reverential reading practices grounded in Puritanism to what many have described with Laura Langer Cohen as the "print explosion of the antebellum years" sparked by a market and industrial revolution. As a culture of devotional reading succumbed to a hastier market of journalism and novels fueled by consumer tastes, Hall explains, "no book, not even the Bible, retained the aura that certain texts had once possessed. Bit by bit, the structure of traditional literacy unraveled as print became abundant, school books were secularized, and the steady [devotional] sellers vanished."[9] Such portrayals often imply a concurrent shift from the sacred to the secular: antebellum Americans "transmut[ed] Protestantism into Victorianism," in Hall's words, while more recent studies of antebellum print culture have told similar "subtraction stories," to use Charles Taylor's term, in which religion seems to fade from history as an active force while capitalist abundance rises.[10] But if an explosive antebellum print culture indeed diversified America's reading landscape and shifted power from the clergy to editors and journalists, the story of religiosity within this shifting landscape is not one of subtraction but of evolution in which Protestant spirituality adapted and assumed more complex forms. In the most obvious instance, traditional religious institutions tapped into new print powers to expand their spiritual reach—preachers began publishing sermons in papers, while something resembling modern mass media was born with the American Tract and American Bible Societies, as David Paul Nord shows.[11]

The antislavery press's reclamation of Puritanism reveals a more complex reaction to the changing nature of print culture in the antebellum public sphere. While America's Congregationalist and Presbyterian churches claimed to be the Puritans' most immediate institutional and doctrinal heirs, the abolitionist press argued that they had abandoned the most vital facet of this heritage in acquiescing to an alliance of printers, planters, politicians, and merchants who increasingly foreclosed abolitionist protest in the public sphere. Goaded by this alliance, many orthodox believers denounced the abolitionist press not only as a threat to the republic's political Union but also as a secular attack by "infidels" upon American Protestantism. In turn the abolitionist press positioned itself as Puritanism's *true* heir—"moral" rather than "ecclesiastical," in B's words—precisely because it challenged the institutional church and its ties to a despotic social order. Abolitionists revived the original spiritual impulses of Protestantism and Puritanism that had ossified via institutionalization and socialization, the argument went, by mobilizing modern print technologies and defenses of free speech for a sacred cause. Inextricably linked ever since Luther declared the printing press "God's highest and extremest act of grace," Protestant spirituality and modern print technology had together progressively democratized the world by deposing popes and kings through the free circulation of dissent, and the abolitionist press made a show of seizing this baton.[12]

In the first decade of the abolitionist movement, Garrison had cemented himself and his paper squarely within this lineage and perfected a style that bolstered his performance of Protestant martyr-prophet, and by the time he would retire the *Liberator* in 1865, his performance had drawn a critical mass of Americans into its imaginative orbit. For aspiring writers awash in an explosion of print and a sense of texts' declining sacredness, the *Liberator* filled a spiritual void by claiming this mantle. At the time of Garrison's death in 1879, Child affirmed his "strong stamp of Puritanism" and fondly recalled "the missionary work of the old Liberator days" when "the Holy Spirit did actually descend upon men and women in tongues of flame." Long after the war, a Boston woman spoke similarly of Garrison as a "savior from a cold and selfish life," more responsible for her "spiritual joy and growth than all other influences combined."[13]

Press and Pulpit in the Public Sphere

This reclamation of Puritan print was first sparked by the collision of Garrison's evangelical convictions with clergy who he felt had ignored its antislavery implications. As Henry Mayer notes, Garrison's platform of moral suasion, immediatism, and come-outerism was "not so much a political tactic as an expression of the evangelical consciousness" first imbibed from his mother's days among New England Baptists. This consciousness was strengthened when Garrison arrived in Boston as an ambitious printer in 1826 just as Lyman Beecher thundered his orthodox cannons at the city gates, intent on reclaiming the Puritan capital from the Unitarian rule of William Ellery Channing.[14] While he admired Channing's learning, Garrison was especially attracted to Beecher's philanthropic energy, and he made a point to attend the preacher's North End services twice a week. Eager to elevate the nation in their own ways, both leaders spoke powerfully to the young man, who soon decided that he could do similar work, not as a traditional preacher but as the organizer of "a new race of editors" who would use the powers of print to "enhance the value of public opinion" by "fearlessly maintain[ing] the truth" in "every moral enterprise." What the preacher did for his congregation the printer could do for a a much larger readership. Such an approach to print was novel in its attempt to harmonize vocations usually considered separate, one sacred and the other secular: while the preacher had been considered a spiritual leader for two centuries, the printer-editor was a younger and greasier species sprung from the partisanship of the 1790s, often considered a sensationalist and opportunistic party tool. Garrison admitted that "for many years, indeed, [the editor's] reputation has been sullied by the conduct, character, and principles of many who have aspired to fill it," but he positioned himself as part of a new generation of editors with "nobler views," using the press the way Beecher and Channing used their pulpits.[15]

After a transformative encounter with Benjamin Lundy in 1828 and the explosive effect of David Walker's *Appeal* in Boston and the South the following year, Garrison grew convinced that slavery was the great sin of his era and that—as with any sin in the evangelical consciousness—no halfway measures would do.[16] Garrison's newfound immediatism lent focus to his vocation as reformer-printer, but it also grated on his more temperate models. As this divergence in tone and tactics became more pronounced, Garrison increasingly conceptualized the role of editor-printer less as an extension of the pulpit's spiritual authority than as its successor, heir to its moral mission if the clergy continued to avoid their duty to purify the public sphere of slavery by clinging to the dead forms of their office. Two concrete problems spurred this ideological shift: the struggle to secure stable venues for speaking and printing, and clerical wagon-circling to shun immediatists from their ranks. Garrison struggled with both in his first antislavery speech on the eve of the *Liberator*'s birth as administrators of churches and town halls, unwilling to risk controversy or property damage, closed their doors to his requests for a venue. Only after Garrison managed to place an ad in the *Courier* that threatened to preach on the Boston Common did he secure a venue through Abner Kneeland's freethinking Universalist Society.[17] After an impassioned address there on the evening of October 15, 1830, he was surprised to gain a zealous convert in the Unitarian minister and well-connected Brahmin Samuel J. May, who eventually became one of Garrison's most valuable allies. ("That night," May reflected, using the same Pentecostal language as Child, "my soul was baptized in his spirit, and ever since I have been a disciple and fellow laborer of William Lloyd Garrison.") The rest of Boston's Unitarians proved less receptive, as did Lyman Beecher and the orthodox. In attendance that night, Beecher attempted to corral Garrison's zeal within the bounds of the American Colonization Society. "If you will give up your fanatical notions and be guided by us," he promised, "we will make you the Wilberforce of America."[18] Having already become convinced that the colonizationist movement was a compromise with a rotten status quo, Garrison quipped that this was the first time Beecher advocated a "gradual abolition of wickedness."[19]

If such leaders could not be convinced to treat slavery as sin, Garrison avowed that he would build an alternate structure for shifting the terms of debate in America's public sphere: he would agitate public opinion directly through an alternative press until it shifted, forcing leaders to concede. "You and I will continue to cry 'woe, woe, woe,'" May wrote eagerly, "until the Channings and Beechers in the land are roused to answer the demand of the people."[20] With support from Boston's black community and the wealthy evangelical Lewis Tappan, Garrison released the first issue of the *Liberator* three months later, on New Year's Day 1831. "My conscience is now satisfied," he declared on the front page, posing his mission for immediate abolition against the moderation of Beecher and Channing. "I am aware, that many object to the severity of my language; but is there not cause for severity?" he asked. "On this subject, I do not wish to think, or speak, or write, with moderation. No! No! tell a man whose house is on fire, to give a moderate alarm," he wrote, perfecting a style of increasing urgency that mirrored the fiery revivalists of the Second Great Awakening, and concluded in pounding prose: "I am in earnest—I will not equivocate—I will not excuse—I will not retreat a single inch—AND I WILL BE HEARD."[21] Thus began a career of capitalization, exclamation, and conflagration that bore a distinct resemblance to David Walker's incendiary *Appeal*, still fresh in many minds.

As with Walker, alarmed citizens soon argued that such incendiarism exceeded the bounds of free speech in its potential to stir up slave revolt and destroy the republic that safeguarded these freedoms. Garrison just as quickly retorted that the right to print and speak freely and harshly on matters of conscience was not merely a constitutional construct dependent on a political union, but a deeper spiritual demand that rested in the authority of God alone, an impulse that had fueled a sacred Puritan heritage that predated, created, and sustained the republic. This struggle over the boundaries of speech in the public sphere quickly reached a boiling point, and the New York City antiabolitionist riots of 1834 were among the first results. Controversies began when Arthur Tappan underwrote the formation of a female antislavery society and made a public statement by sitting in a segregated pew next to Samuel Cornish, the editor of America's first black paper, *Freedom's Journal*. Even more than in Boston, abolitionists were a bothersome minority among New York's wealthy elite, and tensions were doubly high among the city's Irish, who resented the prospect of competition with black workers. When abolitionists planned a celebration of emancipation, riots erupted for three days, targeting black and abolitionist homes, churches, and business. Beginning a trend that would continue until the Civil War, popular periodicals like the *Journal of Commerce* blamed the unrest on abolitionists, while the colonizationist editor James Watson Webb added fuel to the fire in his *Courier and Enquirer* by insinuating that abolitionists were encouraging interracial romances (Tappan, he implied, had left his wife for a black woman). In response, the *Liberator* asked if a new Dark Age was overturning the nation's Protestant heritage. "Has it come to this, that in free America, men cannot express their opinions, because the whole community almost, holds to opposite opinions? . . . Are *an infuriated mob* to act as censors of the pulpit and the press?" one writer asked. "God forbid. Sooner will we fight the battles of the Revolution over again, or dive into the recesses of the wilderness, where we can think, speak and act, according to the dictates of our judgments. . . . So would have said the Pilgrims, the Huguenots, and every other genuine aspirant after liberty." The riots confirmed the antislavery press's sense that it was tending a Pilgrim flame in a moral wilderness.[22]

This mission became personal for Garrison the following year, when the American Antislavery Society organized America's first mass mail campaign, a vast effort to send abolitionist periodicals and pamphlets to leaders in the South. When this mail arrived in the port of Charleston on July 29, 1835, a mob broke into the post office and burned the lot alongside effigies of Tappan and Garrison, cheered on by a crowd of two thousand people. This censorship came to Boston the next month when a mob shut down a speech by British abolitionist George Thompson and nearly lynched Garrison. Once more Garrison immediately turned to his press to mythologize the event as an assault on a sacred heritage of free speech. In his account for the *Liberator* (reprinted frequently in the year to come), Garrison shifted the terms of abolitionism to prod the conscience of apathetic white readers. "The great question to be settled is not whether 2,500,000 slaves in our land shall be either immediately or gradually emancipated," he wrote, but "whether the liberty of speech and of the press, purchased, with the tolls and sufferings and precious blood of our fathers, is still to be enjoyed, unquestioned and complete—or whether padlocks are to be put upon our lips; gags into our mouths, and shackles upon that great palladium of human rights, the press; whether the descendants of the Pilgrim fathers . . . [are] to speak or be dumb, and to walk freely or with a chain upon their spirit." If white Northerners cared little about the rights of black Americans, Garrison hoped to rouse them by repositioning slavery as a threat to their own cherished Pilgrim and Patriot traditions of a free press.[23]

As the clergy remained wary of speaking forthrightly on this increasingly volatile issue, each of these events further radicalized Garrison's sense of Puritanical mission as he increasingly came to consider himself "an apostle of radical Christian liberty in the Miltonic tradition," in Henry Mayer's words. While "the bedrock of his faith remained the Protestant's right of private conscience," he grew frustrated with what felt like a conscious effort on the part of the clergy to suppress his own, and under the influence of John Humphrey Noyes's intense brand of Finneyite perfectionism, Garrison thundered at his former heroes Channing and Beecher in a storm of Puritanical fervor, accusing them of dead formalisms that abdicated their historical charge.[24] When Channing outlined a more staid antislavery argument in his 1835 *Slavery* and denounced the "showy, noisy" tactics of the immediatists, Garrison responded by reprinting in the *Liberator* a celebrated essay that Channing had formerly written on Milton, in particular a passage where he defended the poet's harsh polemic during the English Civil War. While Channing generally read Milton as what he himself hoped to be, in the words of Kevin P. Van Anglen "a high-minded defender of dominant class authority," Garrison cleverly excerpted the passage where even Channing could admit that desperate times required a cutting polemic from Milton.[25] "Liberty was in peril," Channing had written, "and who will blame [Milton] for . . . defending [it] with fervor and vehemence?" Such enthusiasm was appropriate to "those great periods which have been distinguished by revolutions in government and religion," he concluded. In the pages of the *Liberator* such quotes acquired an ironic new resonance within the current struggle with slavery, perhaps the latest of these "great periods." With a clever grandiosity, Garrison quietly praised his movement and himself via Channing's ode to Milton. "At such periods, men gifted with great power of thought and loftiness of sentiment are especially summoned to the conflict with evil. . . . They must and will speak with an indignant energy, and they ought not to be measured by the standard of ordinary minds in ordinary times."[26]

The next summer Garrison similarly attacked Beecher, who proved even more infuriating in a denominational circling of wagons that surpassed Channing's reticence. After Garrison refused his invitation to work as a moderate reformer in his approved benevolent organizations, Beecher had convinced Congregationalist and Presbyterian associations across the North to deny their pulpits to itinerant speakers deemed "dangerous to the influence of the pastoral office and fatal to the peace and good order of the churches." Everyone understood that he meant the abolitionist firebrands rallying around Garrison and his pulpit-paper, and by 1836 every church in Boston had heeded Beecher's call. That year the Massachusetts Anti-Slavery Society was forced to hold its annual meeting in a horse barn, and while Garrison could joke with allies that the movement finally had "a *stable* foundation," he lashed out at Beecher in the voice of Luther and Milton: Beecher's goons were "selling indulgences" and "lulling consciences," aiding the South "in all its turpitude of crime, rather than peril the union between Christ and Belial!"[27] As with Channing, the implication was clear: in the midst of a new Reformation, New England's preachers were failing to live up to their forebears' legacies and were allying themselves instead with Pandemonium.

The link between America's Puritan-Pilgrim heritage and a free abolitionist press reached its apex with the death of the printer Elijah Lovejoy in 1837 after his antislavery press had been destroyed by a mob, moved, rebuilt, and destroyed anew in St. Louis, Missouri, and Alton, Illinois, the year prior. After the first attack, the *Liberator* ran Wendell Phillips's declaration that slavery "chills the blood of the Puritans, till their sons cease to remember that it was liberty to think and speak as we pleased, which planted our rocky hills." Four months later it ran a warning from the Boston merchant George Russell to work "till the principles of our Pilgrim fathers are carried to their full extent" by "erect[ing] the lightning rods of freedom of speech, and freedom of the press."[28] After Lovejoy's death, even Channing found himself unsettled enough to call the public meeting in Boston at which Phillips rose to prominence. Channing insisted that they focus on a defense of free speech and avoid "mix[ing] up the meeting with Abolition," but defending free speech in the abstract while foreclosing actual free speech on real topics of concern was an oxymoron for Garrison.[29] Instead Garrison reprinted a more encouraging report by the Portland Anti-Slavery Society from Lovejoy's native Maine on the occasion of the printer's death: "We consider it the duty of the sons of the Pilgrims, at the hazard of their property and lives, to maintain, and transmit to their posterity, the principles of liberty, pure and free as they were received from the Puritans. Resolved, that we consider every citizen called upon, in a special manner, to use his utmost influence, in every lawful and proper way, to preserve our rights—the liberty of the press, the pen, the tongue."[30]

By the end of the 1830s, the connection between a Puritan heritage and a dissenting antislavery press was secure. It was reused and bolstered in the decades leading to war as the cause faced new threats. Whether addressing the congressional "Gag Rule" barring discussion of antislavery petitions from 1836 to 1844 or continued opposition to the gathering of female antislavery societies, the *Liberator* continued to rally its readers around a revolutionary Protestant heritage of free speech and press.[31] If this connection often coalesced intuitively and spontaneously from concrete conflicts over spiritual authority in the public sphere, it remains to be examined *why* this connection proved intuitive, captivating, and useful.

Harsh Spirits

Most immediately, the Puritan past sanctioned an aggresive style that thrilled allies, angered enemies, and exasperated moderates. Perhaps no movement in American history was so frequently preoccupied with defending its aesthetic as Garrisonians, constantly parrying the charge of "harsh language." Already on the *Liberator*'s very first page Garrison was "aware, that many object to the severity of my language," and while critics argued that this tone risked upsetting a precarious Union, Garrison always doubled down with rhetorical cannonade, even on the eve of war. "If the state cannot survive the anti-slavery agitation, then let the State perish," he wrote, and "if the church must be cast down by the struggles of humanity to be free, then let the church fall . . . consumed by a living thunderbolt."[32]

Nearly fifty years later Lydia Maria Child still felt obliged to defend such bombast to the broader readership of the *Atlantic* in her eulogy for Garrison. "He was dealing with something more formidable than flies, and weapons stronger than feathers were needed," she explained. (Margaret Fuller described the issue with her more characteristic haughtiness: "It is no wonder that he speaks loud, when he has so long been calling to deaf people.")[33] A Puritan heritage widely respected for its plainspeak and its moments of iconoclasm could do much to fit this style into a venerated lineage. By stitching themselves into this history, Garrisonians defended their right to speak and write with as much militancy as they felt necessary.

Here the *Liberator* responded to a broader debate over appropriate style as periodicals grew increasingly central to the American public sphere and increasingly distant from the stateliness of New England's clerical leadership. Even the orthodox American Tract Society consciously rejected the "stateliness of a sermon" to avoid "repel[ling] the general reader by elaborate expositions, or abstract discussions, or incessant exhortations. No; the newspaper requires varied and lively talent in a style of its own . . . brief, tersely written, highly evangelical articles, suited to claim and reward the attention of half a million of readers."[34] As David Paul Nord notes, the resulting product "read remarkably like the sentimental, romantic novels and story papers that the editors deplored," and for this reason, religious editors "never felt at ease with popular genre publishing" and instead "believed that religious truth, however sweetened or simplified, was difficult."[35] A similar mix of acquiescence and resistance to the democratic trends of print marked the abolitionist press, where a desire to garner broader audiences with new styles battled an insistence on the blunt truth of their depictions of slavery and a mission to challenge the nation with the difficult truths of its economy. But a key difference arose in the abolitionist focus on a national rather than personal sin, urging the press into repeated and often personal conflict with the institutional leadership of the American church and state; more specifically, the disunionist and come-outer impulses of Garrisonianism often resulted in sweeping indictments of the institutions themselves, as when Garrison sought to smite church and state alike with "a living thunderbolt." Here especially the Puritans proved useful in sanctioning a style many deemed uncivil in its critique of the church.

The divergent approaches of incendiary Garrison and august Channing are illustrative. In *Slavery*, Channing betrayed an obvious unease not only with Garrisonians' "tone unfriendly both to manners and to the spirit of our religion" but also with their rowdier Jacksonian manner of organization, which diverged from the genteel models of leadership he sought to embody.[36] Channing argued that the American Anti-Slavery Society should have been an "elective" association composed of carefully chosen "men of strong principles, judiciousness, sobriety," in line with the benevolent societies he had built. Instead they "gather together young and old, pupils from schools, females hardly arrived at years of discretion, the ignorant, the excitable, the impetuous," and "very unhappily they preached their doctrine to the colored people." Here was the real threat of Garrisonian bombast: it might spark mobs from polloi kindling, in particular from black readers. "To this mixed and excitable multitude, minute, heart-rending descriptions of slavery were given in the piercing tones of passion," a tactic altogether "unfriendly to the spirit of Christianity" as much as to a stable republic.[37] Channing admitted that mobs were a part of the American Revolution, but this was because a revolution was then needed to throw off a monarchy for a republic; with the republic now established and a constitution that was the marvel of the West, mobs only threatened to destroy a precious experiment in self-rule. The entire dynamic of shifting power from enlightened leaders to impressionable masses was amplified by a press that could deliver the intoxicating Garrisonian style to Americans across the nation. "A newspaper, which openly or by innuendoes excites a mob, should be regarded as sounding the tocsin of insurrection," Channing asserted. "The tone of their newspapers, as far as I have seen them, has often been fierce, bitter, and abusive."[38]

Channing's worries that a print-crazed mob could destroy the republic resembled Plato's fear in the *Phaedrus* that the invention of writing would similarly destroy the dialogic basis of enlightened republican leadership. Against Channing's Hellenic sense of the public sphere, Garrison posed a more Hebraic and indeed Puritanical model. When he responded by reprinting Channing's essay on Milton in the *Liberator*, he highlighted Channing's own recognition that the English Civil War was a crowning example of moments in history when dialogue was insufficient for spiritual reformation and iconoclastic conflict was instead required. "We must not mistake Christian benevolence, as if it had but one voice, that of soft entreaty," Channing formerly wrote and Garrison now quoted, for "that deep feeling of evils, which is necessary to effectual conflict with them, and which marks God's most powerful messengers to mankind, cannot breathe itself in soft and tender accents. The deeply moved soul will speak strongly, and ought to speak so as to move and the working-men and the aristocracy."[39] One wonders whether Channing read his own words back to himself in the pages of the *Liberator*, perhaps blushing, perhaps annoyed. Here was another unwieldy power of print: the ability to revive and recontextualize former statements for purposes beyond the author's intentions. With this tactic, Garrison sanctioned his style not only with the Puritans but with the very words of a respected national clergyman, bypassing dialogue with Channing for a more aggressive and aggravating use of language.

Garrison most fully theorized this style in the essay "Harsh Language." In place of Channing's Habermasian sense of the public sphere as a process best perfected through rational debate, he posed a prophetic-romantic model in which "indignant spirits" goad a nation's apathetic conscience with aggressive rhetoric. "That my language has been rough . . . is true: but why?" Garrison asked, "because any other language would have been inappropriate and ineffectual; because my theme was not a gentle one, about buds, and blossoms, and flowers . . . but about a nation of boasting Republicans and Christians, ruthlessly consigning to chains and slavery every sixth person born in the land. . . . Call things by their right names, and let the indignant spirit find free utterance." Brimming with the language of prophecy, he cast aside objections to this style, for "honeyed accents were tried in vain for years." For precedent he turned again to a familiar genealogy of Old Testament prophets, Reformation dissenters, New England Puritans, and Revolutionary patriots, weaving between the prophet Ezekiel, "the earnest inquiry in 1776," Martin Luther, and the "Pride of New England! / Soul of our fathers!"[40]

At the heart of this style and lineage was a particular "political theology of print," to use Steven Mailloux's term, that hinted at the appeal of the Garrisonian ideology for antebellum seekers.[41] If the story of sacred history was the unfolding of liberty inaugurated by the Reformation, the press played a crucial role in this process as a protagonist in its own right and a potent medium on behalf of liberty in its ability to speak directly to millions of readers. "Thanks to the Printing-Press," Phillips declared in a speech titled "Public Opinion," "wherever you have a reading people, there every tongue, every press, is a power. . . . What gunpowder did for war, the printing-press has done for the mind."[42]

Such idealism was both theological and strategic. Abolitionists were more acquainted than most with the ways in which a dissenting press's idealistic message was nonetheless rooted in and susceptible to material forces—the cost of postage and paper, congressional gag laws passed by blocs invested in the slave economy, the brute violence of proslavery mobs destroying their presses, and more. But the physical press was imagined as the medium of an expansive and dynamic *spiritual* message. The *Liberator*'s paper pages and wooden presses were the vessels for its revelations—like a martyr's body, their material base could be destroyed, but their witness lived on. Writing for the *Liberator* in 1835, one Reverend Waterman asked, "Did the silencing of Wickliffe stay reform? Did the abandonment of the press of the Pilgrims in Leyden, stay the progress of thought?" Will today's truth "dropped, thick as flakes of snow, in our cities, and towns, and western valley . . . lie and rot in the room where it was sterotyped [*sic*], printed, and folded?" If the press was destroyed or the printer killed, "the work goes on. God sustains it."[43] Elevating the press above bullets as Protestantism's superior weapon was also strategic rhetoric: it helped to convince allies that they could overcome formidable material forces. Wendell Phillips declared public opinion and the press the strongest force yet seen by history. "The great statesmen had pledged themselves not to talk on this subject. They have been made to talk," he declared to a cheering crowd, "not by *three* newspapers, which Napoleon dreaded, but by *one*."[44]

This theology of the press grew from and reinforced the Garrisonian belief that slavery was less a political problem than a sin requiring a change of spirit. References to "spirit," "spiritual," and a "spirit of X" abound in the *Liberator*, often attached to nouns that could just as well stand on their own—the spirit of the Gospel, of calculating politicians, of the Constitution, etc.[45] To speak of the "spirit of" something was not uncommon in antebellum parlance, but the *Liberator* relied on the formula to an extraordinary degree, recurring to the phrase nearly six times as frequently as a group of Southern periodicals, three times as frequently as the Free Soil Party's *Emancipator-Republican*, and even more often than the *Congregationalist*, Boston's voice for religious orthodoxy.[46] If measured by recurrence to the term alone, the *Liberator* seems to have been more preoccupied with matters of the "spirit" than other publications, unsurprisingly most concerned with the "spirit of slavery" and the "spirit of liberty/freedom."[47]

After John Quincy Adams used similar language in his congressional battle against the gag laws, denouncing the Slave Power's effort to make "perpetuation of slavery the vital and animating spirit of the national government," the *Liberator* returned to the quote over a hundred times in its thirty-year run; likely Garrison was attracted to it in part because Adams spoke his own language of "spirit."

If this trend of writing about a noun's "spirit" rather than simply the noun itself grew from the Garrisonian tendency to focus on the spiritual root of political problems, this tendency itself grew from Puritan roots. Amid the revolutionary fervor of 1778, Benjamin Rush had attributed this kind of language (as well as its political import) to the Puritans, surmising that "the destruction of our republics can originate only from causes within *ourselves*" and hoping "(to speak in the puritanical phraseology of our Ancestors) to see a republican Spirit yet found out upon us."[48] Of course the meaning of this ethereal word *spirit* shifted from Puritan to Republican to Romantic New England, but it also retained a certain continuity: Rush's "republic spirit . . . within ourselves" and Garrisonians' "spirit of liberty" preserved something of the Puritan belief that a free society's well-being depends as much on—oftentimes *more* on—the inward convictions of its members than on the letter of the law. Emerson clarified how this language of spirit complemented Garrisonians' emphasis on moral suasion above political forms in his speech against the Fugitive Slave Law, calling for individual disobedience to federal law as "no forms, neither constitutions, nor laws, nor covenants, nor churches, nor bibles, are of any use in themselves." Instead, "to interpret Christ it needs Christ in the heart. The teachings of the Spirit can be apprehended only by the same spirit that gave them forth."[49] In the same way, when Garrisonians spoke of the spirit of Christianity, they spoke as individuals with "Christ in the heart," indicting institutions that failed to live up to this internal witness. The converse was true for Garrisonian talk of negative spirit (e.g., the spirit of slavery, war, or revenge) as the wicked or apathetic inner state of individuals who sustained a corrupt order. This is what Chapman meant when she concluded in her history of Garrisonianism that "the machinery of organization, with all its systematized and mechanical helps, must be utterly unequal to obtain emancipation, unless freedom be the moving 'spirit within the wheels,'" paraphrasing the prophetic vision of Ezekiel 1:20.[50]

Speaking of the "spirit within the wheels" of an existing social structure was also a political strategy for destabilizing the ideological implications of words, part of the broader Garrisonian impulse toward linguistic iconoclasm. Alvin Gouldner helpfully defines ideological change as "*a linguistic conversion that carries with it a reorganization of the self,* on the one hand, and an alienation from old social conventions, on the other" (emphasis in the original), highlighting how a conversion to Garrisonian immediatism came with a new vocabulary, inherently antagonistic as it contested or re-defined the ideological implications of words like *liberty, constitution,* and *Christianity,* for instance.[51] When opponents used such terms as they were commonly understood, Garrisonians countered by invoking the *spirit* be-yond the letter of these terms to express their dissatisfaction with the pres-ent vocabulary. "The whole scope of the English language is inadequate to describe the horrors and impieties of slavery," Garrison declared in his defense of harsh language, and "instead, therefore of repudiating any of its strong terms, we rather need a new and stronger dialect."[52] Garrisoni-ans' "harsh language," then, was a necessary cause and effect of the spiri-tual transformation demanded by its immediatism, a means of challeng-ing corrupt institutions on the authority of deeper spiritual convictions and experiences. In *Eikonoklastes,* Milton similarly rejected the thought that King Charles could achieve "a thing so Spiritual" as "the reforming of Religion"—"what kind of Reformation we could expect from him; either som politic form of an impos'd Religion, or els perpetual vexation, and persecution to all those that comply'd not with such a form."[53] Similarly for Garrisonians, aggressive opposition to these false forms was necessary for a true reformation of religion.[54]

The Garrisonian Experience

If one approaches Garrisonian ideology, à la Gouldner, as a new kind of language for desires and dissatisfactions, attention to that language's style reveals its emotional dynamics for antebellum readers—in particular how Garrisonianism responded powerfully to an acute religious restlessness. Garrison's blend of prophecy, romanticism, and the Puritan past—his talk of the "spirit of" the church, the Reformation, the constitution beyond their existing forms—struck the right notes for Americans who struggled to reconcile the spiritual promise of their nation with the material com-placency of its present. One might consider this restlessness an inchoate "structure of feeling," to use Raymond Williams's term, that preceded the embrace of a fully articulated Garrisonian ideology and coalesced within a residual Puritan past and an emergent capitalist present. Within this struc-ture of feeling, abolitionist talk of the "spirit" beyond forms emerged as a conduit between the world as it was and the world as it ought to be in the minds of the restless, a link between individual desire and social agenda.

William James spoke of the need for a "means of adaptation" when one senses a disjunction between the "seen" and "unseen" world that can take an aggressive or passive form; Garrison tapped into and politicized a deep-seated desire to reclaim America's spiritual promise through an aggressive holy war that pitted America as it ought to be against America as it was.[55] Thus could Child and others describe their conversion to Garrisonianism less as a rational adoption of a program than as a discovery of "tongues of flame" in the *Liberator*'s pages.

Others recognized how these structures of feeling made American abolitionism a uniquely enthusiastic and Puritanical experience compared to its French and British varieties. At the 1840 World Anti-Slavery Convention in London, Whittier found that American abolitionism had "little sympathy with anything staid, sober-paced, prosaic, and formula-fettered," while the English were "mere non-conductors" of this more "fervid, imaginative, electric-sparkling abolitionism," impelled by millennial desires that "dream[ed] of setting a whole world free from all kinds of oppression—mental, physical, social, religious and political; millenial fire-shadowings." While the American nursed "an enthusiasm which was to go round the world," his English cousins instead "gave him dull reports . . . with as much coolness and imperturbable self-possession, as if they were engaged in reckoning the interest of the British national debt."[56] American abolitionists waved "Cromwell's 'sword of the Lord and of Gideon'" in a spiritual fervor that startled the British yet attracted spiritually restless American readers toward the promises of the abolitionist press.

One such seeker was James Boyle. Raised Catholic in Ontario, by the 1820s he was noted for his fiery preaching as a Methodist minister in Ohio, Michigan, and upstate New York, where he became acquainted with the revivalist Charles Finney and his even more ardent perfectionist disciple John Humphrey Noyes. In 1833 Boyle accepted Noyes's invitation to New Haven, where they jointly developed the strain of ultra-perfectionism that would influence Garrison. Ever restless, Boyle soon parted ways with Noyes too, moving then to the free-love creed of Theophilus Gates. By the 1840s he had discovered socialism and joined a Fourierist community in Northampton, embraced the New Covenant movement that eschewed all religious organization, and settled later into Swedenborgianism and faith healing. Like others, Boyle found a more focused outlet for this spiritual restlessness in the Garrisonian cause. Boyle was especially taken with its challenge to the American clergy as a revival of Protestantism's more vital legacies. "The spirit with which you are now in conflict is no other than the spirit of priestly domination and sectarian selfishness," he wrote in an excited letter to Garrison, even going so far as to quote Erasmus's answer to Frederick III when he asked why the church hated Luther: "He has touched the Pope upon the crown, and the monks upon the belly."[57] Garrison fueled his new disciple's sense of purpose; "the spirituality of the gospel is not clearly discerned," he averred, quoting at length the Scottish neo-Calvinist Thomas Erskine's portrait of religion as a transformative way of life beyond civil Christianity.[58] In a series of letters, Boyle and Garrison fed each other's neo-Protestant fires. "The distant sound of approaching earthquakes is heard," Boyle wrote; "false prophets and false christs are many." Garrison did him one better: "Out of the ruins of the various religious sects, (for they are all to be destroyed by the brightness of the coming of Christ,) materials of holiness shall be gathered to build up a spiritual house."[59]

Because this affective intensity was channeled toward aggressive and iconoclastic political ends, Garrisonians were deemed Jacobins as often as Puritans by allies and enemies alike.[60] William James later described this variety of religious experience as "saintliness," the fusion of militant will and spiritual protest that linked Cromwell's New Model Army to the "utopian dreams of social justice in which many contemporary socialists and anarchists indulge." Such radicals, James wrote, inherited the Christian belief in the "potentialities of development in human souls." Puritans and socialists alike were "impregnators of the world, vivifiers and animaters of potentialities of goodness which but for them would lie forever dormant." While James felt that these impulses could narrow into fanaticism, they were also a "genuinely creative social force."[61]

In tenor and intensity, this "genuine creation" qualifies Bercovitch's vision of "the American ideology" as a hegemonic Puritan ritual that conserves a national core. One can accept this work as an accurate and even exhilarating portrait of a prominent cultural pattern, yet when approached from a bird's-eye view as "*the* American ideology," it can miss the texture of conflict and antagonistic intensity at the heart of an experience like Garrisonianism. In this respect (and despite appeals to a later and more pliant generation of Marxism), Bercovitch relied upon a classical Marxist definition of ideology as a static reflection of dominant values—"ideology is basically conservative," in his estimation, and useful for this very reason, revealing a central cultural continuity.[62] But to describe Garrisonians' alternative use of the Puritans as little more than a prelude to a new consensus misses the prophetic, "saintly" experience at its core. If one considers ideology not as "false thought" but in the more neutral sense as a consciously adopted set of beliefs that set one at odds with others (Girondin v. Montagnard, Menshevik v. Bolshevik, Tappanite v. Garrisonian), this emotional intensity and its appeal become clearer.[63] One can even agree with Bercovitch that American writers generally "were not subversive at all" without denying the influential iconoclasm at the heart of the Garrisonian experience.[64]

For this reason, opponents often felt that Garrisonianism was rooted less in any principled faith or ideological program than in a select group of individuals' vainglorious desire to experience the role of Puritan prophet, as convinced of their own righteousness as of the nation's depravity; while the Garrisonian style was frequently blasted as "harsh language," the underlying experience was labeled more simply "egotism." The giant word "EGO" crowned the corners of Adalbert Volck's cartoon caricature of abolitionist "worship" built atop a foundation of "PURITANISM." Senator Samuel S. Cox argued that "abolition is the offspring of Puritanism" in reviving "the same selfish, pharasaical, egotistic and intolerant type of character. . . . Swollen with spiritual pride, it complacently assumes to read the designs of Providence as if it was a part of the Godhead!"[65] In an 1852 pamphlet printed by none other than Ticknor, Reed, and Fields in Boston, one "Medico" likewise concluded in his "Review of Garrisonian Fanaticism" that abolitionists were "egotistic snivelers and ranters" whose "holy zeal" was in fact little more than hate: "The main element in the spirit of the movement, it honestly appears to me, is revilism, the principle of hatred to slavery, to slave-holders and their abettors, to the church and to the state, and love to nobody," where "there is no sunny side of life, but all is gloomy, dark. . . . Theirs is the spirit of strife and hatred, yes, bitter hatred to all who disagree with them." Rather than labeling this egotistical hatred "Puritanism" like the Westerner Cox or the Southerner Volck, Medico (perhaps himself a New Englander) used Garrisonians' own language against them. Hatred was "the deadliest spirit . . . which the poet places in his pandemonium of evil" (likely a reference to Satan's comment in *Paradise Lost* that "never can true reconcilement grow, / Where wounds of deadly hate have pierced so deep").[66] Medico proceeded to paint his own rather Miltonic portrait of this spirit rising "as smoke from the bottomless pit, shrouding the sun of heaven, and withering the beauty of earth."[67] Such comments anticipated Henry Adams's slightly more sympathetic observation that "the New Englander, whether boy or man, in his long struggle with a stingy or hostile universe, had learned also to love the pleasure of hating; his joys were few."[68]

The heart of this disagreement concerned the authority and form of religious experience in the public sphere, more specifically the tension between a secularizing nation and its living roots in an intensely experiential and activist variety of Protestantism. Medico asserted that hate-filled Garrisonians were so convinced of their righteousness and their enemies' depravity that they foreclosed the possibility of free speech and abandoned the public sphere by substituting prophecy for debate—thus the frequent charges that Garrisonians were at once making religion too political and politics too religious, threatening to destroy both by forgetting their differences. Occasioned by a newspaper article in which a preacher defended a Garrisonian's comment that fugitive slaves had the right to kill those who would return them to slavery, Medico especially attacked the preacher's belief that "*I am not responsible* to you, (editor) or even to the public, for what I preach, but only to God" (emphasis original). Medico retorted that such antinomianism left the nation at an impasse: if one preached treason or violence, as many believed the Garrisonians did, "have not the public any right to object?"[69] This antinomianism tended toward the dissolution of the church as much as of the state in Medico's mind, and despite Garrisonians' claims that they continued the true spirit of the gospel and the Reformation against the "pretenders to Christianity" in America's Protestant churches, true Christianity in fact consisted in avoiding a Garrisonian spirit of hate and assuming love for one's enemies, forgoing individualistic antinomianism for the bonds of church and community. But the "pernicious influence of the Liberator" instead spread a destructive hatred.[70]

From the inside, of course, the Garrisonians' prime motive wasn't a "pleasure of hating" in and of itself but the hatred of *sin* as sin; they had assumed the aggressive and bothersome duty to make their countrymen see a national institution *as* a sin. (To say nothing of the prevalent hatred for abolitionists that usually took more violent forms.) When "B" praised the *Liberator* as Puritan, for instance, he quoted Emerson: "The doctrine of hatred is to be preached as the counteraction of the doctrine of love, when that pules and whines." For James, saintliness was not egotistical hatred but "the moral fighting shape," the need for witness with teeth.[71] Here indeed was an impasse, for the experience at the heart of the Garrisonian ideology—at the heart of any radical ideology—was a sense that the public sphere had grown so stagnant that it required a foundational transformation. In imaginations shaped by a strong Protestant heritage, this change would come less through rational debate than through a clash between transformed and complacent spirits. It remains up for debate whether abolitionists were correct in this approach and how much it contributed to the impasse that the nation reached in the 1850s over slavery, but the appeal remained for contemporary readers. James especially hinted at the nature of this appeal: the sense of a conversionlike awakening that made one an active participant in a new chapter in sacred history, a warrior for a noble cause.

Thus could Garrison conclude in "Free Speech and Free Inquiry" that opponents saw his mission as a "spirit of hate," quite simply, because their own spirits remained unawakened to a new chapter in Providence. To Garrison's mind, when writers like Medico asserted antiabolitionists' equal right to free speech, they were making a duplicitous argument less for true free speech than for the majority's right to suppress new revelations that threatened a retrograde status quo. "Of all the reformers who have appeared in the world, whether they were prophets, the son of god, apostles, martyrs or confessors," he wrote, "not one of them has been exempt from the charge of dealing in abusive language . . . of aiming to subvert time-honored and glorious institutions, of striking at the foundations of the social fabric, of being actuated by an irreligious spirit." He maintained, as he had since the *Liberator*'s first days, that "the charge has ever been false, malicious, the very reverse of the truth."

Further, theirs was an inherently sacred mission precisely *because* it challenged the foundations of the American social fabric, the heart of their sacred Protestant heritage. "Luther and his coadjutors were represented as the monsters of their times" for the same reason that critics reviled Garrisonians as hate-filled devils, praising past reformers from a safe distance while ignoring similar work in their own era. The present

> places Luther, Calvin, Penn, in the calendar of saints with comfortable ease because they who hunted, like wild beasts, the reformers of the 15th and 16th centuries, are crumbled to dust, and we stand upon their ashes, and brand them freely and bravely as a band of cowards and persecutors. Why should we not? We have no trade at stake. . . . But what are we doing in regard to the impostures, the crimes, the wrongs of our own times, and our own country? Are we grappling with them, with any thing like the boldness of those whose sepulchres we are proud to build?[72]

Those who ostensibly honored the Protestant past often missed its vital ongoing mission, while those who left it behind for new revelations in fact fulfilled it. Garrison amply praised Lowell's poem "The Present Crisis" as a powerful statement of this dynamic: "We can and must transcend our predecessors . . . 'we ourselves must pilgrims be, launch our Mayflower.'"[73]

This sense of participating in the latest dispensation of sacred history offered Garrisonians a level of purpose that rivaled that of traditional Christian institutions and experiences. Maria Weston Chapman described the initial years of Garrisonianism as "days like those of Wat Tyler, of Wycliffe, of Knox, and Luther" in offering a sense of spiritual purpose so powerful that it could even replace traditional Christianity and scripture.[74] After a funeral, Chapman found more comfort in the cause and the *Liberator* than in the Bible and traditional religious structures. "I cannot refer thus to any opinions of faith, as the words are commonly understood. But the thing, whatever it is, that makes us forget ourselves in our fellow creatures—*that* remains, when the personal presence of our other self is resumed," she wrote to James Russell Lowell, double-underlining that *"The Cause has been the paraclet to me"* as (much like Child) she fell back on the language of Pentecost and a new linguistic dispensation of the Holy Spirit. "I never shall forget the moment when the dawn broke upon me after a night of watching by the dead—and I stretched out my hand to the Liberator lying on the table," she continued, "'I shall not be able to read it' I thought—I shall care for nothing again. But I opened it & found to my astonishment that all *that* faithful friend of excellence was untouched by death."[75] To the reprobate this appeared as so much infidelity, but to the transformed Garrisonian elect it was nothing less than the work of salvation in a new age.

Miltons *Manqués*

How art thou fallen from heaven, O Lucifer, Son of the Morning! how art thou
cast down to the ground, who didst weaken the nations!"—This undoubtedly
gave Milton the first thought of Satan's rebellion, and war. . . . Nothing gives
greater weight and dignity to Poetry, than Prophecy.

—Timothy Dwight, *"On the History, Eloquence, and Poetry of the Bible,"* 1772

Pilgrim ghosts again haunted James Russell Lowell in 1863, though for
more painful reasons than when he first conjured Captain Standish in
1845. Then he had enlisted in a holy war against slavery. Now the war was
real and had claimed two beloved nephews.[1] By popular demand, Lowell
returned to his most famous creation, the homespun Yankee abolitionist
Hosea Biglow, but only with the deepest reservations, wondering whether
his youthful antislavery zeal had hastened his nephews' death. "I've seen
ye, an' felt proud, thet, come wut would, / Our Pilgrim stock wuz pithed
with hardihood," Hosea reflected of nameless youth off to war, yet sometimes "my sins / Come drizzlin' on my conscience sharp ez pins." Seeking
solitude in depression, Hosea slips among the pines and thinks on "the
Rebellion, then o' Hell," wrestling with his nation's "self-blow-up" until
he drifts to sleep (lines 175–79). In his dreams he meets a Pilgrim ancestor with simple advice on the present conflict. "Smite 'em hip an' thigh!"
the Pilgrim bellows, "an' let every man-child die! / Oh for three weeks o'
Crommle [Cromwell] an' the Lord! / Up, Isr'el, to your tents an' grind the
sword!" Such zeal had appealed to a young Lowell, but now Hosea rebukes
the holy warrior. "Thet kind o' thing worked wal in ole Judee, / But you
forgit how long it's ben A.D.," he responds, hesitant "to start Millennium
too quick," for "now I'm gittin' on in life, I fin / It's a sight harder to make

up my mind" (287–92; 261–67). Despite these doubts, Lowell gave the last word to the Pilgrim. "Ef you want selvation, cresh it dead,— / An' cresh it suddin," he declares, and "brought his foot down fercely, ez he spoke, / An' give me sech a startle thet I woke." The poem was a rallying cry to finish the war, but it revealed Lowell's deeper doubts.

Such a public display of uncertainty signaled a new distance from the ardent optimism of Lowell's Unionist peers and even anticipated the postbellum skepticism of the "Metaphysical Club," which would come to view abolitionist certitudes as a recipe for violence.[2] In this respect he especially parted ways with his former rival for the title of America's leading abolitionist poet, John Greenleaf Whittier. Early in life both men juggled political and poetic ambitions with a conscience that demanded reform, and both embraced abolition as a cause that could harmonize these desires through a vocation modeled on Milton's. But while Whittier continued to beat the abolitionist drum into the 1850s and the war, Lowell increasingly doubted his mission, a failed Milton wondering if his violent brew of Puritan spirits had been more potent than he realized.

By 1855 Lowell and Whittier's aggressive neo-Puritan style had grown so popular that even the gentle Whittier could be mistaken for a Cromwellian military chaplain by zealous disciples like Charlotte Forten. The year prior, this seventeen-year-old admirer had left her renowned family of black abolitionists in Philadelphia for the integrated Higginson Grammar School in Salem, Massachusetts, thrilled as an aspiring poet and reformer to arrive at the frontline of the abolitionist imagination.[3] Forten had read so much Whittier that when a friend recited "some exquisite lines" from an unknown author, she suspected that he had written them as well, even though they in fact came from *The Saint's Everlasting Rest* (1649) by Richard Baxter, chaplain to the New Model Army.[4] If wrong, Forten's guess displayed an affinity with Whittier and Lowell's antislavery verse. To those who found themselves distracted from heaven, Baxter's advice was simple: "Use watchfulness, and violence with your own imaginations." Though a professed pacifist, Whittier wielded a similar violence with his imagination for nearly two decades in verse that chided the nation for its sin and called upon Americans to enlist in spiritual warfare.[5] "Quaker as he was," one critic reflected, "every word was a blow as uttered by this newly enrolled soldier of the Lord."[6]

Whittier and Lowell reveal the power and risk alike within the abolitionist imagination's tendency toward spiritual warfare and metaphoric violence, for their verse was an exemplar of the abolitionist imagination as a whole, the most renowned results of Garrison's weekly poetry column for the *Liberator*, a venue that first sparked their prophetic fires and in later

decades encouraged a generation of black, working-class, and female poets like Forten and Frances Harper. By the time Forten moved to Massachusetts in 1855, she recognized and savored this aesthetic.[7] Garrisonian
oratory and verse "were half battles" that "excited me to such a degree of
enthusiasm," she wrote, reminded of Martin Luther, "to a higher, nobler
impulse than that of *physical* resistance; to a stern *moral* resolve of stern-
est *moral* warfare" that "renews one's strength; make one feel equal to any
labor, for the ennobling of mankind." Before the end of the year, Forten
had decided that she too would make her mark as an antislavery writer,
and two months later, she published her first poem in the *Liberator*, praising Garrison via his own favored conceit of moral battle: "Thou, who so
bravely dost her [Lady Abolition's] battles fight / With truer weapons than
the blood-stained sword, / And teachest us that greater is the might / Of
moral warfare, noble thought and word."[8] After a short year of studying the
abolitionist imagination, Forten, like hundreds of others, had zealously
enlisted in its regiment of poet-prophets, eager to march with Lowell and
Whittier to Baxterian rhythms.

Forten's embrace of prophetic antislavery verse reveals how even poets
from nonwhite and non–New England backgrounds could draw inspiration from an imaginative landscape where the Puritan past and abolitionist present joined in holy war through frequent and particular linkages.[9]
This popularity has not been adequately explained due to New Critical and
(later) critique-driven methodologies that have emphasized the aesthetic
and political failures of antebellum verse, antislavery poetry charged with
its most egregious sins. If sentimental and "aesthetically worthless" at best
or plagued by "the fantasies of white abolition versifier" at worst, this archive nonetheless merits attention, argues Marcus Wood, for its popularity
and influence. If "history is never what happened, but what a given society
decides it wants to believe has happened," antislavery poets especially fed
a desire for a revival of the heroic spiritual legacies in the Protestant past.[10]
As Michael C. Cohen has recently argued, American antislavery verse was
less a product of sentimentalism than has been assumed; its performances
of nonconformist prophecy, martyrdom, and holy war were in fact often
reactions *against* sentiment and sympathy.[11] "Sympathy!—the sympathy of
the Priest and Levite," Whittier seethed, "does it hold back the lash from
the slave, or sweeten his bitter bread? Oh, my heart is sick—my soul is
weary of this sympathy." These kinds of prophetic performances no doubt
carried the risks noted by Wood, but why, then, did they move antebellum
Americans so forcefully?[12]

This revival of Miltonic prophecy and warfare in abolitionist verse stemmed foremost from mixed feelings toward the rising dominance of a market economy and new forms of secularization. Economic growth offered poets a wider audience and higher profits than ever before but also reinforced the feeling that American energy was stumbling into a spiritless present. The emergent forces of romanticism and German higher criticism rebelled against this declining spirit by attributing near-divine powers to poets, simultaneously humanizing scripture and apotheosizing the poets. But they also fragmented former foundations of belief.[13] In both instances, poets felt new powers unmooring them from traditional sources of meaning. In turn, they heard new reverberations from the Puritan past. One was a discordant indictment as literary ambition labored uneasily under Puritan legacies of iconoclastic conscience. "The Puritans divorced the Church from Art, and, as far as they could, crushed the poetical element out of religion," Lowell complained, yet he retained the suspicion that poetry could distract from more serious moral and spiritual matters.[14] In an essay read by Forten, Whittier similarly complained of the Puritan propensity "to crack the voice of melody" as "sworn enemies of the Muses," yet he concluded in deference to their "noblest of historical epics on the rough soil of New England" which "lived a truer poetry than Homer or Virgil wrote." Both men clarified a broadly felt tension between art and religion, artifice and action, beauty and duty that they felt could be traced to an ambiguous Puritan legacy.[15] They were not entirely off the mark. Of course the Puritans respected poetry, as these Milton-worshiping descendants well knew, yet Baxter's command to "use violence" with the imagination was one of many instances of an inheritance in which imagination and beauty were approached with disciplined caution regarding the spiritual risks of artifice and ambition.[16]

Like others, Lowell and Whittier seized upon abolition as an outlet for this tension, a mission that might harmonize their romantic poetic ambitions with the "truer" heritage of Puritan conscience and action. As it gained popularity, their antislavery verse in turn assumed a particular "social life," to use Michael C. Cohen's helpful phrase, for many readers who felt a similar tension.[17] If abolitionists responded to secularization in lyceum lectures, female antislavery societies, and newspapers that claimed the Puritan past for themselves, antislavery poets seized an especially prophetic authority as the mission of abolition offered a spiritual and moral justification for devoting oneself to poetry, counteracting the secular potential of romantic verse, a booming print market, and aesthetic ambition with a heroic battle to fulfill the nation's sacred heritage. Whittier and Lowell were the foremost among many drawn to the cause as a way to synthesize art and duty via the prophecies of holy war. Ironically, some of Lowell's best poetry would arise from regrets later in life regarding the violence implicit in this project.

Liberator Poetics

Whittier published his first poem in the Newburyport *Free Press* while it was under the editorship of William Lloyd Garrison, who so loved the piece that he made a thirty-mile journey to congratulate the nineteen-year-old poet and later offered him a job editing the Boston temperance journal *National Philanthropist*. Whittier responded with eager ambition, publishing over fifty poems in the next year while working his way up to the editorship of the *New England Weekly Review*, a leading Whig periodical. This early success drove his ambition in competing directions, pulling him between a passion for poetry and a zeal for reform. "It shall be my endeavor to merit that name which I consider of all others the most worth of our ambition,—the friend of man," he assured Garrison in 1828, but in a few years he changed tack, praising poetry as "something holy and above the fashion of the world." He soon changed tack once more, declaring that "the world shall know me in a loftier capacity than as a writer of rhymes."[18] On the one hand, Whittier was flush with romantic passion for poetry's divine powers "above the world." On the other hand, a desire for worldly distinction could quickly flip poetry's otherwordliness from holiness to irrelevance.

In the meantime, Garrison's conversion to immediatism catalyzed the *Liberator* and its weekly poetry column. In the canonical verse and original work he chose to publish, Garrison followed an intuitive sense of how poetry related to reform. If not explicitly antislavery, all of the poems he chose tended toward the cultivation of spiritual reflection, key to his faith in moral suasion. These values shaped the *Liberator*'s poetry column into a space for aesthetic debates about the canon and its relationship to reform. Before Lowell and Whittier became staple presences, the introspective lyrics of Wordsworth and Coleridge were favored guests, as was the devotional verse of Felicia Hemans. As we would expect, most of the poets who made appearances possessed satisfactory antislavery credentials, though less righteous versifiers slipped in enough times to stimulate debates on the value of good poetry written by immoral poets. The revolutionary yet impious Byron appeared often enough (especially his line "Who would be free themselves must strike the blow") for Lynn abolitionist Alonzo Lewis to pen his own poetic evaluation: "Mighty spirit! did thy lyre / To themes of nobler thought aspire . . . / How would my spirit rush to greet / Thy muse, with praises pure and sweet!"[19] (If Byron had good poetry and bad morals, Lewis was one of several who reversed the mix.)

A head above the rest was Milton, "a primal site for the articulation of the basic right to liberty of all humans," as Wood notes, whose "centrality to abolition thought and writing is a terrain waiting to be mapped."[20] In the *Liberator*'s prose and poetry, like the abolitionist archive at large, *Samson Agonistes, Paradise Lost*, and Milton himself appear so frequently as to become stable points of reference. For one example, the image of Ithuriel's spear—used in book 4 of *Paradise Lost* to dispel Satan's toadish disguise—appears over fifty times in the *Liberator* as shorthand for unmasking the slave power. When Lowell reflected that the American Anti-Slavery Society "never looked so sublimely as now . . . refus[ing] to fling away its impenetrable moral buckler," he saw them wielding the weapon: "Almost every man has in his bosom respectability, which has been detected by and has writhed under the Ithuriel-spear of pure abolitionism."[21] For Whittier and Lowell in particular, Milton would prove to be an anxiety-inducing forefather, but for Garrison and the *Liberator* more broadly, he bolstered antislavery verse's propensity for prophecy, apocalypse, and holy war. If much of Garrison's earliest poetry exemplified conventional spiritual introspection, he soon embraced these prophetic intensities as a more captivating rhetoric for audiences raised on Bunyan and Milton, able to tap into the imaginative heritage of Protestant history and instill in readers a romantic sense that they were as capable today of spiritual greatness as the heroes of Reformation and republican England. In the *Liberator*'s fourth issue, for instance, Garrison echoed Walter Scott's portrait of the English Civil War: "My slumbering energies, awake! / No longer idly play the sluggard, heart, . . . Be not slain by Indolence's dart! / But in the noble strife be first to lead, / And for the rights of man e'en dare to bleed."[22] The poem's message and language resemble a scene from *Peveril of the Peak* (1823), written not long prior by one of Garrison's favorite writers. In this story set during the "Popish plot" of 1678, Major Bridgenorth, an aging Roundhead veteran, reflects on the heroic energies roused by the English Civil War. "Society knows not, and cannot know, the mental treasures which slumber in her bosom, till necessity and opportunity call forth the statesman and the soldier from the shades of lowly life to the parts they are designed by Providence to perform. . . . So rose Oliver—so rose Milton," he tells young Peveril, who responds that "it must be a noble sight . . . to behold the *slumbering energies of a great mind awakened into energy*" (emphasis mine); this is almost certainly the source of Garrison's own use of "slumbering energies."[23] Gar-

rison, the poor son of an absent father, would have certainly been drawn
to this portrait of "lowly life" rising to providential heroism through the
awakening of inward energies.[24]

Excited by the possibilities of a providential fight, Garrison anticipated
his own future imprisonment the next month with a "Prison Sonnet"
declaring, "A martyr's crown is richer than a kings!"[25] By the end of the
year Garrison's Foxean fervor had burned up his conventional sonnets in
the fires of martyrdom and holy war. "For love or fame I can no weapon
wield," he wrote, "but test my spirit at the blazing stake, for advocacy of the
rights of man."[26] Just below this poem, one of the Liberator's many "sacred
odes" to freedom, this one by "L," likewise urged a revival of reformational
history: "When freedom rose, / Waked from her sleep of years / . . . pointing to religion's shrine, / Her sons she bade repair, / . . . Announced with
thunder and with flame, / In accents all sublime."[27] This prophetic style
especially proved popular in its tendency to draw a clear providential arc
from an ambiguous present. "'Twere a vista dark / As midnight," wrote
Englishman John Bowring (one of the first living foreigners whom Garrison published), "could this wearied mortal eye / Thro' the dim mists that
veil futurity / Discern not that heaven-bright, tho' distant spark, / Lighted
by prophecy."[28]

In one of the most remarkable poems published in the Liberator's first
year, William J. Snelling's "Song, Supposed to be Sung by Slaves in Insurrection" radicalized all of these tropes by putting them in the mouths of
slaves who took them seriously. "Will southern nullifiers do us the favor to
read it to their slaves?" Snelling opened tauntingly. "The negro wakes . . .
And wins with bloody hand his right" and like "Sampson girds him for
the fight": the slaves turn Garrison's calls for holy war literal as they become Miltonic-Hebrew warriors in real time.[29] Already in its first year, the
Liberator's poetry column had landed on the "violent imagination" that
would excite future poets and readers for decades, one that revived a Protestant heritage of freedom in "accents all sublime," prophetic "thunder
and flame."[30]

Puritan Prophecies

Whittier and Lowell would soon perfect these conceits as they found a fire
in the Garrisonian mission. Garrison was in fact energizing his poetry column with this prophetic purpose just as Whittier received a blow to his
own, suffering a nervous breakdown in 1833 after he lost a bid for a Massachusetts congressional seat. Garrison wrote to his former protégé with

perfect timing, urging Whittier toward abolition with a zeal that proved to be infectious for a young man with scattered ambitions. "The cause is worthy of Gabriel," he wrote, "yea, the God of hosts places himself at its head. Whittier, enlist! Your talents, zeal, influence—all are needed."[31] Whittier enlisted, again with ravenous ambition. In the next two months he read everything he could acquire on the topic of slavery and published his conclusions at his own expense in *Justice and Expediency*, a work that took imaginative as much as ideological guidance from Garrison. Despite his belief that "abolition must convince every candid mind, that it is neither visionary nor dangerous," Whittier himself tended toward the visionary and seemed to revel in the prospect of slavery reaching a breaking point.[32] "Let the Christian remember that the God of his worship hateth oppression," he proclaimed, quoting Exodus and Isaiah, for "woe unto us, if we repent not, as a nation, in dust and ashes."[33]

Justice and Expediency burned most of the bridges that might have returned Whittier to a career in politics and weighted his new poems with a sense of purpose. Poetry must now be "consecrated to the sacred interests of religion and humanity," he wrote to a friend; otherwise it is "a criminal waste of life."[34] This outlook accounts for the excessive zeal of Whittier's early antislavery verse (swarming with exclamation marks) but also its improvement over his earlier tepid imitations of Byron. *Poems Written during the Progress of the Abolition Question* (1837) gained energy and focus from the Garrisonian aesthetic, even improved upon it. For instance, Whittier invigorated the abolitionist trope of New England pride with the homespun vigor and country air that would popularize his later verse. His much-loved "The Yankee Girl" imagined abolitionist dissent as a plain New England girl at her spinning wheel, rebuking a "haughty Southron" and his offer to free her from her supposed Yankee degradation "with a scorn in her eye which the gazer could feel, / And a glance like the sunshine that flashes on steel" (lines 23–25). Other works buoyed the Garrisonian pride in Puritanism ("Is the old Pilgrim spirit quenched within us?") with what would become Whittier's characteristic panoramas of the New England landscape, often culminating in the voice of a free folk: "from all her wild, green mountains: / From valleys where her slumbering fathers lie / . . . Loud as the summer thunderbolt shall waken / A PEOPLE'S VOICE!" ("A Summons," lines 32–44).

Such tropes remain shot through with Whittier's early desires to represent New Englanders—now poetically if not politically—and he returned to them continuously as they met with popular acclaim. His much-loved "Song of the Free" synthesized all of these tropes, opening in the dactylic foot of classical elegy: "Pride of New England! / Soul of our fathers! / . . . Where's the New Englander / Shamefully cowering? / Graves green and holy / Around us are lying." The dimeter speeds as it shifts from elegiac shame about forgotten graves toward an enemy who can revive their fighting spirit: "Back with the Southerner's / Padlock and scourges! / Go—let him fetter down / Ocean's free surges!" (lines 1–16). More tightly than others, the poem binds Puritan history, the New England landscape, and abolitionist dissent into a sublime romantic whole: "New England's own / Free sons and daughters! / Free as our rivers are / Ocean-ward going / . . . Speak as the tempest does, / Sterner and stronger / . . . Startling the haughty South / With the deep murmur: / 'God and our Charter's right, / Freedom forever" (lines 39–46). Ending on the Puritan charter, Whittier rooted his romantic dissent in New England history as much as its countryside and folk.[35] If self-righteous and simplistic, the popularity of these poems testifies to their effectiveness as propaganda, a fact that leavens the critiques since leveled against them.[36]

These poems especially moved readers by fusing cherished New England myths and images into a compelling mix of conscience and verse. By 1842, Whittier found that his poems had grown so popular as to prompt heaps of imitators, and his editor Isaac Knapp homed in on the peculiar appeal of his verse: its "electrifying *estro* joined to high and powerful conceptions of moral beauty and sublimity . . . because the writer 'lives as a life what he apprehends as a truth.'" Knapp recognized that the public especially admired Whittier for infusing his poems with a plainspoken moral message, that the moral was indeed part of their exciting pleasure. Knapp further testified to the way beauty and morality blended for his antebellum audience when he hoped that Whittier's poetic work on the "battle-field of Christian Freedom" would awaken readers to "the beauty of abolition principles."[37]

A cheeky nineteen-year-old Lowell needed some years and an antislavery lover before he could be convinced. In his "Class Poem" delivered to fellow Harvard undergraduates in 1838, he sniped gleefully at abolitionists and their radical ilk, roasting the transcendentalists as "misty rhapsodists . . . Flapping their half-fledged wings in Reason's face" and abolitionists as "canting fanatics" who demonized the South from a safe distance. If he admitted his sympathy for the slave ("Still thank God ! some pilgrim blood remains / To stir the lazy current of our veins"), the young Lowell's model for reform remained the calmer work of William Ellery Channing. And beyond reform lay the higher calling of "Poetry! best gift to mortals given."[38] But like many recent graduates, four years later Lowell found himself drifting, moody and aimless after law school. He found poetry and purpose alike when he fell in love with the devout abolitionist Maria White. Lowell returned to the abolitionist imagination in the fervor of first love.

While Whittier's response to the Garrisonian stimulus was intuitive, Lowell's deeper critical faculties drove him "more seriously than any of his contemporaries, except possibly Whitman, to set a definite aim for himself as a poet."[39] As a self-aware (and ultimately failed) experiment, Lowell's early ambitions especially clarify the ways in which abolition could both help and hinder poets struggling to discern their vocation. In particular, Lowell was eager to understand the relationship of the poet to American society at large. He discovered an agreeable model in Shelley's defense of the poet as legislator and prophet alike, but while Shelley subordinated the religious to the poetic, Lowell's mystic temperament and religious heritage pursued the idea down more spiritual avenues.[40] Lowell even testified to experiencing a mystic "revelation" in which his poetic vocation descended upon him like tongues of flame. "I never before so clearly felt the spirit of God in me and around me," he reflected, and then "I spoke with the calmness and clearness of a prophet." Lowell clarified the revelation's meaning: "Poets are the forerunners and prophets of changes in the moral world" who "utter truth to be sneered at . . . which become religion to posterity."[41] (Such ideas were remarkably similar to those being developed at the same moment by Emerson in "The Poet," where he declared all religions "the ejaculations of a few imaginative men.")

Abolitionism arose for Lowell as the most promising cause for the American poet-prophet hoping to change "the moral world." To see the aesthetic boost that he, like Whittier, achieved in this new mission, one can compare any of his earliest works to "Prometheus." Consider an early sonnet that flops bloodlessly from its opening line, "Our love is not a fading earthly flower," shaking every saltwater drop from the conceit ("To us the leafless autumn is not bare") before flailing toward the expected yet tangled end: "For nature's life in love's deep life doth lie."[42] For all its flaws, "Prometheus" at least has an intensity that shakes off these conventions. In a free-verse dramatic monologue, Lowell's transcendentalist titan declares his triumph over Jove's tyranny as a martyr to the eternal ideal of freedom, "a power and a memory, / A name to fright all tyrants with, a light / Unsetting as the pole-star" (lines 132–44). Lowell rightly felt that it was his best poem yet, "over-running with true radicalism and antislavery." Even more explicitly than Whittier, he nearly confessed to using abolition as a moral gloss on his ambition: "I only mean to use my ambition as a staff to my love of freedom and man. I *will* have power and there's the end of it."[43]

Charged with a vocation and a cause worthy of his titanic ambition, Lowell had hardly finished "Prometheus" before he began elaborating its ideas. Likely taking inspiration from Carlyle's recent work on the Lord Protector, Lowell's "A Glance behind the Curtain" moves from myth to history as it imagines Oliver Cromwell at the edge of the Atlantic on the eve of the English Civil War, urged by Hampden to flee Britain for the New World. Instead, sensing history growing ripe with Providence, Cromwell delivers another free-verse monologue (like "Prometheus" thrice as long as it should have been) and declares his decision to stay and seize a sacred destiny. Needless to say, Lowell's Cromwell is more Tennyson and Carlyle than orthodox Puritan, though he aims the Protector at more progressive ends than either sage would have preferred. As Cromwell reflects on men "mocked at by the world they love, / Haggling with prejudice for pennyworths / Of that reform which their hard toil will make / The common birthright of the age to come," he concludes that they could never sustain their challenging mission "but for this same prophecy, / This inward feeling of the glorious end" (288–98). If in "Prometheus" Lowell performed the role of a lone titan screaming at tyrants, he better achieved the role of prophet in "A Glance Behind," speaking to his own people as God's mouthpiece, peeling back the curtain of history to show a nation that Providence still speaks. The poem's greatest success is its ability to foster a sense of historical liminality and present potential, inspiring the now with both a sense of destiny and a reason to act. "He who waits to have his task marked out / Shall die and leave his errand unfulfilled," Cromwell warns, transforming the New England errand from communal covenant into individual earnestness when he concludes that "our time is one that calls for earnest deeds" (lines 208–11). Even more explicitly than in "Prometheus," "A Glance Behind" confessed Lowell's ambitions by ending abruptly and awkwardly on Milton, asserting the union of Protector and poet as men of action alike. Proclaiming a Shelleyian faith that "the poet's lyre demands / An arm of tougher sinew than the sword" (lines 322–33), Lowell prophesied his own role as poet-prophet and effectively announced his campaign "to become the Milton of the abolitionist cause."[44]

While Whittier's poems were gaining popularity, Lowell's second proclamation garnered less attention than the first, which raises the question of how an abolitionist Milton could lead a nation that did not read him. Revealingly, Lowell's next work descended from titan heights and the Cromwellian sublime for the cute "Stanzas Sung at the Anti-Slavery Picnic in

Dedham," an imitation of Whittier's freedom hymns awash in New England pride that lacked even their modest charms. He tried the formula again with "Rallying Cry for New England against the Annexation of Texas," where the only memorable line again arose from his knack for joining past and present: "Grey Plymouth rock hath yet a tongue, and Concord is not dumb, / And voices from our fathers' graves, and from the future come." Though the line was frequently quoted in later abolitionist works, Lowell seemed less than proud of the work, signing it anonymously as "A Yankee."[45] The failure of Lowell's imitations reveals a different temperament and faith from Whittier's, whose antislavery verse was bolstered by a deep love for the quiet countryside. Whittier's freedom hymns roused yeomen by dramatizing these genuine feelings, but Lowell's attempts to unite the poet and the legislator needed to experience disillusionment with actual legislators before his prophecies could go beyond performance and acquire real fire.

A stimulus came in 1845 when Congress welcomed President Polk's surprise announcement that the Republic of Texas had agreed to his secret proposal of annexation. Shocked at the subterfuge of Polk's scheme for more slave territory and Congress's capitulation, Lowell achieved a far more potent rallying cry in "The Present Crisis," a poem that dramatized an idealist faith chastened yet unconquered. Here Lowell's acute sense of historical liminality gained depth through elegiac shading as he wrestled with the ways in which history is often a string of setbacks, cowardice, and bloodshed.[46] "The slave, where'er he cowers, feels the soul within him climb," it begins, "As the energy sublime / Of a century bursts full-blossomed on the thorny stem of Time" (lines 1–5). Lowell gave a ghastly underside to the organic conceit: before freedom can blossom, "a corpse" claws up into human consciousness and "crawls round unburied," reanimated by unnatural necromancers who sustain dead legacies (15). Lowell channels the voices of Isaiah, attacking such dark arts as a desecration of Providence that eventually reaches a breaking point: "once to every man and nation comes the moment to decide . . . God's new Messiah, offering each the bloom or blight" (21–23). If the undead are doomed to die again, the living must still choose which historic role is theirs for eternity, necromancer or gardener.

History itself thus becomes the drama of salvation as these crises become "new Messiahs" that (echoing Christ's parable in Matthew 25) sort "the goats upon the left hand, and the sheep upon the right" (24). The new elect arise as those "chosen heroes . . . that stood alone . . . and down the future saw the golden beam incline / To the side of perfect justice." More directly and explicitly than in "Prometheus" or "A Glance Behind," Lowell assumes the voice of the prophet—"Hast thou chosen, O my people, on whose party thou shalt stand, / Ere the Doom from its worn sandals shakes the dust against our land?"—but his divine authority now rests less in the Promethean self-assertion of the solitary romantic and more in the dramatic historical development of humanity itself, the "instincts" and "swift flash of right or wrong" in "mankind . . . one in spirit" (16–17). The poem especially draws energy from dramatizing this new elect as a moral minority within a present where progress seems dim. The triumph of right becomes more sublime because of this persecution, and the poem's core (and its most frequently quoted stanzas) channels this impulse to inspire present action: "Truth forever on the scaffold, Wrong forever on the throne,— / Yet that scaffold sways the future, and, behind the dim unknown, / Standeth God within the shadow, keeping watch above his own." More powerfully than in "A Glance Behind," "The Present Crisis" makes progress feel both inevitable and contingent, spurring action with destiny.

"The Present Crisis" was Lowell's first critical and popular success alike, to be quoted by abolitionist, socialist, and civil rights publications for a century to come. Its popularity arose in part from its greater degree of abstraction, not beholden to particular figures like Cromwell and Prometheus. It also spoke more powerfully to the average activist, who needed only to be on the right side of history, as opposed to a promethean romantic. But the popularity of "A Present Crisis" in its immediate moment also stemmed from Lowell's bringing his flair for historical liminality to the popular Garrisonian trope of Pilgrim pride. "We ourselves must Pilgrims be, / Launch our Mayflower, and steer boldly through the desperate winter sea," it concludes, transforming a common Garrisonian trope into a revolutionary historiography: "Nor attempt the Future's portal with the Past's blood-rusted key" (lines 86–90). Marcus Wood rightly asserts that "if abolition had a single poetic anthem then this was it," for it perfected the Foxean and neo-Puritan conceits that had become central to the Garrisonian imagination.[47] Lawrence Buell finds "a curious but typical doublethink" in the poem's conclusion, as "the present stands indicted for its bondage to the past, yet it may save itself by building a Utopia based on a vision from the past."[48] Rather than doublethink, this is better understood as a prophetic vision of history, what Walter Benjamin called *Jetztzeit*, a sense of "now-time" in which past and present fuse in a vision of historical plenitude, "blast[ing] a specific era out of the homogeneous course of history" to enable "a revolutionary chance in the fight for the oppressed past." It achieves what Fredric Jameson called "the emotion of great historiographic form," the feeling one gets when historical necessity and possibility alike have been marshaled into a providential arc.

Lowell transformed history into a wrathful "great avenger" and positioned himself as its mouthpiece, led "into the wilderness" to be "baptized in fire, a prophet and reformer."[49] Only then could a poet hope to reach what Milton called "that pure fame which alone can claim 'The perfect witness of all-judging Jove.'" Lowell claimed something strikingly similar to Milton's vision of verse as "a human version of the divine record" rooted in "the chronicles of conscience," in William Kerrigan's description, an intensely "arduous conception of poetry" as "artistic creation, inseparable from the account to be rendered to God, takes place under the shadow of ultimate judgment."[50] If the adamant Milton could bear this prophetic sense of poetry, the more puckish Lowell would find it increasingly irksome.

Comedy

"The Present Crisis" was the apex and the conclusion of Lowell's performance of Miltonic prophet, a high note on which to conclude a role that quickly grew unsatisfying and unsustainable. Oracular monologues soon become predictable, and Lowell's growing desire to unite the poet and the leader of men strained against the role of lone prophet; the one rallied a majority, the other reassured a persecuted minority. Most simply, the calling was a poor fit for Lowell's personality. Where Whittier's abolitionist fire was sparked by his love of the New England shire, Lowell drew energy from stylistic peacocking as satirist and humorist. An editor later reflected that all of his work revealed "the play of the two characters that met in Lowell's nature, the humorist and the moralist." While the latter attempted to subdue the former in a mission to become an antislavery Milton, Lowell found the absurdities of antebellum politics driving him back to the satirical barbs and feathers of his "Class Poem."[51] Just two weeks after "The Present Crisis" appeared in the *Courier*, Lowell again took to its pages with "An Interview with Miles Standish," strategically published just in time to lampoon the annual Forefathers' Day toast to the Pilgrims, narrated by the kind of frivolous Yankee poet who might attend just such a dinner more for the madeira than for the memorial.[52] If silly, "An Interview" is a noteworthy development in its ironic distance and dramatic conflict: the narrator is no longer a Cromwellian prophet but the kind of dilettante that Lowell could imagine resisting these voices in good part because he had worked to suppress that voice within himself for the role of prophet, and not altogether successfully. "An Interview" accepted and worked with his inner class clown by pitting it against the inner prophet and the Pilgrim ghosts that haunted him.[53]

The start of the Mexican War in May 1846 accelerated this development. Disgusted by the ease with which the country slipped into a war for slave territory—and likely annoyed that his Prometheus, Cromwell, and Standish hadn't made enough of a splash—Lowell experimented with a drastically different voice. "I imagined to myself such an upcountry man as I had often seen at antislavery gatherings," he later reminisced, "capable of district-speech English but always instinctively falling back into the natural stronghold of his homely dialect when heated."[54] The result was Hosea Biglow, a homespun Jonathan from the fictional village of Jaalam, Massachusetts who wrote protest verse in the Yankee vernacular. Lowell sent the first of such verse to the *Courier* anonymously, assuming the guise of Hosea's proud father Ezekiel on the (real) occasion of a recruitment officer's visit to Boston to enlist young men in the war effort. "Wal, Hosea he com home considerabal riled," Ezekiel explains to the editor, and wrote his indignation into verse. After the local Parson Wilbur declares his verses "True grit," Ezekiel sent them on to Mr. Buckingham at the *Courier*, hoping for publication. The real Buckingham was delighted to oblige "Ezekiel," printing his letter alongside Hosea's verse that June. *Courier* readers encountered the same trochaic meter and syncopated rhythm of "The Present Crisis," though it gained a cocky jaunt in Hosea's vernacular. "Thrash away, you'll *hev* to rattle / On them kittle drums o' yourn," Hosea taunts the recruiter, for "Taint a knowin' kind o' cattle / They is ketched with mouldy corn." Where Lowell's former work attacked slavery from a high-prophetic mode, Hosea allowed him to deliver the same critique in a more popular Jacksonian style, spiced with a populist humor, Yankee common sense, and misspelled vernacular to revitalize the Garrisonian tactic of New England pride. Hosea aroused New Englanders against an overreaching region as he asked, "Aint it cute to see a Yankee / Take sech everlastin' pains / All to git the Devil's thankee, / Helpin' on 'em weld their chains?" (lines 17–21; 65–68).

Lowell likewise Yankeefied his propensity for prophecy. "Ez fer war, I call it murder . . . / I don't want to go no furder / Than my Testy ment fer that," Hosea writes, for "Ef you take a sword an' dror it, / An' go stick a feller thru, / Guv'ment aint to answer for it, / God'll send the bill to you" (lines 33–36; 45–59). In a stanza that reveals the full potential and pitfalls of this style, Hosea offers a definition of human rights that is powerful in its simplicity, pocked as it is with the bad grammar and racial slurs of the average New England farmer. "Chaps thet make black slaves o' niggers / Want to make wite slaves o' you," Hosea declared, but "Laborin' man an' laborin' woman / Hev one glory an' one shame. / Ev'y thin' thet's done inhuman / Injers all on 'em the same. // 'Taint by turnin' out to hack folks / You're agoin' to git your right. / Nor by lookin' down on black folks / Coz you're put upon by wite" (lines 69–84). Lowell's decision to mar Hosea's noble sentiment with racial slurs, more difficult for modern readers, was partly a concession to vernacular humor but also emphasized his belief that a divine principle could shine through even flawed minds, that "high and even refined sentiment may coexist with the shrewder and more comic elements of the Yankee character."[55]

This mix of unpolished vernacular, brash Yankee defiance, and simple antislavery principle proved wildly popular with readers. After Hosea's creation, Lowell saw his verse "copied everywhere," in genteel and working-class circles alike, passed around in parlors and "pinned up in workshops," frequently quoted "and their authorship debated." When one reader guessed that James Russell Lowell was the author, Lowell was especially amused to overhear a second protest that the verse was too *good* to be his.[56] Hosea's popularity continued to grow as Lowell published new installments in the *Courier* over the course of the war, attaching his name to the series after its third installment to claim his praise.[57] "Lowell deserves pride of place" in any antislavery canon because of *The Biglow Papers* alone, Marcus Wood posits, "the most successful transatlantic abolition writing . . . superseded in mass public response" only by *Uncle Tom's Cabin*.[58]

But as Hosea's "true grit" began to take off, Lowell worried that his success had made a joke of abolition, that he ran "the risk of seeming to vulgarize a deep and sacred conviction." Perhaps for this reason, Lowell returned to his inner Puritan preacher after the third installment by introducing the character of Reverend Homer Wilbur, an amiable caricature of the genteel Cambridge clergy to which Lowell's father belonged. A learned and sensible Whig (and overeager to demonstrate both), the Reverend dignifies Hosea's homespun sense.[59] As Lowell gathered the Biglow pieces into a single volume in October 1848, he expanded the Parson's role to editor of Hosea's verse, a continual presence in the single volume as he introduced, concluded, and supplemented each of Hosea's poems with more polished prose. The Parson's Latin-addled windiness contrasts humorously with Hosea's vernacular even while it bolsters his common sense with sharper satire. In the second paper, for instance, the Parson can rebuke the argument that the Mexican War is waged "for the spreading of free institutions and of Protestantism" more deftly than Hosea. (If so, why not fill bombs with "copies of the Cambridge Platform and the Thirty-nine Articles," he suggests, "a mixture of the highest explosive power . . . to those who sit in the darkness of Popery." Wilbur then flips the argument on its head: "earnest Protestants have been made by this war,—I mean those who protested against it.")[60] The genteel Wilbur also helped Lowell justify the ungentlemanly sting of his satire, in particular its naming of names. "A bad principle is comparatively harmless while it continues to be an abstraction," Wilbur explains, but while he laments having to attack real people, the greater risk is compromising with sin so as to avoid hurt feelings. "It is one of the cunningest fetches of Satan, that he never exposes himself directly to our arrows, but, still dodging behind this neigbour or that acquaintance," where "he holds our affections as hostages, the while he patches up a truce with our conscience." Humor and satire are justified when weaponized in the abolitionist holy war with Satan.

Of most interest for Lowell himself, the Parson let Lowell publicly introduce a theory about American culture and politics which the *Biglow Papers* had brought to his mind: if reimagined in creative ways attuned to the spirit of the time, New England's Puritan heritage might cease to be an aesthetic burden and instead become a powerful resource for a progressive democracy. The introduction to the single volume, written in the Parson's voice, sketches many of the ideas that Lowell would polish in his important 1855 *Lectures on English Poetry*. Wilbur admits that Puritanism produced an iconoclastic culture, but also one that bolstered a moral democracy. "New England was not so much the colony of a mother country, as a Hagar driven forth into the wilderness . . . that they might have the privilege to work and pray, to sit upon hard benches and listen to painful preachers as long as they would," he concedes jokingly, yet the result was an "earnest-eyed race . . . who had taught Satan to dread the new Puritan hug." The Parson describes Lowell's own vision for the aesthetic of the *Biglow Papers*: the New England errand created a "strange hybrid"—"such mystic-practicalism . . . cast-iron-enthusiasm, such sour-faced-humor"— that persists in Hosea and more closely resembles the vital culture of Elizabethan England than the modern British people. New England, he argues, is "nearer than John [Bull], by at least a hundred years, to Naseby, Marston Moor, Worcester, and the time when, if ever, there were true Englishmen," for while "John Bull has suffered the idea of the Invisible to be very much fattened out of him, Jonathan is conscious still that he lives in the world of the Unseen as well as of the Seen. To move John you must make your fulcrum of solid beef and pudding; an abstract idea will do for Jonathan."[61] Lowell would later elaborate these ideas, but in 1848 they already offered a justification for fitting his satire into a genealogy of Puritan morality and Anglo art alike.

After the publication of *The Biglow Papers* in 1848, Lowell's former prophet-poet identity splintered irreparably as his imagination ran in different directions toward one of his most productive years: beyond *Biglow* were editorials for the *National Anti-Slavery Standard*, his lauded satire of antebellum poets in *A Fable for Critics*, the mystic romance *The Vision of Sir Launfal*, and a new collection of verse. If such disparate projects "represented the disintegration of that carefully unified poetical and personal identity which he had tried to achieve during his early search for the 'heroic' life," they also freed Lowell to perfect new styles.[62]

Into the 1840s Whittier too had grown warier of the presence of Puritan iconoclasm and Garrisonian militancy in his verse. *Voices of Freedom* (1846) would be his last and best use of the prophetic style. Poems like "Moral Warfare," "The Branded Hand," and "Massachusetts to Virginia" remain among the best poems to smoke from the Garrisonian gun, but like Lowell, Whittier began to find its barreled focus confining as he sought forms of beauty beyond reform. As he reread early Puritan accounts of settlement, he was struck by their inability to perceive the beauty of the New World as they felt overwhelmed instead by a "desert and frightful wilderness" in need of reforming.[63] Whittier increasingly recognized this militancy in himself. "I have still strong suspicions," he wrote, that "something of the grim Berserker spirit, has been bequeathed to me." The feeling had since "found new and better objects" in "what Milton calls the martyr's 'unresistible might of meekness,'" he reflected, as his boyhood knights were replaced with figures like Luther, Henry Vane, Mary Dyer, Thomas Clarkson, and, revealingly, George Fox rebuking Cromwell and his soldiers. Above all, Milton at his life's end "approaches nearly to my conception of a true hero," Whittier said, "sick, poor, blind, and abandoned of friends," yet a dissenter to the last. Like Milton, Whittier resolved that he would continue "to tell the very soil itself what its perverse inhabitants are deaf to," but the shift in emphasis was already evident: Whittier felt less like a captain in the New Model Army and more like a lonely prophet on the ropes against a growing tyranny.[64] In the face of an apathetic majority, moral warfare had grown tiresome, and Whittier at times admitted as much. If his antislavery poetry's "rough picture overwrought appears," he explained, it is "not of choice, for themes of public wrong / I leave the green and pleasant paths of song" but because "Before my soul a voice and vision passed, / Such as might Milton's jarring trump require."[65] Less successfully than Lowell, Whittier tried to leaven the abolitionist mission with comedy in poems like "Haschish" and "Letter from a Missionary," a Biglowesque satire of a Kansas preacher complaining of "Yankee abolitionists . . . Each face set like a flint of Plymouth Rock." Whittier's comedy did leaven his poetry in noteworthy works like "Skipper Ireson's Ride" and "The Barefoot Boy," but like Lowell he found comedy improving his poetry and mood in part because it distanced him from abolitionist prophecy.[66] Alongside the comedic, a tragic vision especially bolstered their poetry, though in different ways as Lowell grew to doubt his youthful antislavery zeal while Whittier embraced the Civil War as its fruition and ultimate victory.

Tragedy

Like all abolitionists, Whittier was especially shocked by Daniel Webster's "Seventh of March" speech that lent crucial support to the Fugitive Slave Act. And like his peers, flush with imaginative holy wars, Whittier tended toward demonization in "Ichabod" (Hebrew for "inglorious"), casting Webster as a new Miltonic Satan, a "light-bearing" Lucifer now felled by pride. "So fallen! so lost! the light withdrawn / Which once he wore! / The glory from his gray hairs gone / Forevermore! . . . he who might / Have lighted up and led his age, / Falls back in night . . . A fallen angel's pride of thought, / Still strong in chains" (lines 1–4, 27–28). Unlike his peers, Whittier's demonization was more tragic than prophetic, fueled by "surprise and grief" more than holy anger. "Revile him not, the Tempter hath / A snare for all; / And pitying tears, not scorn and wrath, / Befit his fall" (5–8), he concluded, pitying Webster as "A bright soul driven, / Fiend-goaded, down the endless dark" (14–15) by wicked peers. He concludes by urging his readers to "Pay the reverence of old days / To his dead fame; / Walk backward, with averted gaze, / And hide the shame!" (33–36), just as Noah's sons did upon discovering their father drunk and naked. "Ichabod" bends abolitionists' favored Miltonic tropes toward a tragic lense befitting the shame of the once great Webster.

Lowell's poems were chastened by far more personal tragedies. The success of *Biglow* was cut short when Lowell's mother and infant daughter died within months of each other, the start of a "waste land of emotional aridity" that tumbled toward its nadir in 1853 with the death of his wife Maria, the woman whose love had impelled him toward abolitionism in the first place.[67] Between a nation stumbling daily closer to crisis and the death of the women he most loved, Lowell's antislavery fire faded to dull coals. A merciful distraction arose when he accepted a commission to deliver the prestigious Lowell Institute Lectures on the topic of English poetry. As he worked for the next year to fill the series, the calmer task of rereading the Anglo canon and honing his criticism further confirmed his shift away from the role of poet-prophet as he found himself most admiring writers who least fit that role. He noted that Chaucer and Shakespeare were no reformers, and privately he reflected that "the sole advantage of Restoration was that it took Milton out of politics." The work solidified a belief that had been fermenting since 1849, that "the poetical has nothing to do with morals . . . but imagination *has*."[68] In this same vein, the lectures aim like *Biglow* to incorporate New England's heritage of Puritan conscience into the broader, richer aesthetic tradition of English poetry. As he'd begun to do with Parson Wilbur in *Biglow*, Lowell relocated his audience's Puritan heritage firmly within the cultural greatness of Tudor and Stuart England: "the most truly imaginative period of English poetry," he argued, was bookended by Spenser and Milton, the same period in which "the English mind culminated" and made a "great heave and yearn toward freedom in politics and religion" via Puritan and Parliamentarian dissenters.[69] For this reason, despite their iconoclasm, the Puritans could be lauded as key contributors to England's cultural greatness, allies rather than enemies of the nation's greatest imaginations: "Shakespeare had been dead five years, and Milton was eleven years old, when Mary Chilton leaped ashore on Plymouth Rock," he noted, "as if Shakespeare, sprung from the race and the class which colonized New England, had not been also ours! As if we had no share in the puritan and republican Milton, we who had cherished in secret for more than a century the idea of the great puritan effort, and at last embodied it in a living commonwealth!"[70] In a clever way, Lowell not only reaffirmed his audience's genteel Puritan pride but also implied the converse: their Puritan conscience need not be the "sworn enemy of the muse" as Whittier charged.

Of course many holes can be poked in Lowell's history: the Puritans often *were* the enemy of certain kinds of art just as Spenser, Shakespeare, and Milton all stood in a mixed relationship with their Nonconformist contemporaries. In reality the lectures crafted a usable past that justified Lowell's leaving behind the role of antislavery Puritan-prophet for that of the poet. What sets Lowell apart from his peers is that he *admitted* his vision of the past was constructed. "To make a people capable of great things . . . make an alliance with their imaginations," he advocated: "for this kind of thing any past will do, if you can only make men believe in it." Because a nation "lives to feel a past behind it, to have its rear guarded by an illustrious ancestry," Lowell concluded that "it will have heroes even if it has only shadows to make them out of, and *is obliged to wink a little to believe in them"* (emphasis mine).[71] Lowell urged his audience to recognize that their nation was above all the product of its past language and culture, and that this heritage, like its constitution, was constructed and open to reconstruction and reimagination based on the needs of the present. Unsurprisingly, Lowell felt that poets and critics played a favored role in this project by shaping culture into narratives that could move people, and the lectures were his own attempt to do so, to reimagine his New England heritage away from the prophetic vision of the Puritan past that had once roused him, to coax his audience to exchange its moral militancy for poetic greatness.

While the lectures earned Lowell the old Harvard post of his friend Longfellow, a usable past of poetry over prophecy became increasingly out of touch with the national mood when the tensions of the 1850s exploded into real war. Ironically, the pacifist Whittier's *In War Time* (1864) would better represent the nation by beating the war drums, albeit tempered by a tragic vision, horrified by the violence. "The future's gain / Is certain as God's truth; but, meanwhile, pain / Is bitter," it opens, driven back to apocalyptic imagery: "The firmament breaks up. In black eclipse / Light after light goes out. One evil star, / Luridly glaring through the smoke of war, / As in the dream of the Apocalypse, / Drags others down." The conflict was nearly a "suicide" by "fires of hell" and "furnace blast" as "God recast[s] / And mould[s] anew the nation." On the cause and aim of this pain, Whittier never wavered: "What gives the wheat-field blades of steel? . . . Hark to the answer: Slavery!"[72] In a revealing image, he literally demonized slavery (if not slaveholders themselves), imagining the present war as an exorcism that racked the body politic. "God lifts to-day the veil, and shows / The features of the demon! / North and South, / Its victims both," he wrote, "What though the cast-out spirit tear / The nation in his going?"[73] The tragic aspects of the war give *In War Time* more heft than some of Whittier's antislavery verse but did little to shift his fundamental tendency toward moral warfare. Nor did the war even seem to pose any major challenges to Whittier's cheer. Two years after the war, he vacationed in *The Tent on the Beach* and described himself blithely as "a dreamer born, / Who, with a mission to fulfil, / Had left the Muses' haunts to turn / The crank of an opinion-mill, / Making his rustic reed of song / A weapon in the war with wrong." That path seems not to have troubled him in the least as "He rested now his weary hands, / And lightly moralized and laughed, / As, tracing on the shifting sands / A burlesque of his paper-craft" (lines 97–104). The tone is melancholic only insomuch as it colors Whittier's nostalgia for a time when "the common air was thick with dreams."

Whittier perfected this mood the next year in *Snow-Bound* (1868), his most successful work commercially (earning a $10,000 profit) and critically, a genuinely good poem centered on two men remembering a moment from their childhood when their family, now mostly gone, gathered round a fire to trade stories amidst a snowstorm. Published just three years after the war, *Snow-Bound*'s appeal is best understood if one approaches it as a national eulogy, an effort to comfort more than challenge. Not that the poem skirts around death or hides Whittier's interpretation of the war's cause; it remembers "when all the land / Was clay in Slavery's shaping hand" and abolition "a far-blown trumpet [that] stirred / The languorous, sin-sick air," just as Whittier is equally forthright in his vision for the future, honoring the war dead as "freedom's young apostles" who "uplift the black and white alike . . . and substitute / For Slavery's lash the freeman's will." Similarly, the character of a schoolmaster, a different kind of apostle for freedom, quietly embodies Whittier's hopes for Reconstruction as a chance for Northerners to enlighten what he saw as a backward region. But these infrequent statements float in a pool of pleasanter memories, and even the most explicit antislavery remarks soon give way to vague hopes for reconciliation, "North and South together brought . . . / Harvest[ing] the fields wherein they fought"—a common postbellum sentiment but also, as Albion Tourgee dramatized in his best-selling *A Fool's Errand* (1879), unrealistic.[74] The nocturnal snowstorm and its warring shades of black and white (a less than subtle symbol for the postbellum nation) contrast sharply with the domestic fireside. "Shut in from all the world without," narrator and readers alike are "content to let the north-wind roar," for as "cider simmered" and "apples sputtered . . . what matter how the north-wind raved?" His mission accomplished, the antislavery Puritan hangs up his guns and comforts the war-wounded with hearthside cider.[75]

As a bachelor, Whittier only had two nephews eligible for war, and both of them survived.[76] The conflict was far more personal for Lowell, a sociable and twice-married man from a large family. The youthful zeal that had given birth to his prophecy was depleted by the bloodshed of the war, brought home in the death of his nephews. Thus when Lowell resurrected Hosea Biglow and Parson Wilbur by popular demand in 1863, it was with extreme hesitancy. By 1865 the toll had come to three nephews, three cousins, and more family friends dead, and Lowell confessed in the *Biglow Papers*' penultimate installment that he couldn't go on with the show. "Sence the war my thoughts hang back / Ez though I wanted to enlist 'em," Hosea remarks, as if haunted by the notion that each of his antislavery poems was a regiment of boys sent off to war.[77]

Reflecting a personality long split between the moralist and satirist, the second Biglow poems careen even more wildly between hope and dread as Hosea wrestles with a deep depression. "Where's peace?" he asks as former pleasures that "filled my heart with livin' springs" now "seem to freeze 'em over; / Sights innercent ez babes on knee, / Peaceful ez eyes o' pastur'd cattle, / Jes' coz they be so, seems to me / To rile me more with thoughts o' battle."[78] The piece culminates in a heartbreaking anguish for his departed nephews:

> Rat-tat-tat-tattle thru the street
> I hear the drummers makin' riot,
> An' I set thinkin' o' the feet
> Thet follered once an now are quiet . . .
> . . . Why, hain't I held 'em on my knee ?
> Did n't I love to see 'em growin',
> Three likely lads ez wal could be,
> Hahnsome an' brave an not tu knowin'?

Struggling with something resembling survivor's guilt, Lowell concluded, "'Tain't right to hev the young go fust, / All throbbin' full o' gifts an' graces / Leavin' life's paupers dry ez dust / To try an' make b'lieve fill their places."[79] In the midst of such reflections, he confessed via Hosea, "I . . . half despise myself for rhymin'," and ended with this image—as if in anticipation of *Snow-Bound*'s nostalgia: "Snow-flakes come whisperin' on the pane / The charm makes blazin' logs so pleasant, / But I can't hark to wut they're say'n', / With Grant or Sherman ollers present."[80]

Lowell set aside this raw confession and spent the last months of the war diving into two research projects on New England history, a detailed study tracing New England vernacular to sixteenth-century England (what would become the introduction to the second *Biglow Papers*) and "New England Two Centuries Ago," a review of the third volume of Palfrey's *History of New England* and four volumes of Puritan primary sources published by the Massachusetts Historical Society.[81] This odd and drastic shift in topic was partly, like his lectures, a distraction from the death of loved ones. And yet there was something significant in Lowell's persistent decision to return to New England history in such moments of personal and political crisis. In these works he admitted that the Puritans were the source of Americans' "capacity for enthusiasm" and their "skirmishing habit of thought," inherited from "that element of English character which was most susceptible of religious impressions."[82] He went so far as to admit that the Cromwellians forced the "religious element of Puritanism" into politics—precisely what abolitionists were accused of doing. In a review of Thoreau's works six months later, he seemed to turn this charge on his younger self. Reflecting on the days of his youth, he wrote that "everybody had a mission . . . an assurance of instant millennium," days in which "the belated gift of tongues, as among the Fifth Monarchy men, spread like a contagion." By deeming American reformers new Fifth Monarchy Men—the very group he had once denounced as the rotting, "putrefactive" final stage of "Puritanic fermentation"—Lowell chastised his own youthful ambitions to be a Miltonic poet-prophet, which after the bloodshed of war now appeared less like righteous anger than like a millenialist bender that had aggravated the conflict. If he wanted to believe in the Puritan and Parliamentarian experiment that culminated in American democracy just as much as he believed in "vinous" Spenser and "acetous" Milton, with three nephews dead, he also was "obliged to wink a little to believe in them."[83]

And yet he could not rest content with winking alone nor with simply abandoning the Puritan conscience that remained his birthright. Instead he careened in his favored liminal spaces between despair and hope, between his present skepticism and his old propensity for prophecy. If his retrospective on transcendentalism was filled with critical irony toward the puritanical zeal of his youth and his peers, it also sincerely concluded that "the Puritanism that cannot die, the Puritanism that made New England what it is, and is destined to make America whats it should be, found its voice in Emerson" and the reformers to whom he was a "sleeping partner." Similarly, despite deeming reformers new Fifth Monarchy rot, "New England Two Centuries Ago" also made it a point to denounce those who would throw out Puritan conscience with its zealotry. In reference to the strained relations between the Union and Britain, Lowell emphasized "a curious parallel" in Restoration England's heavy-handed treatment of its New England colonies and modern English elites' antipathy toward New England's antislavery "enthusiasm."[84] It was a quiet but unmistakable rejoinder to the common British belief that their Puritanical cousins had blown up their republic in another fit of fanaticism. He refuted this belief with a clever (if again selective) reading of colonial history: the chaos of the English Civil War never touched the New England colonies because they were never directly ruled by a corrupt monarchy, he argued, returning to his favored metaphor: in America the Puritanic "fermentation had never gone further than the ripeness of the vinous stage. Disappointment had never made it acetous, nor had it ever putrefied into the turbid zeal of Fifth Monarchism and sectarian whimsey." In so many words, he was arguing that nineteenth-century America, like seventeenth-century Britain, faced a chaotic civil war not because of Puritanical zeal but because of a corrupt nobility.[85] In fact, he argued that New England democracy and the antislavery movement that claimed its promises was the best result of this Puritanic "fermentation," for "the English Puritans pulled down church and state to rebuild Zion on the ruins, and all the while it was not Zion, but America, they were building . . . the first experiment in practical democracy." Here too Lowell spoke as much of the nineteenth as the seventeenth century, critiquing an Anglo-Confederate alliance of gentry as the graver threat to republicanism than Puritanical antislavery enthusiasm. In fact, Puritanical abolitionism "develop[ed] the latent possibilities of English law and English character."[86] Lowell's incessant recurrence to the Puritan past were not mere distractions but returns to the source of his moral imagination in its worst and best facets.

After Lowell vented his doubts about the war in the second *Biglow Series*, he reaffirmed his faith in Puritan conscience with his "Ode Recited at the Harvard Commemoration," among his best works. Shortly after the war's end, Lowell was asked to deliver an original poem in memory of Harvard graduates killed in the conflict—his own nephews among them. Feeling a heavy responsibility, he finished after a two-day writing binge just in time for the commemoration on July 21, 1865. The poem was overshadowed by Emerson's more memorable performance, but it remains a striking tribute and a fitting conclusion to the author's struggle with his responsibilities as a poet to his nephews and his nation. The ode's opening echoes the humility of the Gettysburg Address: "We seem to do them wrong, / Bringing our robin's-leaf to deck their hearse / Who in warm life-blood wrote their nobler verse" (lines 4–6). Where Julia Ward Howe's "Battle Hymn of the Republic" purposely equivocates on whether the "fiery gospel writ in burnished rows of steel" is scripture, the truth of antislavery literature, or the soldiers themselves, Lowell unequivocally places all "truer poetry" in these fallen soldiers who "shaped in squadron-strophes their desire, / Live battle-odes whose lines were steel and fire" (9–10), lending his verse to a much humbler task: "to buoy up . . . the common grave of the unadventurous throng" (12–13).

Lowell's praise for these true poets begins in language that is stately, Roman, and secular. He lauds the vital core of Harvard that "could thy sons entice / From happy homes and toils . . . Into War's tumult rude" (lines 31–33), not mere academic study but the sterner and "deeper teaching of her mystic tome" (17), nothing less than the "Veritas that lurks beneath / The letter's unprolific sheath, / Life of whate'er makes life worth living" (37–39). But this sacrifice to the mystic tome soon sparks a shift in Lowell's language back toward the prophetic language that marked his earliest work and forms the climax of the Ode. Harvard's fallen sons follow Truth "where all may hope to find / . . . with danger's sweetness round her. / Where faith made whole with deed / Breathes its awakening breath / Into the lifeless creed" (57–62). And just as in early antislavery works like "A Glance Behind" and "The Present Crisis," the ode skillfully cultivates a prophetic sense of "messianic time," of historical liminality as the poet binds past, present, and future into a plenitude, asking what will "make the next age better for the last? . . . / Something to live for here that shall outlive us?" (68–71).

To be certain, the ode diverges sharply from Lowell's earliest prophecies in the space it devotes to doubt, especially for a momentous public elegy: "The little that we see / From doubt is never free; / The little that we do / Is but half-nobly true" (74–77). In some of its most striking language, the poem teeters toward nihilistic despair: "Life seems a jest of Fate's contriving, / Only secure in every one's conniving / A long account of nothings paid with loss, / Where we poor puppets, jerked by unseen wires, / After our little hour of strut and rave, / With all our pasteboard passions and desires" (80–85). But the poem vents these doubts in order to redirect them toward something more permanent, stronger for its ability to withstand such skepticism. "Ah, there is something here / Unfathomed by the cynic's sneer," Lowell declares without the slightest wink, "To claim its birthright with the hosts of heaven" (88–96).

The prophesied "something" is nothing less than the Puritan conscience of Lowell's youth, but one now matured, more aware of its cost and pain, the ways it haunts and hurts a degenerate world: "A conscience more divine than we, / A gladness fed with secret tears, / A vexing, forward-reaching sense / Of some more noble permanence; / A light across the sea, / Which haunts the soul and will not let it be, / Still glimmering from the heights of undegenerate years" (lines 101–7). Lowell reaffirms this conscience even as he emphasizes how it haunts and goads humanity "not down flowery meads" but "up the steep, amid the wrath / And shock of deadly-hostile creeds / . . . By battle's flashes gropes a desperate way" (110–16). While his antislavery peers had long embraced abolitionism out of a desire for heroic, fighting "true religion" akin to the Puritanism of old, Lowell repledged his allegiance yet reminded his youthful self and his ardent comrades of the costs involved. Now their "war of tongue and pen / Learns with what deadly purpose it was fraught" (126–27), and "the soft Ideal that we wooed / Confronts us fiercely, foe-beset, pursued" and demands,

"Give me thy life or cower in empty phrase" (131, 135). The line is an aggressive challenge to everyone who, like young Lowell, eagerly attacked slavery with imaginative holy wars without giving much forethought to the lives that might be lost in real battle. For this reason, another key difference emerges between the ode and Lowell's early prophecies: it is no longer he that is the prophet, but his fallen nephews who laid down their lives for Truth: far better than him, such men show "God's plan . . . Limbed like the old heroic breeds" (143–46). Lowell concludes with a return to the full prophetic language of his youth: "Bow down, dear Land, for thou hast found release! / Thy God, in these distempered days, / Hath taught thee the sure wisdom of His ways, / And through thine enemies hath wrought thy peace! / Bow down in prayer and praise!" (150–54). But there is one key difference: the prophecy is an elegy, the prophets now dead.

FIVE

La Belle Puritaine

The Sword often serves to chastize the Church for their Apostacy . . . when Christians have enjoyed long Peace and Prosperity.

—Amos Adams, *"The expediency and utility of war . . . a discourse before, and at the desire of the Ancient and Honourable Artillery-Company, at Boston,"* 1759

In an 1826 Forefathers' Day sermon at Plymouth, "The Spirit of the Pilgrims," the Reverend Richard Storrs used language that was striking for a Congregationalist minister. The Pilgrims and Puritans, he declared, had passed on a "spirit of free inquiry" that trumped creeds and institutions, for "the difference between the Hindoo and the merely nominal Christian, are entirely circumstantial and unimportant" without the "heartfelt conviction" that drove their fathers to liberate England and plant America in their protest against "the virulence of the carnal heart . . . intrenched too firmly within the walls of an established church." Though himself a minister in a church that had been recently disestablished in Connecticut (and remained threatened in Massachusetts), Storrs instructed his audience "to imbibe a portion of their spirit." He underestimated the potency of the spirits he served.

Storrs and his audience felt no risk in such language to their identity as conservative guardians of the Puritan errand; the spirit of the Pilgrims was neither "the wild spirit of fanaticism" nor "a cold and speculative system of theology" but, as for Lowell, a conscience "inflexibly maintained" and grounded in "the divine law."[1] Yet how one interpreted this law and the Puritan errand proved to be an increasingly unstable affair in the decades to come as abolition especially threatened the standing of the American clergy and church, the Puritans' most direct institutional heirs. Much of

Storrs's language could have been mistaken for the transcendentalist and abolitionist impulses already boiling into a threat against orthodoxy. By 1840 the Reverend Jonathan Ward spoke for many when he feared that Garrisonian critiques of the clergy forced Americans to choose between church and abolition. Worse yet, they claimed this same "Spirit of the Pilgrims" in their mission to "destroy the influence of ministers."[2]

Ward was likely thinking of his renowned colleague the Reverend Lyman Beecher, a portent for how American churches would struggle under the abolitionist challenge. Throughout the 1820s and 1830s Beecher had risen steadily as the nation's most promising ministerial heir to the Puritan errand in a time of growing disestablishment and democracy, reimagining his forefathers' errand as a union of Protestant churches and benevolent institutions that would spread New England civilization across the nation. But by 1840 Lyman's ambitious plans had capsized in the growing storm over slavery, buffeted on one side by antiabolitionists within his own denomination and on the other by Garrisonian abolitionists whose shrinking faith in the church culminated in their formal separation from the "Tappanites" and their church-based antislavery work. Before and after this rupture, the many ministers like Beecher who opposed slavery yet cherished the church faced the worrisome task of sailing existing religious institutions, traditions, and beliefs between the Scylla of Garrisonian anticlericism and the Charybdis of slavery. None made it through unscathed. Major denominations split into Northern and Southern branches, while members of the orthodox lapsed into Garrisonian "infidelity," disillusioned with the church's indecision on the issue. All parties claimed "the spirit of the Pilgrims," but ministers especially felt the strain of its radical potential. If the abolitionist reclamation of Puritanism was a response to anxieties about secularization, the clergy were particularly anxious as they watched their cultural authority decline, their denominations disestablish, and their congregations consider the arguments of abolitionists who claimed the spirit of the Pilgrims in opposition to the nation's "dead" churches.

In the decades to come, Lyman's talented children Reverend Henry Ward Beecher and Harriet Beecher Stowe would inherit their father's mission to reimagine the church's Puritan errand for new times. But where their father could revise the theology and institutions of the "Forefathers" from an abstract distance, Henry and Harriet faced the more intimate challenge of reimagining the legacies of their literal father. As they balanced loyalty to Lyman's legacy with their sense of its shortcomings, they wrestled with a stronger anxiety of influence. Out of these mixed feelings grew their vision of what Stowe would describe as *la belle puritaine*, the lovelier facets of Puritanism as a communal way of everyday life that were over-looked by its other antebellum claimants, in particular Garrisonians, whom she felt distilled Puritanism into an anticlerical mythos for radical iconoclasm, "Old School" Presbyterians who let it rust into conservative inaction, and moderate "New School" ministers like their father who fell into the middle as the nation polarized on slavery, content to parse the Pilgrim spirit into a system of "New Divinity" and a network of benevolent societies. Disliking all three options, Beecher and Stowe hoped to reunite the nation around their own "beautiful Puritanism" as a moderate and church-based antislavery alternative. And yet in its effort to create a common ground on which the nation could return to its Puritan roots, this "Belle Puritaine" ended with little that was distinctly Puritan in any sense. In fact, the further Henry and Harriet moved away from their father's Puritanism, the more adamantly they explored and insisted on their own Puritanness. Here was perhaps the best example of how deeply abolition destabilized the Puritan errand and its clerical descendants, aggravating the tension between Pilgrim spirits and Pilgrim institutions: those who held most creatively and fiercely to both ended up "Puritan" only by the greatest stretch of imagination.[3]

Beecher's Pilgrim Spirit

In 1826 the Reverend Lyman Beecher resolved to reclaim Boston from the Unitarians and restore its status as the capital of Puritan America. The first *belle puritain* in the Beecher line, he planned to use captivating style, modern communication technologies, softened doctrine, and vigorous benevolence societies to create a distinctly modern Puritan church suited to a democratic nation. Where he had once opposed efforts to disestablish the Congregationalist Church in Connecticut, he famously changed his mind after disestablishment passed in 1818, deciding that a loss of state support would energize America's ministers for a national campaign of revival and reform. He especially planned to dethrone the Unitarians with a regiment of benevolent societies that would squelch national sins like dueling, drunkenness, and slavery. Each of these reform efforts were assumed to be projects emanating from the church itself, but the delicate question of slavery quickly became the stickiest part of this mission, and one that Beecher ultimately failed to resolve on two fronts. First, he never convinced the young William Lloyd Garrison that his mission might best be accomplished if it was accommodated to the church's existing efforts. More disastrously, he fueled Garrisonians' anticlericism by failing to unite the churches themselves around a forthright response to slavery. This would prove to be a recurring struggle for early orthodox reformers and their Tappanite successors in the decades to come. While Garrison claimed the Puritan mantle for a bold and focused immediatist platform, Beecher and his orthodox allies wavered as they failed to agree upon what exactly their forefathers would have them do about slavery.

The *Spirit of the Pilgrims* especially reveals this quandary. Two years after Reverend Storrs's sermon of the same name, Beecher and other colleagues became convinced that their mission, like most in the early republic, required a paper. The *Spirit* ran monthly from 1828 to 1833, for a time edited by Beecher himself. The fact that dignified clerics were now participating in a medium traditionally considered below their station was itself a small admission that the pulpit had declined in cultural authority: "The mass of mind which is now awake to investigate and feel," Beecher wrote, "renders the pulpit unequal, and a new means of enlightening and forming public sentiment indispensable." A primary motivation for the paper was to convince Bostonians that orthodoxy could be an enlightened affair. Here too like Storrs "they did not hold themselves responsible to the letter for those doctrines as stated in the creeds of the Reformation" but esteemed "the expectation of 'farther light' as the glorious privilege of the New England churches." Yet such a venture was precarious from the start in its effort to remain open to Storrs's "spirit of free inquiry" but not so open as to fall from a sacred inheritance nor damage the Puritans' institutional legacies. "The time has come," Beecher concluded, for "a united and simultaneous effort to rescue from perversion the doctrines and institutions of our fathers, the fairest inheritance ever bestowed by Heaven upon men." In these and subsequent writings, Lyman and the contributors to the *Spirit* made clear that the journal's name was no mere rhetoric but a deep desire to preserve "the religion and institutions of our fathers . . . all the great designs which God has to answer by planting our fathers here."[4] Article after article exhibited a deep concern for how to best retain New England's Puritan and Pilgrim inheritance, where it needed preservation and where it ought to be updated to better fit new times.

On slavery, the *Spirit* never achieved a united stance. Early on it praised the neo-Edwardsian divine Samuel Hopkins (whom Lyman's daughter Harriet would later dramatize in *The Minister's Wooing*) as "one of the first men in this country who boldly set his face against the African slave trade, and engaged in systematic efforts for its suppression," while another article waffled on whether the slow progress of the colonization movement was providential or a purposeful scheme to delay emancipation, as early critics like Garrison charged.[5] In the same issue another writer took a different approach, arguing that Colonizationists and Immediatists were not as opposed as they claimed to be.[6] This indecision seemed to bother contributors all the more because of an implicit understanding that slavery would be a defining issue for the future of America and a key chance for the clergy to restore their role as the nation's spiritual leaders. One writer argued that while New England had declined in political importance, "she is destined, if not unfaithful to herself, and to her God, to exercise a higher, and a nobler influence . . . in learning, morals, and religion," especially on the issue of slavery, "big with fearful destiny, for the alleviation and removal of which, I am persuaded, the spirit and the men of New England must take lead." The author was light on strategic details, halfheartedly siding with the Colonizationists.[7]

Underlying this predicament was a deeper indecision about the political demands of the Reformation and the Puritans on the present, another instance of uncertainty concerning shifting boundaries between the sacred and the secular. The Reverend John Crosby repeated the familiar Whig argument that any revolution not rooted in religion was doomed to the excesses of the French Revolution, but he also anticipated Emerson and Garrison's converse argument that Protestant heritage sometimes demanded revolution. "The birth of English & American liberty," he argued, "was kindled at the Reformation as we have seen by *religion*. Portions of it have since been smothered" while others "raged with violence" before "subsiding into a steady flame," but one thing was certain: Unitarian calm could never spark any fire whatsoever. It remained for the orthodox to tend the Puritan flame. "It was the religion of the Puritans, which swept away the institutions of despotism," he concluded, and "what would the *Puritan* have been—what would they *have done* for British & American liberty, had they been urged by nothing more powerful than that system of natural religion, which some of their descendents have mistaken for the gospel of Christ!"[8] On the other hand, another writer drew a more literal model from Pilgrim separatism by concluding that American politics had grown so corrupt that religion should withdraw entirely from it, should "be preserved from the *mania* of party zeal, and stand aloof from the conflicts of ambition, and the din of political controversy."[9] The Reverend Joel Hawes took a more moderate position in his defense of Congregationalism as the best way "to strengthen and perpetuate our civil institutions." While he could concede that the Puritans were wrong to enforce a Congregationalist state church, they were right to regard "piety as the prime qualification for all places of public trust," and "all who possess the spirit of the Pilgrims must prefer those candidates for places of power and trust, who appear to be under the influence of *true and vital religion.*"[10] All agreed that America would be saved by its Pilgrim spirit, but none agreed on what these effervescent spirits entailed in practice.

The creation and near implosion of Lane Theological Seminary reveals how this volatile pilgrim spirit spilled beyond and threatened clerical authority and institutions. Bankrolled by the Tappan brothers in 1828, this hopeful "Princeton of the West" aimed to spread New England culture and the steady Tappanite mix of "New School" Congregationalism and moderate antislavery activism. All agreed that Beecher was a perfect candidate for the seminary's first president on all fronts. He eagerly accepted, outlining his vision for college and nation in *A Plea for the West* (1835), a call for the clergy to combat Catholicism by extending Protestant institutions across the continent. Like his ministerial colleagues, he emphasized a particularly Puritan union of sacred and secular in which American republicanism was founded on and preserved by Protestantism's revolutionary potential. "The republican tendencies of the Calvinistic system," he wrote, "have always been on the side of liberty in its struggles against arbitrary power," and "through the puritans, it breathed into the British constitution its most invaluable principles, and laid the foundations of the republican institutions of our nation . . . and fought, and suffered through the revolutionary struggle."[11] But this revolutionary Puritan spirit soon inspired more radical abolitionists to confront Lyman himself with the arbitrary power of slavery. In 1834 his gradualist approach to the issue appeared increasingly craven to a new generation of young seminarians electrified by Garrison and led by the charismatic Theodore Dwight Weld, himself the son of a Connecticut Congregationalist minister and a proud descendant of a revolutionary Puritan.[12] These "Lane Rebels" worried school trustees as they staged debates on Immediatism and undertook mission work among Cincinnati's black population with an attitude of equality that troubled white residents. Beecher tried and failed to mediate between positions that grew irreconcilable: after he simultaneously refused to expel the students and consented to harsh administrative retaliation, he was publicly humiliated when most of the Rebels departed anyway, leaving Lane on the brink of collapse.[13]

Perhaps still bitter with Beecher, Weld would later snipe at the violence of "our Puritan fore-fathers" as evidence that Americans were more than capable of slavery, but among his allies and disciples, the Puritans and Pilgrims were more often reclaimed from Beecher.[14] The Lane Rebels eventually accepted an invitation to join Oberlin College, recently established as a biracial and antislavery alternative whose founders compared the school's establishment to Plymouth Rock; the Rebels insisted that *they* were the true Pilgrims.[15] When preachers complained that Oberlin and the Rebels had divided their congregations, one of Weld's disciples, Reverend John Keep, rebuffed the charge of schismatism by insisting that their antislavery congregations followed "the purest form of the Puritan fathers."[16] The entire episode was an omen for later Tappanite efforts to unite churches against slavery, and in some cases it confirmed the clergy's suspicion that abolitionism not only split up congregations and denominations but even drove individuals away from organized religion altogether. In the most prominent instance, Weld himself became one of many abolitionists who grew so disillusioned with the church's response to slavery that he abandoned institutional Protestantism.[17] Through and beyond the Tappanites, "ecclesiastical abolitionism" made progress among scattered separatist congregations. Certain groups punched above their weight, like the Presbyterian-descended Oneida Institute under the direction of Gerrit Smith and Beriah Green's "animating mix of Puritan discipline, religious warmth, and zealous abolitionism," an institution that would train Henry Highland Garnet, Alexander Crummell, Amos Beman, and other black leaders, clerical or otherwise.[18] Yet under the leadership of Beecher and his allies, major Northern Presbygationalist denominations as a whole failed to achieve unity, a "painful but portentous adolescence" dogged by "political caution and sectarian loyalties," in the words of Timothy Smith.[19] Some felt that this failure was nothing short of disastrous. "I verily believe that, if Lyman Beecher had been true to Christ and to liberty in that trying hour," concluded an early historian of abolition, "the whole course of American history in regard to slavery would have been changed, and that the slaves might have been emancipated without the shedding of blood."[20] Ironically, Lyman's son Henry was about to become the Tappanites' most influential leader.

Henry's Puritan Bluff

Into the 1840s, the Tappan brothers joined with other wealthy New England transplants in New York to establish an antislavery Congregationalist church that would become one of the nation's most influential: Brooklyn's Plymouth Church (once more named for the Pilgrims). The same Tappanites who had lured Lyman Beecher to the West succeeded in luring his son Henry back East after he had proved his talent for fresh approaches in Indianapolis, swelling the size of his congregation by combining his father's sensitivity to public opinion with a warmer "Gospel of Love" that tempered

Lyman's neo-Edwardsianism and deemphasized the increasingly unpopular facets of Calvinism. Just as Lyman beautified Puritanism, Henry further renovated his father's *belle puritaine*. In the words of Debby Applegate, "under Lyman's influence, the Beecher children yoked the Puritan legacy of a strong social conscience to a modern mastery of persuasion and public opinion, keeping their fellow citizens riled up, inspired, and entertained."[21] Alongside this promising combination was Henry's track record on slavery that suggested he might aid the Tappanite cause where his father had failed. During the Lane Rebellion he sided with his father, but by 1839 he had rejected his father's Colonizationism and Garrison's Immediatism alike.

With his new congregation of wealthy yet idealistic Tappanites, Henry could afford to be radical. Increasingly inspired by Emerson's transcendentalism and the revolutions in Europe, he amplified his reformist bona fides by performing the role of the Protestant revolutionary. For his first Thanksgiving sermon at Plymouth Church, Henry made the expected Beecher argument that slavery's greatest evil arose in destroying the kind of free society bequeathed to America from the Puritans, but he diverged from his father when he declared that only spiritual warfare would settle the issue. Christ "came not to send peace on earth, but the sword," after all, and "the most radical book on earth is the Bible."[22] This occasional delight in performing the role of the radical was not without substance. Beecher especially came to national attention during Bleeding Kansas, when he helped organize Free State settlers from the Beechers' ancestral Connecticut and raised funds for their armament, smuggling rifles through enemy lines in crates of "Bibles." These "Beecher's Bibles," as the rifles came to be called, marked the rising Brooklyn preacher as something more than an armchair preacher, if no John Brown. Critics derided Beecher's Brooklyn congregation as the "Church of the Holy Rifles," while his more ardent beneficiaries in Kansas later christened their church the "Beecher Bible and Rifle Church" without a hint of irony (the congregation still holds Sunday services today). In his widespread pamphlet "Defence of Kansas," Beecher defended these actions with a manifesto that proclaimed a radicalized version of his father's faith: the survival of a free society descended from Puritan New England now demanded revolutionary Protestant resistance in the West. Here Beecher agreed with more liberal figures like Child, Higginson, and Parker: Kansas was the plain upon which a holy war would be decided. He grew apocalpytic, quoting Revelation: "'A great mountain, burning with fire, was cast into the sea; and the third part of the sea became blood.' So will armed Slavery be cast into Kansas."[23]

As with other abolitionists, this impulse toward prophecy and Puritanical holy war was especially loosed with the Civil War when the prospect of real battle was baptized with antislavery potential and the patriotic prospect of thumping Southern rebels. After South Carolina's secession, Beecher delivered a jeremiad that traced the present storm back to irreconcilable social systems symbolized in the *Mayflower* and the slave ship, "two seeds of the two systems that were destined to find here a growth and strength unparalleled in history . . . Puritan liberty and Roman servitude."[24] Though he professed to "love every drop of Puritan blood that the world ever saw," Beecher chastised the North's fall from this sacred heritage in its growing complicity with slavery, its "gradual corruption of the moral sense, so that property and self-interest dominate the conscience."[25] Sounding every bit the Puritan parson, he held before his audience a future of either disaster or peace: the outcome depended on a present reckoning with sin.[26]

When the prospect of peace was dashed with the firing on Fort Sumter later that year, Beecher donned his Puritan battle armor in a sermon two days later. Though the present looked dark, he sketched a heritage of embattled Protestant prophets overcoming great odds through courageous faith. From Luther to the Dutch Revolt to the English Revolution, he proclaimed, in "every one of these instances darkness and the flood lay before the champions of truth," yet victory came through a courageous commitment to sacred principles. "Now our turn has come. Right before us lies the Red Sea of war. It is red indeed," Beecher concluded, but "by the memory of the fathers; by the sufferings of the Puritan ancestry . . . by what we are and what our progenitors were,—we have a right to walk foremost in this procession of nations toward the bright future."[27] From the start, Beecher maintained that the war ought not be merely for Union but for emancipation, to actualize "the principle of man's rights based upon the divinity of his origin . . . embodied (thanks to Puritan influence) in our Constitution."[28] When Union fervor had declined a year later after a string of stalemates, Beecher defended the abolitionists as they "who labor to bring back the voices of the founders of this Union; the men whose faith touches the original principles of God's Word; the men that are in sympathy with Luther; the men that breathe the breath that fanned the flame of the Revolution; the men that walk in the spirit of the old Puritans."[29] Hoping to fan up British support for the Union the next year, he asked a London audience to "pray for the North as you would have prayed for the Covenanters, for the old Nonconformists, for the old Puritans, for Christians in any age whose duty it became to resist unrighteousness."[30] (He never seemed to consider that Londoners might not share his admiration for the Puritans.)

Yet before the war, Henry had rarely claimed the Puritan mantle so zealously, while during and after he amply counterbalanced his Puritan war drums with a more frequent tendency to smooth discord with a gospel of love (most evident in his unflagging devotion to President Johnson during Reconstruction). This zigzagging between conservative and radical impulses was partly due to a restless and inconsistent temperament and partly due to Henry's driving desire to be liked: he was a revolutionary only insofar as he could count on support from his Tappanite allies at home and the like-minded across the nation. But there was more to this imbalance than a temperamental pursuit of popularity. Elsewhere Henry elaborated a more conscious defense of this tacking as a necessary part of negotiating an old Puritan tension: balancing the dissenting individual conscience with the stability of the institutions that protected its rights, revived anew in the Garrisonian-transcendentalist propensity for antinomianism and the preservation of a sound Union. Even in his first Thanksgiving sermon Henry tempered his defense of radicalism with a Tappanite jab at Garrisonian anticlericism, proclaiming that "any great and constant Progress rests chiefly upon one Association, THE CHURCH."[31] In a later address called "Man and His Institutions," he gave a nod to the Jacksonian and transcendentalist spirit of the times by praising individuality as a God-given strength, but he maintained that "a man without institutions is a fountain without an egress; like a soul without bodily members to work with." Institutions were a way of helping a moral vision broaden beyond and outlast its original seer, a way to discipline the nation for the spiritual warfare at hand: "We can not meet the drilled and disciplined battalions of evil with a scattering guerila warfare. We must institute Justice, Truth, Love, Peace, Purity."[32] Here too his institutional vision was rooted not only in the church but in the broader New England traditions from which it grew. Sounding much like his father, he called on his listeners to join him in "rear[ing] along the vast intervals and valleys of the West a civilization as deep, as wide, as compact of social refinement, of intellectual culture, of moral richness, as that which hovers in their memory of dear old New England."[33]

Revealingly, Henry described this balance between cherished New England institutions and innovative individuality as a father-son relationship. "They are not antagonistic; they are co-operative," he said: "the parent protects the weakness of infancy and leads the son up to his manhood. That manhood, in turn, takes the weakness of age into its arms, and the old man is strong in the cradle of his son's bosom!"[34] Here was Henry's idealized vision of his own relationship with his father and everything Lyman represented culturally and historically. For good reason, much of the scholarship on the Beechers emphasizes the strain between Lyman and his children as they struggled to free themselves from his Calvinism. Robert Ingersoll was not entirely off when he concluded that Henry "was born in a Puritan penitentiary, of which his father was one of the wardens." But Lyman and the Puritan heritage he represented were less a prison for his children than a hegemonic affair, all the harder to escape because they had convinced themselves of much of its historical greatness.[35] One ought not take Henry at his word when he proclaimed himself "the son of a Puritan, and a Puritan myself" who "would have burned at Oxford, and fought with Cromwell," but one should take seriously the desires behind such bluff.[36] That is, Henry did not want to see his Gospel of Love as a fall from his spartan Calvinist ancestry, as in Ann Douglas's telling.[37] Instead he tried his hardest to see it much as Lyman saw his own decision to soften and popularize neo-Edwardsian theology: the preservation of a sacred inheritance by reforming and refreshing its spiritual vigor for new times. Moreover, he felt that such a process was demanded by the inheritance itself, a reforming of Reformation. Here Lyman and Henry were in the company of Emerson and Phillips, though they expressed this belief in more traditional institutional venues.

Yet the zeal with which Henry claimed the Puritan mantle during the war suggests afear of abandoning this inheritance entirely. After spending much of the 1850s putting distance between his orthodoxy and his father's Calvinism, Henry was perhaps surprised by 1861 to see how successful he had been both theologically and financially, and the success came (as it often did in New England) with nagging worries about a lapse from ancestral faith precisely because the ancestral was the paternal for Henry. Where the abolitionist crusade offered restless Unitarians a chance to revive a more intense strain of religiosity, war was Henry's chance to perform the faith of his fathers rather than admit the simpler truth: he was no Puritan. Such an admission would have been nearly unthinkable for someone whose father had devoted his life to sustaining a Puritan legacy that included filiopiety as a core facet, for someone who had committed himself to the same institutional legacies if not their theology. While Henry would go where he wanted in his private beliefs, he nonetheless couched these changes in bald assertions of his own Puritanism, performances with some substance yet performances nonetheless. Henry never seemed to recognize this tension, much less resolve it, nor perhaps could he so long as he remained invested in the Congregationalist institutions descended from his forebears. Ironically, his sister Harriet had better success in imagining what a lovely and useful Puritan heritage might look like in antebellum America precisely because her gender denied her a leadership role in these institutions. As a novelist, she was free to imagine the Puritans however she pleased.

"Bands of Reverence" after Uncle Tom

Denied the pulpit, Harriet Beecher Stowe found that the struggle with slavery aggravated her ambivalent relationship with her Puritan ancestry and its institutional descendants even more than for her brother Henry, supported by those institutions. Like Henry's preaching, *Uncle Tom's Cabin* found an enthusiastic reception in 1852 partly because its warmer vision of Christianity spoke to a new generation eager to escape the dour legacies of Calvinism; readers cheered as the flinty Puritan conscience of Ophelia (a familiar type for many) softened under love, and they welcomed the novel's advice to simply "feel right" on slavery, espousing the "sympathies of Christ" beyond the severity of the Calvinist God. Stowe similarly appealed to a broader evangelical readership by distinguishing herself from Garrisonian radicalism, believing that abolition could emanate safely from the church itself. "Let the church of the north receive these poor sufferers in the spirit of Christ" to cultivate "the educating advantages of Christian republican society," she concluded, and the black race would achieve liberty. It was a page from the Beecher playbook, elevating Christian institutions as the safeguard of the republic. And yet despite her respect for these institutions, Stowe threatened them with a wrathful Jehovah if they ignored her sympathetic Christ. In *Uncle Tom's* final sentences she shifted abruptly from right feeling to terrific jeremiad: America would quake with divine revolution should the churches fail to cultivate right feeling. In an age "when nations are trembling and convulsed," Stowe wrote, "O, Church of Christ, read the signs of the times! Is not this power the spirit of Him whose kingdom is yet to come?" If the church failed, its "injustice and cruelty shall bring on nations the wrath of Almighty God!" Puritan Ophelia speaks alongside sentimental Tom, Garrisonian anticlericism alongside Tappanite evangelicalism.

Garrison himself struck at this ambivalence shortly after the novel's release. With her newfound fame, Stowe needed to clarify her position within the broader abolitionist movement. The church-based Tappanites were the more natural fit, but Stowe also felt indebted to the Garrisonians as the movement's trailblazers, even as she worried about their harsh critiques of the church. Stowe wrote to Garrison to see how he might respond, confessing her fear that his anticlericism "will take from poor Uncle Tom his bible

& give him nothing in its place," might destroy the progressive potential of the church by overemphasizing its failures.[38] In his reply—published in the *Liberator* as a response to an anonymous "friend"—Garrison sniped at Stowe's weak points. On her wish to see the *Liberator* circulated only among the intelligent (lest uneducated readers like Tom "lose their Bible"), Garrison was blunt: "So says the Romish Church," he chided, sure to sting a proud Puritan Beecher. Garrison claimed Protestantism for his own anticlericism, denying any middle road between papal infallibility and individual Protestant conscience: "each one can determine only for himself" the merits of scripture and the church, "for on Protestant ground, there is no room for papal infallibility." Thus Garrisonian critiques of the church were "not necessarily heresy,—unless the great Protestant right of private judgment be heretical, as Papal Rome says it is."[39]

Garrison's reclamation of Protestantism worked. Stowe's (private) response met Garrison in the middle and revealed an unsettling of former beliefs. She admitted that her sense of heresy had softened. (She had read Theodore Parker's works and discovered in them "a fair view of the modern form of what people have generally denominated 'infidelity.'") Yet she still worried that the *Liberator*'s "general tone and spirit"—its "hasty assertions, appeals to passion"—would especially "break the bands of reverence and belief."[40] In true Beecher fashion, she worried that the Garrisonian challenge to American churches threatened social anarchy in weakening these "bands" of communal belief for an antinomian riot of individual conscience. Put otherwise, Stowe was, like Henry, sensitive to the old Puritan tension between individual dissenters and the church that guarded their sacred right to dissent, and she rightly sensed how much Garrisonians revived the antinomian impulses of Protestantism. More troubling yet, Stowe did not know how to bypass Garrison's invocation of this very Protestant heritage to support his antinomian tendencies. As proud of her Puritan heritage as Henry was, she lauded its tendency "to challenge and dispute all sham pretensions and idolatries of past ages,—to question the right of kings in the State, and of prelates in the Church."[41] Garrisonians lived up to this spirit better than any, and Stowe partially admired them for it.

The threat of this new antinomianism is a common thread in Stowe's post-*Tom* writings as they seem to meander from travel memoir to a tale of a black revolutionary to quaint portraits of New England in the final days of Puritanism. Each work wrestles with anxieties raised by Garrison's challenge to the church and the quandary left unresolved in *Uncle Tom's Cabin*: why did most individuals and churches continue to feel *wrong* on slavery, unable to unite in antislavery "bands of reverence"? In response, Stowe's fiction grew preoccupied with religious "nature" and "nurture": how individuals might be predisposed toward certain spiritual sensibilities, and how the church—the historic Puritan church in particular, as well as the republican culture which she believed it produced and safeguarded—had strengthened or aggravated these dispositions with its own antinomian and iconoclastic tendencies. Stowe initially believed in Americans' capacity to feel rightly, but personal and political experience soon undermined this faith and prompted a sustained search for spiritual cohesion within democracy's spiritual disarray. Ultimately Stowe's high estimation of Europe in *Sunny Memories of Foreign Lands* (1854) and her dire diagnosis of American individualism in *Dred* (1856) drove her back to the Puritan past in *The Minister's Wooing* (1859) and *Oldtown Folks* (1869), where she counteracted Garrisonian antinomianism with a lovelier vision of Puritan heritage that might forge antislavery bands of reverence.

When Stowe first wrote to Garrison, she had just returned from her first visit to Europe, a tour to promote *Uncle Tom's Cabin* and aid the antislavery cause. The journey sparked what Carolyn Karcher calls her "sociological" quality and her first full-scale examination of Puritanism's role in American culture at large.[42] She wrestled with these thoughts in *Sunny Memories of Foreign Lands*, a lighthearted travel memoir that grew into a comparative study of nations' merits. Stowe's Puritan biases arose often and forcefully; hiking the Swiss Alps, she found herself annoyed that the scenery was interrupted by begging and goitered Catholics. "The fact is, they are poor," she concluded, "because invention, enterprise, and intellectual vigor—all that surrounds the New England mountain farmer with competence and comfort—are quenched and dead, by the combined influence of a religion and government whose interest it is to keep people stupid that they may be manageable." In Cologne she laughed at "the rottenness of the Romish system" behind the backs of relic-venerating priests.[43] Like many orthodox Congregationalists, Stowe likewise concluded that the French revolutions had failed where the American had succeeded because, in a word, they lacked Calvinists, for Catherine de Medici "drained France of her lifeblood" when she drove the Huguenots from France.[44] Europe never fully undermined her Beecher belief that republicanism required Protestantism's "religious democratic element."

Yet other observations qualified these biases. At the ruins of Melrose Abbey in Scotland, stripped of its art and sporting the scars of Cromwellian cannons, Stowe reflected that "New England's earnestness and practical efficiency," good as it was, came with "a crushing out of the beautiful,—which is horrible. Children are born there with a sense of beauty equally delicate with any in the world, in whom it dies a lingering death of smothered desire and pining, weary starvation. I know, because I have felt it."[45] For this reason Stowe was smitten with France's aesthetic splendor and its "passion for the outward and visible."[46] Pitched between these pros and cons, Stowe wondered whether the aesthetic vitality of Catholic nations were separable from their antidemocratic flaws. "I thought of the ignorance and stupid idolatry of those countries where this ritual is found in greatest splendor," Stowe reflected, "and asked whether these are the necessary concomitants of such churches and such forms, or whether they do not result from other causes."[47] That is, Stowe wondered whether an ideal society could combine the aesthetic vitality of France with the religious earnestness and democracy of New England.

Stowe discovered a new America upon her return, one that seemed intent on blowing itself up with the anarchic and iconoclastic excesses of its democratic Puritan heritage. A week after Stowe's reply to Garrison, Senator Stephen A. Douglas reignited tensions around slavery by proposing the Kansas-Nebraska Act. After four months of bitter debate in Congress, the bill became law and Bleeding Kansas soon erupted. When fighting reached its fiercest in 1856, Brooks caned Sumner, Brown executed proslavery settlers, and Stowe's own brother Henry sent his "Beecher's Bible" to aid the cause. With every passing month Stowe's call for "right feeling" looked more naive. If she had once worried that Garrison took away Tom's Bible, Stowe now encountered a different problem: under pressure, American Protestantism had armed everyone with a riflelike Bible and no grounds for adjudication between opposed beliefs. The specter of slave revolts especially stoked this fear: Had not Turner taken up arms under divine visions? Was he not—as writers like William Wells Brown, Frederick Douglass, and Henry C. Wright themselves implied—the most obvious reincarnation of the Puritan warriors that Henry and Harriet lauded?

Stowe clarified these worries in her second novel, Dred: A Tale of the Dismal Swamp (1856).[48] After Frederick Douglass and Martin Delany publicly expressed their distaste for Uncle Tom's passivity, Stowe imagined Dred, the son of slave rebel Denmark Vesey and himself a Puritanical slave who sees signs everywhere, studies scripture, and speaks in Hebraic jeremiad as he prepares for armed revolution in the name of a wrathful God. Stowe pitches between moralistic prescriptions against Dred's violence and sympathetic descriptions of how he arrived at such feelings, emphasizing that his religiosity is less fanaticism than the expected result of forcing a sensitive spiritual nature into an oppressive social structure. Dred is "by nature" heroic, literary, and religious—Stowe's ideal Christian, yet one who has been twisted into violence by slavery. As Dred carries Vesey's Bible through the Dismal Swamp, isolation amplifies his "impassioned nature" and drives him to the words of the Old Testament prophets. Yet Stowe worried about his reading of scripture even as she understood it. "As the fierce and savage soul delights in the roar of torrents," she wrote, "so is it in the great answering volume of revelation. There is something there for every phase of man's nature; and hence its endless vitality and stimulating force."[49] Beginning with prescription, Stowe rejected the "savage soul" reading the Bible toward revolutionary ends even as her Protestant faith in scripture conceded its "endless vitality" for all people, even volatile slaves like Dred. Warily, Stowe admitted the radical implications of this faith, for "even in cold and misty England, armies have been made defiant and invincible by the incomparable force and deliberate valor which [scripture] breathes into men"—especially meaning the militant legacies of her Puritan ancestry in the English Civil War. When a book as unwieldy as the Bible was read by a man of Dred's history, circumstance, and "nature" (which for Stowe included race), the result was even more explosive: "planted back in the fiery soil of a tropical heart, it bursts forth with an incalculable ardor of growth."[50] Stowe understood Dred's nature and nurture only to worry that this mixture made him a Cromwellian army of one.[51]

The Dismal Swamp thus becomes not only Dred's tangled home but a symbol of his soul and a metaphor for American religion writ large, vital yet chaotic, a landscape where plants and people, "from the singularly unnatural and wildly stimulating properties of the slimy depths from which they spring, assume a goblin growth."[52] In stark contrast to the atmosphere of *Uncle Tom's Cabin*, *Dred* imagines a world where religious experience filters through individual natures and threatens to sprout in goblin growth if left uncultivated. As an established church and a centralized clerical authority fade from American democracy, varieties of religious experience multiply just as social means of negotiating between them diminish. In this respect Stowe anticipated Lincoln's observation that the North and South "read the same Bible and pray to the same God, and each invokes His aid against the other" as another eruption of Garrison's Protestant insistence on individual conscience, what Christian Smith calls "pervasive interpretive pluralism."[53] Without a shared religious culture to cultivate these individual experiences, society tangles into a dismal spiritual swamp where plants choke one another. *Dred* vents this suspicion most forcefully in its portrait of a revival camp meeting, the novel's center and the dramatic conclusion to its first volume. As the revival erupts into glossolalia, howls, and contortions, Stowe emphasizes her simultaneous repulsion and attraction toward this spiritual vitality as her hero and heroine dislike the revival's spectacle but insist on sympathy toward other believers' experiences. Here too she is a Beecher, trying to mediate between Old and New Lights.

Yet in a new vein of pessimism foreign to *Uncle Tom's Cabin*, Stowe is unflinching on the revival's failure to awaken Americans to the evils of slavery. The crude slavehunter Ben Dakin is brought to tears during a sermon yet remains unrepentant toward his brutal occupation, just as the preaching of humble and slaveless Father Dickson proves far less popular with the crowd than that of the slaveowning Father Bonnie.[54] Most of the believers in her democratic collage seem consigned to wrong or right feelings on slavery by temperament and social context, factors that long predate the narrative's opening. As a Puritan insistence on individual conscience erupts into America's swampish spiritual landscape, Stowe fails to harmonize this chaos, even worrying that "there is no such thing as absolute truth" within such a world, revealing what Gail K. Smith deems deep "anxieties about interpretation and epistemology."[55] A lynch mob chases the noble antislavery planter out of South Carolina while Stowe abruptly kills off Dred and her heroine, her prescription for "right feeling" overwhelmed by her description of America's democratic yet chaotic religious landscape. Fresh from Europe, Stowe was feeling as never before the anarchic potential of her individualistic and iconoclastic Puritan heritage. When the novel's hero asks the clergy why they don't denounce slavery, they respond, "We leave that thing to the conscience of individuals."[56] This shot at Garrison casts both abolitionists and proslavery clerics as symptoms of a greater spiritual malaise: in an increasingly individualistic and anti-institutional religious culture, mutually opposed religious experiences are doomed to clash without a common church's ability to gather individual natures into a social whole with bands of reverence. Ultimately, *Dred* clarifies the problem that Stowe would aim to answer in her two best historical novels, *The Minister's Wooing* and *Oldtown Folks*.

La Belle Puritaine

Shortly after *Dred*, Stowe's worries about religious nature became personal when her son Henry drowned while a student at Dartmouth without the conversion experience expected of true believers within the family's neo-Edwardsian tradition. Stowe confronted her anxieties about religious nature with a newfound desperation in *The Minister's Wooing* (1859), the first of several novels set in eighteenth-century New England. The novel tracks the devastation of the Puritan maiden Mary when her love James, good-hearted yet temperamentally averse to the requirements of Edwardsian religion, dies at sea. Writing from her own anguish, Stowe detailed James's mother's "ecstasy of despair" as she agonizes over the fate of her son's soul under the demands of Calvinism. (Stowe memorably describes Jonathan Edwards's sermons as a "refined poetry of torture.") In an existential pit, Mrs. Marvyn recovers only through the simple faith of the former slave Candace, who like Uncle Tom sweeps aside Calvinism to proclaim Christ's simpler love. Mrs. Marvyn sheds "healing sobs and tears" as all are freed from the terror of election. Even the (real) neo-Edwardsian divine Samuel Hopkins admits the power of this "gospel of love" when he concedes his engagement to Mary after James reappears alive.

The novel is often read biographically as Stowe's rejection of her father's theology, but it is even more a perceptive analysis of Calvinism's strengths and weaknesses. Where *Sunny Memories* and *Dred* vented Stowe's worries about the iconoclastic and anarchic potential of Protestantism, *The Minister's Wooing* traces the problem to a specific trait of New England Puritanism: it demanded a particular kind of religious experience and failed to accommodate individuals temperamentally unsuited to such experiences. Where abolitionists praised a Puritan refusal to compromise with evil, Stowe—closer than any to a living Puritanism—felt an inhumane ideological rigidity that failed to see how nature and nurture shape individuals. Just as Dred inherits his mystical disposition from his father, Mary "inherited a deep and thoughtful nature, predisposed to moral and religious exaltation," while James, conversely, feels predisposed against Edwardsian piety despite his best efforts to become its ideal Christian: "They tell me it's because I'm a natural man, and the natural man understandeth not the things of the Spirit. Well, I am a natural man,—how's a fellow to help it?"[57] Voicing Stowe's own opinions, James rebuffs the procrustean prescriptions of the Reverend Hopkins. "All the metaphysics of your good Doctor, you can't tell how they tire me," he complains; "I must have real things,—real people."[58]

In demanding a one-size-fits-all individual religious experience, Stowe also felt that Puritanism undervalued the potential for *relationships* to woo individuals toward faith. While Dred's radicalism is aggravated by his isolation, *The Minister's Wooing* continually pairs couples in which one's inherited piety stimulates the other's lack; Mary awakens the spiritual faculties of James, parallel to the experience of her own father and mother, Cerinthy Ann and her clerical beau, and Mr. and Mrs. Marvyn. "As to every leaf and every flower there is an ideal to which the growth of the plant is constantly urging, so is there an ideal to every human being" that others can help or hinder. That is, edifying relationships can counteract the spiritual "goblin growth" of *Dred*. To climb out of this swamp, Stowe fastened upon the biblical story of Jacob's ladder to heaven as a metaphor for the ways in which relationships can form a spiritual trellis and guide certain natures toward their ideal selves: God places the ladder's base "in human affections, tender instincts, symbolic feelings, sacraments of love, through which the soul rises higher and higher, refining as she goes" until "the soul knows self no more." Stowe minces no words in declaring that Edwardsian theology "knocked out every round of the ladder but the highest, and then, pointing to its hopeless splendor, said to the world, 'Go up thither and be saved!'"[59] In contrast, when James faces death at sea, he takes comfort in a vision of the biblical ladder and discovers divine love via Mary's love for him. Though he rightly senses that Dr. Hopkins "would have called that all selfishness," James reaffirms Stowe's own feelings: "One man alone on the great ocean of life feels himself a very weak thing. . . . We are held up by each other more than we know."[60]

Where Edwardsian individualism ignored relationships' ability to cultivate uplifting growth, its iconoclasm ignored art's power to do the same and thus knocked out the rung of beauty in the ladder to heaven. "Had [Mary] been born in Italy," Stowe writes—certainly thinking of her time in Europe—"she might, like fair St. Catherine of Siena, have seen beatific visions"; had Dr. Hopkins "been born beneath the shadow of the great Duomo of Florence . . . his would have been a soul as rounded and full in its sphere of faculties as that of Da Vinci."[61] Before her Calvinist breakdown, Mrs. Marvyn pines for aesthetic experience as she sits in the "rattle-windowed meeting-house," fantasizing Stowe's trip through Europe as she imagines Raphael's paintings, Mozart's Miserere, and France's cathedrals.

Yet a critique of Edwardsian individualism and iconoclasm was far from a wholesale rejection of America's Puritan heritage, the cornerstone of the Beecher faith. Instead Stowe—much like her brother and father—ultimately frames her critiques as attempts to preserve the better qualities of a lauded heritage in changing times. Before and after *The Minister's Wooing*, Stowe continued to prize this heritage, as she made clear in "New England Ministers," a review written for the *Atlantic* the year before the novel. "The doctrine that a minister is to maintain some ethereal, unearthly station," she argued there, "is a sickly species of sentimentalism, the growth of modern refinement, and altogether too moonshiny to have been comprehended by our stouthearted and very practical fathers. With all their excellences, they had nothing sentimental about them."[62] It was striking praise coming from America's leading sentimental author. Stowe even honored this trait in Edwards and Hopkins, despite the ways in which their theology had plagued her during her son's death. As she first professed in *Sunny Memories*, Stowe again concluded that their emphasis on God's sovereignty beyond that of any king cultivated "the strong mental discipline needed by a people who were an absolute democracy." She emphasized the direct implications this had for current reform efforts: like her father and brother, "the pastors of New England were always in their sphere moral reformers," and thus even "profitable and popular sins, though countenanced by long-established custom, were fearlessly attacked."[63] *The Minister's Wooing* built on this Puritan pride in several ways beyond its depiction of Reverend Hopkins's (historically real) stand against Newport's lucrative slave trade. The novel incorporates Stowe's praises in "New England Ministers" nearly verbatim when it reminds readers that they owed their democracy to an increasingly unpopular Puritan heritage. In the preface to the novel's British edition, Stowe wrote that the novel grew from her "reverential tenderness for those great religious minds . . . and for those institutions and habits of life from which, as from a fruitful germ, sprang all the present prosperity of America." She grew vituperative when she considered that readers might not care about the theological subtleties of Calvinism: "It is impossible to write a story of New England life and manners for a thoughtless, shallow-minded person."[64]

Like her brother, Stowe asserted her own Puritan identity at the very moments when she felt most critical of and distant from it. But unlike Henry, who was confined to delivering single sermons at a time, Stowe's fiction allowed her to dramatize these competing values simultaneously. This drama is especially evident in the frequently studied depiction of Mrs. Marvyn's Calvinist despair in *The Minister's Wooing*. Stowe titled the chapter "Views of Divine Government," most immediately in reference to the doctrine of election, but she also hinted at political governance and the Puritans' legacy for American politics therein. As if to soften the blows she was about to strike against Edwardsianism, Stowe opened the chapter with a paean to the Puritan errand as a harbinger of democracy. Before readers encounter Mrs. Marvyn's anguish, they read her praise for the Puritan impulse to "dispute all sham pretensions and idolatries of past ages,—to question the right of kings in the State, and of prelates in the Church." As Mrs. Marvyn's curse of Puritan despair is prefaced by the blessing of Puritan democracy, the chapter is less a rejection of Puritanism than an astute analysis of its positive and negative effects on individuals as a historical and social force. Ultimately Stowe concluded that Puritanism energized reverent natures like Mary's, repelled irreverant natures like James's, and acted as "a slow poison" on sensitive natures like Mrs. Marvyn's. She emphasized this mixed bag in the strongest language possible: "While strong spirits walked, palm-crowned, with victorious hymns, along these sublime paths, feebler and more sensitive ones lay along the track, bleeding away in life-long despair."[65] Puritanism was indeed the spartan, uncompromising conscience that abolitionists lauded, but its very rigidity had destructive social implications for those who hoped to hold together a diverse community.

As Stowe had first wondered in France, *The Minister's Wooing* ultimately imagined a relationship that preserved Puritanism's strengths and purged its poisons: Mary's friendship with Madame Virginie de Frontignac, a lively stereotype of French vivacity and Catholic beauty. Through Mary's puritan earnestness, Virginie awakens to higher spiritual aspirations, adopts New England's "simple, homely ways," and comes to admire their religion, "sublime, but a little glaciale."[66] Conversely, Virginie awakens Mary to aesthetic delight and the passion of the heart. Together, Virginie and Mary combine the best of France and New England. "There they were," Stowe reflects, "the Catholic and the Puritan, each strong in her respective faith, yet melting together in that embrace of love and sorrow." When James returns and Mary ignores her true feelings out of a Puritan sense of duty toward her engagement with Hopkins, Virginie proclaims what antebellum readers fed up with the dour legacies of Calvinism were certain to feel: "Mais c'est absurde!" Mary's rejoinder is revealing in the arc of Stowe's career: "I should hope that God would help me to feel right." This was precisely Stowe's goal for America at large in *Uncle Tom's Cabin*. But by 1859 Virginie proclaimed the truth that Stowe had accepted after *Dred*: individuals often can't help how they feel. "I am very much afraid He will not, ma chere," Virginie says.[67] Instead it is up to beauty and love to guide one another like Jacob's Ladder toward our ideal selves and new bands of reverence. What one character calls Mary, "la belle puritaine," aptly encapsulates Stowe's aims with the novel as a whole: the Puritan is softened by French sensibility while the belle is strengthened by New England independence.

To imagine a beautiful Puritanism between two friends was one thing, quite another to consider how these bands of reverence might gather an increasingly diverse nation at large. This question became all the more pressing as the Civil War splintered the nation and Reconstruction aimed to put it back together. After the outbreak of the war, Stowe oscillated between public proclamations of its millennial purpose and private fears for her enlisted son Fred: the conflict was both "the *last* struggle for liberty" and "that awful wine-press of the Wrath of Almighty God."[68] In spring 1862 the question of religious cohesion came even closer to home when Stowe's three daughters and her sister Catherine were confirmed as Episcopalians, a tradition that was becoming increasingly attractive to Stowe for its communalism and aesthetic bounty; by comparison, Calvinism "shut the little children out of the fold of Christ," she wrote to Catherine, while Episcopalianism "take[s] the children into the church to be trained."[69] As the war ground on, Stowe settled on the American home as a source of a communal religiosity that might counteract the rigid individualism of Puritan conscience with warmer bands of reverence. In her *House and Home Papers* (1864) and *Chimney-Corner* (1865) series for the *Atlantic*, "sprightly" collections of "household sermons," Stowe declared women's ability to cultivate homes that produced "all heroisms, all inspirations, all great deeds."[70] While Lydia Maria Child and Maria Weston Chapman argued for women's own right to Puritan militancy, Stowe grew increasingly eager to imagine how familial, communal, and social bonds could cultivate this religious vision in a more stable fashion and along more traditional religious and gender lines. Into Reconstruction, this interest became a matter of practical concern. While Henry disastrously and inexplicably sided with Andrew Johnson even through the lowest points of his battle with Congress, Stowe sided with the latter as she considered that "it may be the design of God to set aside this old aristocracy in the reorganization of society at the south and to bring up the *common people* as in New England."[71] Stowe began the book that she hoped would be her masterpiece, a vision of the New England hearth and village as a model of religious community for the splintered postbellum nation.

Grandmother Mather

With *Oldtown Folks* (1869), Stowe felt that she achieved not only her masterpiece but a Beecherite blueprint for reuniting America with new Puritan bands of reverence. "It is my resume of the whole spirit and body of New England," she wrote to *Atlantic* editor James T. Fields, for "I have something I really want to say . . . an object in this book, more than the mere telling of a story."[72] Through a fictional portrait of eighteenth-century New England as the "seed-bed of this great American Republic, and of all that is likely to come of it," Stowe weeded the tangled swamps of *Dred* and shaped the trellised relationships of *The Minister's Wooing* into a national garden— grown from a fertile Puritan past yet cultivated and rid of its deficiencies.[73] Modeling the fictional village of "Oldtown" on her husband's hometown of Natick, Massachusetts, Stowe imagined an entire community of belles puritaines knit together not solely by Puritan doctrine or church but especially by its everyday gemeinschaft, softer bands of reverence to unite and comfort rather than restrict and repress.

Oldtown's communalism was especially sparked by Horace Bushnell's Christian Nurture (1847), a work that stirred controversy among his fellow Congregationalist clergy by rejecting the doctrine of original sin for the power of communal religious nurture.[74] "All our modern notions have taken a bent towards individualism," Bushnell lamented, in which American political and religious life had slowly dissolved communal identity by viewing "persons as distinct units." This tendency overlooked "the idea of organic powers and relations," he noted, which are foremost in "a national life, a church life, a family life."[75] Each of these identities spoke powerfully to Stowe's Beecher heritage and personal temperament, and she seized upon the book's ideas as a way out of the individualistic swamp of American Protestantism writ large. She imagined Oldtown as a portrait of what Christian nurture might look like on a daily basis, rippling outward from family to church and nation, Bushnell's "organic powers and relations."

Stowe accentuated Oldtown's unifying "organic power" with a rich variety of individual religiosity incorporated into village life. Some of Stowe's best characters are the result, all of them "full of contradictions and inconsistencies," from Grandfather Badger, the apathetic Arminian, at once the sharpest and dullest of all Oldtowners; to Sam Lawson, the endearing village do-nothing who leisurely talks theology as others talk horsetrading; to Ellery Davenport (modeled on the historical Aaron Burr), who channels his ancestral Calvinism into godless Byronic radicalism when he is not baiting orthodox relatives or philandering with French girls. Stowe's crowning portrait is Grandmother Badger: between reciting Michael Wigglesworth's "Day of Doom" to grandchildren and welcoming the needy into her kitchen, she is both an "ardent disciple of the sharpest and severest Calvinism" and "the most pitiful, easy-to-be-entreated old mortal on earth." The loose plot further emphasizes the centrality of community as it follows the process by which two orphans and a fallen Puritan maiden reincorporate into Oldtown.

Stowe insisted that her work did not romanticize the New England village but realistically depicted its ability to unite a variety of religious experiences. "My mind [is] as still and passive as a looking-glass," she noted in the introduction, "that you should see the characteristic persons of those times, and hear them talk. . . . All speak in their turn, I merely listen."[76] This posture of detached listening was an attempt to both acknowledge Garrison's emphasis on individual conscience and restrain it within a unifying community, yet Stowe protested too much, for she of course did not "merely listen" but actively imagined Oldtown as a unifying way of life. If *Oldtown* admitted that individual "temperament gradually, and with irresistible power, modifies one's creed"—as Stowe had concluded by the time of *The Minister's Wooing*—it also emphasized how "every individual is part and parcel of a great picture of the society in which he lives and acts," a conscious Bushnellian effort to counterbalance modern individualism.[77] Fitted into the arc of her post-*Tom* career, *Oldtown* aimed to solve Stowe's early worries about religious nature by imagining an ideal social framework that might nurture them into an organic whole. Though unique individuals, Oldtowners are united by *Oldtown*.

Stowe enlisted none other than Cotton Mather to round out her historical portrait of a beautiful Puritan community, contrasting him favorably to the hyper-individualistic Jonathan Edwards. Even more explicitly than in *The Minister's Wooing*, Stowe indicted Edwards for "making his own constitutional religious experience the measure and standard of all others," thus creating a generation of young people "who were not merely indifferent to religion, but who hated it."[78] By contrast, Stowe praised Mather's support for the Halfway Covenant—the mid-seventeenth-century decision to relax standards for church membership—as a more humane alternative to Edwards's (and the early Puritans') demands for individual sainthood, fostering "much sympathy on the part of the children and young people with the religious views of their parents." In Bushnell's framing, Edwards devalued religion's organic and communal facets, in particular the ability of church and family to nurture and unite a variety of perspectives, and was wrong to view the Halfway Covenant as a capitulation to declining faith. In Stowe's estimation, such a covenant in fact aided the church by fostering empathy for ancestral and communal faith, while Edwards's effort to repurify the church by doing away with this covenant "succeeded in completely upsetting New England from the basis on which the Reformers and the Puritan Fathers had placed her."[79] Mather, on the other hand, was given "the greatest possible compliment" when Stowe called him "that delightful old New England grandmother" who, like Grandma Badger of Oldtown, united family and village around hearth and church.

While Lawrence Buell has highlighted antebellum historiography of Puritanism as a key battleground between Congregationalists and Unitarians, Stowe wove, like Lyman and Henry, between the ultra-orthodox, their cultured despisers, and iconoclastic Garrisonians in her uniquely domestic portrait of a beautiful Puritan community, even going so far as to rely upon literal Yankee genetics. Just as Mary's reverence is inherited from her father, "genealogy is a thing at the tip of every person's tongue" in Oldtown, where a "solemn air of intense interest" floated around matters of kinship, usually preserved by women. *Oldtown* aims to counteract the modern excess of "masculine" individualism with feminine guardianship of kinship. "In our present days, when every man is emphatically the son of his own deeds, and nobody cares who his mother or grandmother or great-aunt was," the narrator laments, few understand Oldtown's "intense feeling of race and genealogy."[80] Here too Bushnell's *Christian Nurture* was a likely influence in its disturbing vision of Protestant bio-imperialism: if organic communities were crucial to religion's longevity, Bushnell imagined a "heavenly colony" that incorporated or overran unholier races "by a kind of ante-natal and post-natal nurture combined" as the world was "taken possession of by a truly sanctified stock."[81] Though she refrained from Bushnell's extremes, Stowe implicitly rooted her community of belles puritaines in Anglo-Saxon blood ties (the French are welcome; the Irish are out of sight).

Although racial outsiders like Native and black Americans have a protected place in Oldtown, it is as wards to be assimilated into Oldtown ways. As an old Indian mission, Oldtown features Natives who linger at the town's edge but join with whites for Sunday service. Both the geographic and social center of Oldtown, the church, like Grandma Badger's kitchen, gives space for modest diversity anchored in a cultural core. In her sketch of a typical Oldtown service, Stowe depicts a variety of Natives but interjects her own prescriptions for integration. "Mild, intelligent, and devout," Deacon Ephraim is "the perfect model of the praying Indian formed in the apostolic traditions of the good Eliot," while his wife Keturah retained "the wild instincts and untamed passions of the savage." Here too, as in *The Minister's Wooing*, Stowe's point is that such a community can woo areligious individuals toward a superior Puritan faith. Stowe disregards Native culture as she lauds those Oldtowners "who had wisely forsaken the unprofitable gods of the wild forest," but she also hints that modern religion has given up on such individuals: the Native Dick Obscue, for instance, a "leering, lazy, drinking old fellow," appears regularly at Oldtown service but "was of a class which our modern civilization would never see inside of a church." The situation is much the same for the variety of African Americans who join in worship. In Stowe's rendition, Africans worship alongside Natives, white farmers, and first families as "one fold," but they are quietly consigned to a side gallery and live as a separate community at the edge of town. Stowe wants Oldtown to be a diverse yet unified community, but its racial dynamics are integrationist at best, rooted in Anglo culture and kinship.

Here *Oldtown* responded to Stowe's doubts concerning the prospects of freed slaves in Reconstruction society. In her *Chimney-Corner* piece "A Family Talk on Reconstruction," published shortly after Lincoln's assassination, Stowe vented her fears through the pessimistic Theophilus. Ex-slaves will prove "idle and worthless," he prophesies, because of their upbringing in a culture of slavery which "taught them that liberty means licensed laziness, that work means degradation," while whites "will hound and hiss at him for being what they made him." Alternatively, Stowe expressed her hopes through Christopher Crowfield. This prognostication may be correct for much of the South, Crowfield concedes—sneaking in a racist aside that "left to themselves, [Africans] tend downward"—but adds that "when the free North protects and guides," ex-slaves will and already do flourish.[82] Like many Northern Reconstructionists, Stowe made no efforts to hide her chauvinism toward the South and her paternalism toward African Americans. If freedmen succeeded, it would be as wards of Oldtown.

Stowe's "romantic racialism" has been amply documented since Fredrickson, but less noted is her desire to imagine a harmonious social order for racial differences that grew with her career.[83] Where Lyman once deemed black Americans a "permanently alien and unassimilable element of the population," both of his children were more hopeful even as their emphasis remained on assimilation.[84] Henry argued that America's greatness stemmed in part from its racial mixture. "Such blood mingled with ours, if educated and Christianized, will give stamina, variety, genius," he maintained, and though many in his audience would have drawn the line at white-black relationships, Henry at least theoretically considered the possibility; but like his father, he maintained that America's growing diversity presented a danger if it were not bound together in "a spirit of true religion and of that patriotism which true religion inspires."[85] Elsewhere he employed his romantic racialism for moderate antislavery critique. "We boast of the Anglo-Saxon race; and if bone and muscle, and indomitable sense of personal liberty, and a disposition to do what we please, are themes for Christian rejoicing, then the Anglo-Saxon may well rejoice," he concluded: "there are sins that belong to races," and these "belong to our stock."[86] Similarly, while Stowe maintained a belief in certain strengths and weaknesses ingrained in every race, she not only wielded this belief for abolitionist critique but aimed to imagine a social order that could harmonize rather than separate these differences.

So while Oldtown was paternalistic, tribalistic, and chauvinistic, it was also a more progressive counterpoint to other visions for Reconstruction. Stowe's ideal community not only assimilated minorities but also cultivated white citizens who fought for their rights. *Oldtown*'s loveliest portrait of Puritan folk life, a sketch of a typical Thanksgiving, joins purposefully with the book's most explicitly political episode, a struggle against slave-hunters. Stowe lulls readers into a charming description of a typical New England Thanksgiving as family traditions bring together the entire community. Amidst a pile of pies and dishes, even "the jolly old oven entered with joyful sympathy into the frolic of the hour," just as Oldtown's outliers gravitate toward Grandma Badger's kitchen for a grand supper blessed by "the national hymn of the Puritans." For readers who felt adrift within modern society, Stowe offered respite in this performance of Puritan community. But she also emphasized the holiday as an active part of New England's vigorous democracy, sanctified by the Parson's political sermon and the Governor's benediction on the Commonwealth. The holiday's politics become explicit when its festivities are interrupted by a band of slavehunters who steal the children of Nancy Prime, a free black citizen. The chapter titles this attack "The Raid on Oldtown" as a whole, and white Oldtowners indeed spring at once into action to intercept the kidnappers, as if this were the natural result of warm Puritan community and its crowning Thanksgiving rituals. If Lowell was disgusted by lush Forefathers' Day suppers, Stowe's Thanksgiving feast offered an abolitionism rooted less in Garrisonian iconoclasm than in a warm community that fostered the social ties and heroic right feeling that Stowe had struggled to find since *Uncle Tom's Cabin*.

Both of Stowe's New England novels have been charged with peddling in nostalgia, and justly so. Her depiction of Oldtowners rushing to rescue kidnapped blacks is as historically wishful as her multiracial congregations and homespun gemeinschaft, just as her portraits of Edwards and Mather are at best selective and at worst heretical for reasons that she understood better than most; Mather himself feared that the Halfway Covenant was a concession to declining faith, just as Edwards would have found Stowe's church little more than an Anglican social club for civil Christians. And yet if nostalgia is defined as escapist, the charge sticks less. When Ann Douglas derided sentimentalist writers and their mollified clerical fathers for what she called "the escape from history" into a "triumph of sentimental, local, antiquarian, 'social,' and, loosely speaking, religious history," she granted that "Stowe is the only major figure who could be said to have devoted her finest talents to the historical novel."[87] Both *The Minister's Wooing* and *Old-town* engaged squarely (if quietly) with one of the most pressing problems of the moment, the conundrum that undid her father: how to cleanse the stain of slavery from America's social fabric without tearing it apart.

Stowe hoped that her community of belles puritaines might point the way forward, but she underestimated how tiresome the Puritans had become for an industrializing and diversifying nation. After *The Nation* was founded in New York in 1865 to challenge the cultural supremacy of New England, it reflected much of the nation's postbellum mood in its nasty review of *Oldtown Folks*. "It is some years since our New Englanders have even been a little tedious," the critic began, tired of the "Puritan parson, and the Puritan deacon, and the Puritan tithing-man; and the Puritan Thanksgiving, and 'Lection cake, and May Training; and the Puritan 're-vivals.'"[88] Many blamed the war on puritanical abolitionists, and Stowe's Thanksgiving felt too little too late.

SIX

The *Mayflower* and the Slave Ship

The uninstructed Negroes about your houses, appear like so many Ghosts and Spectres. You may, without being Fanciful, imagine that like so many Murdered Ghosts, they look very Ghastly upon you, and summon you to answer before the Tribunal of God.

—Cotton Mather, *The Negro Christianized* (1706)

Commissioned by Congress in 1888, John F. Smith created a map of the United States that charted the abolitionist imagination. Growing across the North and South were two trees, respectively straight and gnarled. One bore the fruits of *Intelligence, Industry, Virtue,* and *Peace* while the other sliced the southeast with the thorns of *Avarice, Ignorance, Secession,* and *War.* One stretched toward *Immortality* beyond the San Francisco Bay while the other died in *Hades,* central Texas. The first was "God's Blessing Liberty," rooted in a Bible at Massachusetts and stamped with the date 1620, the year in which the *Mayflower*—pictured just off the coast—landed at Plymouth. The second was "God's Curse Slavery," sprouting from a dollar with the same date at Jamestown, where lurked a menacing slave ship.[1] Simplifying the complex problem of American slavery into a millennial clash between the *Mayflower* and the slave ship, Smith illustrated how abolitionists' reimagination of roots drew battle lines and forced the nation to choose sides.

The simplicity of this vision was potent, but it was also simplistic, overlooking how roots tangled and origins mixed upon closer examination. "Origin stories confer upon politics the permanence of nature," writes Joanne Wright, "abstracted from the messiness and complexity of actual politics. Indeed, to be persuasive as stories they must be simple."[2] Consider an 1839 Forefathers' Day Address by Robert C. Winthrop, Massachusetts

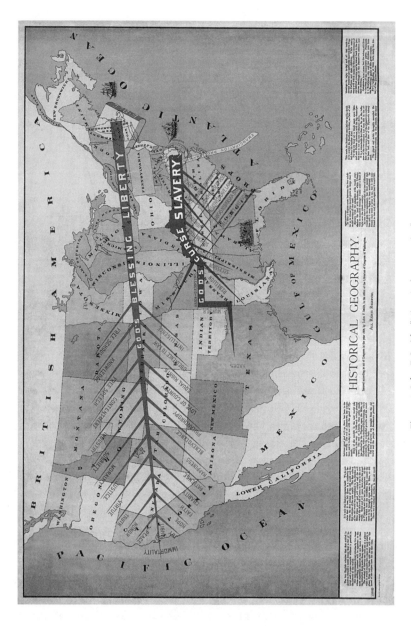

Figure 2. John F. Smith, "Historical Geography," 1888

congressman and descendant of John Winthrop. To prove his claim that "the Colonies of Jamestown and Plymouth had nothing in common," Winthrop turned to the *Mayflower* and the slave ship, "two fate-freighted vessels, laboring under the divided destinies of the same nation . . . like the principles of good and evil advancing side by side on the same great ocean of human life."[3] Winthrop wished for some "some angel arm" to time-travel and "arrest, avert, dash down, and overwhelm its accursed compeer! But it may not be." He simplified America's most vexing problem into opposed origins and destinies only to substitute fantasies of divine intervention for actual politics.[4]

Further, Winthrop did not seem to mind that sinking the slave ship would have drowned the twenty slaves aboard, and this reveals another way in which origin stories were abstracted from political complexities: the Jamestown slave ship was not merely a symbol of spiritual evil but also the source of the first African people in British America, a group fighting to define American and African American origins on their own terms. James McCune Smith, for instance, complained to Frederick Douglass that the "literary world" was forever lauding the *Mayflower*, "repeating the dose, ad nauseam, of that 'solitary ship,'" while overlooking the slave ship and the diasporic people that had risen from it. "I presume when we blacks get a literature, we may speak with pride of that other 'solitary ship' which landed some hundred Africans in the James river," he quipped, noting that the Jamestown slave frigate "kick[s] up a bigger dust in the year of grace 1852, than ever the May Flower did."[5] In this respect, the slave ship could not be exorcised from America's past with the defeat of slavery but remained alongside the *Mayflower* as a part of the nation's origins as long as African Americans insisted on their own Americanness. This may have been precisely what Winthrop feared. Perhaps he wished that God would sink the slave ship to free America not only from slavery but also from the problem posed by a free black people defining themselves on their own terms. In particular, could a nation imagined to grow from certain unifying Anglo and spiritual roots cultivate itself into a multiracial republic? Or would it splinter as different races cultivated different roots?

Paul Gilroy urges us to see the slave ship as the central symbol of modernity's emergence from "routes" rather than "roots," from the exchange of people, material, and ideas on the Atlantic rather than static national traditions, but Winthrop and McCune Smith remind us that the *Mayflower* and the slave ship emerged as important and increasingly entangled roots in the antebellum American and African American imagination.[6] While abolitionists' revolutionary reading of the Pilgrim-Puritan past was often spearheaded by white New Englanders like Winthrop who were often proud blood descendants, the question of color remains: what did the the Pilgrims and Puritans mean, if anything, to those who had arrived at America by way of the slave ship rather than the *Mayflower?*[7] Black writers responded to this origin story with striking frequency, and—perhaps more surprisingly—seldom with McCune Smith's dismissiveness. Though they utilized the Puritans and Pilgrims less frequently and more variously than white allies did, they reveal the importance of this origin story in the very breadth of their interpretations. Whether black writers tended toward integration or separatism, Garrisonianism or nationalism, domestic activism or emigration, Pilgrim-Puritan origins remained a persistent presence in their discourse. Many wrote with seemingly genuine admiration for and investment in the Puritans' legacy. Others invoked "Pilgrim liberty" more strategically as a way to goad white audiences with their own professed values. Emigrationists even cited the Pilgrims as a reason for black people to *leave* America. McCune Smith was among the rarer few who critiqued the *Mayflower* outright. What almost no major black writer of the period did was ignore the Pilgrims and the Puritans altogether. This national origin story was unavoidable for black writers given its pervasiveness among their white abolitionist allies and America at large—most prominently in George Bancroft's *History of the United States* (1834–78), a likely inspiration for Winthrop's *Mayflower*-slave ship juxtaposition and a narrative that traced a providential arc from liberty-loving Puritan roots to American destiny.[8]

Amidst these diverse engagements with the Puritan past, these writers shared a common tactic: they resituated Puritan origins within histories of African glory and American slavery, claiming American identity by revising it. Precisely *because* the Puritans had become central to American identity by the antebellum era, African American writers reimagined this origin story as one tool among several in their own claims for American citizenry. Various connections have been drawn between the Puritans and early black writers, including a revised tradition of typological identification with Israel, captivity narratives, and, most frequently, the "black jeremiad."[9] In addition to these scholarly genealogies, African American writers themselves wrestled with their spiritual genealogies in an effort to reconcile their investment in American and Protestant identity with an emergent sense of black roots. A growing number of scholars have demonstrated the importance of origins for antebellum black writers in conversation with dominant Euro-American traditions, including classicist studies of antiquity, engagement with Enlightenment aspirations toward "universal history," and

hermeneutical debates over biblical history that, for instance, invoked Ethiopian and Egyptian glory to refute arguments for black inferiority, warned
nations of the rise and fall of empires, or refuted justifications of slavery
based on the "Curse of Ham."[10] These efforts were crucial to an emergent
sense of black identity, but they also intertwined in complex ways with
black writers' investment in American Protestantism and its vision of history. Bruce Dickson Jr. has argued that religion was among the most important sites for "the development of the complex issues of voice and authority, appropriation and attribution, that were to constitute the background
for the emergence of African American literature" in the colonial era, a development that "allowed for the possibility of an entrance by black people
into an intellectual setting, a realm of thought, and a world of skills that
might otherwise have been defined as exclusively white."[11] This observation
is all the more true for the first decades of the nineteenth century, when
(among other influences) American Protestantism shaped early conceptions of black origins.

In short, black writers claimed America in part by reimagining its Protestant genealogies; rather than merely appealing to dominant American
narratives of Pilgrim-Puritan origins, black writers reimagined these narratives to even more surprising ends than their white abolitionist allies had
done, tracing the spiritual legacies of America's Pilgrim roots backwards to
Africa and forward to "Christian warriors" like Touissant Louverture, Nat
Turner, and ultimately the black soldiers of the Union Army. To speak in
the antebellum language of historical plantings, graftings, and harvests,
black writers radicalized abolitionists' revolutionary Puritan genealogy by
tracing it backward to black roots and forward to fugitive slaves and revolutionary black soldiers. Here were radical fruits of a destiny both American
and black, traceable to the *Mayflower* and the slave ship alike.

The Clash of the *Mayflower* and the Slave Ship

The evolution of the *Mayflower*–slave ship conceit after Winthrop's 1839
speech itself reveals what Dickson calls "the complex issues of voice and
authority, appropriation and attribution" as black and white abolitionists
reused and revised the image into the 1840s. Something about the *Mayflower* spoke to the future Presbyterian minister and former slave Henry
Highland Garnet, who likely read Winthrop's speech while studying for
the ministry in Troy, New York, when it was reprinted four months later
in the black periodical the *Colored American* (edited by Garnet's associate
and fellow Presbyterian New Yorker Samuel Cornish).[12] Garnet delivered

his first major address the next month at the seventh annual meeting of the American Anti-Slavery Society, a speech that established many of the foundational arguments for black citizenry that would be reused in the coming decades by black writers from a variety of ideological backgrounds, from Douglass to Delany and Nell. Garnet opened his speech by praising the Pilgrims and Puritans for "building up in this new world an edifice within whose walls the most extensive liberty should abide," establishing "the foundation of this government" with "the most solid materials." He noted that "the true American patriot" honored "the moral sublimity of the spirit of the pilgrims," for "their very sails were swelled by the breath of liberty" that would inspire "the broad foundation of republican institutions" in 1776.[13]

But Garnet then pivoted from the promises of an ideal America as embodied in its founding myths to the hypocrisies of America as it actually existed, establishing the tactic that would be utilized more famously by Douglass in "What to the Slave Is the Fourth of July?" To do so, he employed the *Mayflower* less to dramatize two opposed spiritual empires (à la Winthrop) than to establish a common religious and political heritage that, if followed faithfully, granted black Americans full citizenry. He began his speech with the Pilgrims and Patriots, he explained, to emphasize his faith in the essential goodness of America's foundations; what he critiqued was "the base conduct of their degenerate sons . . . guilty of the basest hypocrisy" in denying citizenry to blacks who had proved their dedication to the nation repeatedly. Anticipating William Cooper Nell, he cited blacks' war service in the Revolution and the War of 1812. Anticipating Martin Delany, he cited blacks' agricultural labor, cultivating a wilderness into a bountiful land. Anticipating nearly all black writers of the antebellum period, he cited blacks' devotion to the religious foundations of American society. If "the spirit of our institutions lays it down as a primary duty of Americans, to acknowledge the moral Government of God in all our affairs," Garnet noted, black Americans were not only key participants but even persecuted ones, prevented by slaveholders from practicing Christianity to its fullest extent. Garnet grouped these tactics to emphasize his belief that America's foundations were good but inadequately developed. "Seeing this self same soil which now yields the bitter fruits of slavery in such abundance, in days that have passed, yielded other fruits," he stated, "we ought to blame the culture, not the soil," as if anticipating the two trees of Smith's map, liberty and slavery, alike growing in good soil, but one a wicked weed. The effect of Garnet's rhetoric was potent and clear: black Americans lauded the nation's founding values, claimed them as their own, and, in the familiar fashion of the jeremiad, used them to indict a fallen present. In taming the wilderness, defending the nation, and cultivating its religiosity, black Americans had stood alongside the Pilgrims from the beginning.[14]

But as the militancy of Garnet's abolitionism rose in response to the rising tensions of the 1840s, he aimed this historical vision toward more aggressive ends in his better-known *The Past and the Present Condition, and the Destiny, of the Colored Race* (1848), among the first comprehensive attempts at joining Protestant historiography and an emergent black historical consciousness.[15] When a reporter covered an early lecture version of the book, he was again struck by Garnet's return to the two ships: "He spoke with much power and effect . . . of the landing of the 101 Puritans on dreary Plymouth rock, at the same period when a Dutch vessel landed 20 Africans at Jamestown. What an infamous coincidence! What discordant sounds!"[16] The version that Garnet himself published in *Past and Present* was more militant. In 1620, he wrote, again invoking the two ships, "the angel of liberty hovered over New England, and the Demon of slavery unfurled his black flag over the fields of the 'sunny south.'"[17] Compared to Winthrop's speech, Garnet's added a significant detail in the unfurling of slavery's black flag: where Winthrop ended on the vague hope that this empire would eventually die out, Garnet's language hinted that only battle would unseat this empire. Most importantly, the rest of *Past and Present* centered on black Americans themselves as the most important party in the two ships, destined to play a leading role in this sacred history.

It seems likely that Garnet's militarized vision of the *Mayflower* and slave ship in turn influenced major white antislavery figures. Shortly after *Past and Present*, antislavery congressman Joshua Reed Giddings echoed Garnet's rhetoric in a speech at the 1848 convention of the incipient Free Soil Party. Speaking to a multiracial political bloc that had grown increasingly radicalized on the issue of slavery during the volatile 1840s, Giddings too sailed the two ships toward more revolutionary ends, the pair illustrating how "two antagonistic principles have gone on, shooting their roots downward, and bearing fruit upward, till we found ourselves surrounded by an overshadowing power—moulding our laws—guiding our armies, and absorbing the North into her Maelstrom of rain and death."[18] Giddings imagined an unfinished version of Smith's map, one in which the wicked tree of slavery threatened to choke America's better liberty tree.

Giddings in turn revealed that Winthrop's struggle to reconcile the *Mayflower* and the slave ship only grew with tensions within and between black and abolitionist communities into the 1850s. For instance, the *Mayflower* and the slave ship tossed amidst rifts that rose between black abolitionists who remained dedicated to Garrison's integrationist platform and a growing voice of black nationalists and emigrationists who emphasized the need for racial independence—not to mention the many figures like Garnet, Douglass, and McCune Smith who straddled lines and changed over time. The same year that McCune Smith complained about the *Mayflower*, in fact, the "father of black nationalism" Martin Delany sailed the Pilgrim ship and the slave frigate toward less American and more ethnocentric ends in *The Condition, Elevation, Emigration, and Destiny of the Colored People of the United States* (1852). Like Garnet, Delany noted that "the African captain, and the 'Puritan' emigrants, landed upon the same section of the continent at the same time" to emphasize that blacks had cultivated America as long as the Pilgrims and thus deserved citizenry.[19] But unlike Garnet, Delany argued that the black race had been denied these rights for so long in America that they could only hope to acquire them elsewhere, in effect by smuggling American principles out of a corrupt homeland like new separatists.

Yet the year after Delany used the *Mayflower* and the slave ship to support emigration, the novelist and orator William Wells Brown employed them for a Garrisonian argument. Writing from Britain, Brown devoted a chunk of his influential novel *Clotel* (1853) to one of the most dramatic renditions of the two ships to illustrate the antislavery power of "pure religion." Brown often lampooned religious hypocrisy, but he also revered the rarer power of what abolitionists (quoting James) called "pure religion and undefiled" in the character of Georgiana Peck, fresh from an education where she "had the opportunity of contrasting the spirit of Christianity and liberty in New England with that of slavery in her native state" of Mississippi.[20] Georgiana challenges her father's proslavery religion with pure religion and converts her freethinking suitor, wielding feminine influence like the heroines of Stowe whom Brown admired, a power that he traced in some of his most vivid writing to a sublime Puritan inheritance—I quote at length to illustrate its extent and drama. In 1620

we behold one little solitary tempest-tost and weather-beaten ship. . . . That is the May-flower, with its servants of the living God, their wives and little ones, hastening to lay the foundations of nations in the accidental lands of the setting-sun. Hear the voice of prayer to God for his protection, and the glorious music of praise, as it breaks into the wild tempest of the mighty deep, upon the ear of God. Here in this ship are great and good men. Justice, mercy, humanity, respect for the rights of all; each man honoured, as he was useful to himself and others; labour respected, law-abiding men, constitution-making and respecting men; men, whom no tyrant could conquer, or hardship overcome, with the high commission sealed by a Spirit divine, to establish religious and political liberty for all. This ship had the embryo elements of all that is useful, great, and grand in Northern institutions; it was the great type of goodness and wisdom, illustrated in two and a quarter centuries gone by; it was the good genius of America. But look far in the South-east, and you behold on the same day, in 1620, a low rakish ship hastening from the tropics, solitary and alone, to the New World. What is she? She is freighted with the elements of unmixed evil. Hark! hear those rattling chains, hear that cry of despair and wail of anguish, as they die away in the unpitying distance. Listen to those shocking oaths, the crack of that flesh-cutting whip. Ah! it is the first cargo of slaves on their way to Jamestown, Virginia. Behold the May-flower anchored at Plymouth Rock, the slave-ship in James River. Each a parent, one of the prosperous, labour-honouring, law-sustaining institutions of the North; the other the mother of slavery, idleness, lynch-law, ignorance, unpaid labour, poverty, and duelling, despotism, the ceaseless swing of the whip, and the peculiar institutions of the South. These ships are the representation of good and evil in the New World, even to our day. When shall one of those parallel lines come to an end?[21]

Bringing the two ships to life with vivid sights and sounds in the present tense, Brown connects this vital legacy not to black nationalism but to Georgiana's moral witness. The novel's final lines conclude on Hebraic prophecy that urges readers, like Georgiana, to "proclaim the Year of Jubilee throughout the length and breadth of the land of the Pilgrim Fathers."

James McCune Smith used the ships for something between Delany's nationalism and Brown's Garrisonianism when he responded to an 1854 speech on the Kansas-Nebraska Act by Theodore Parker which invoked the two ships to cast the struggle in Kansas as a fight for the future of America's sacred Pilgrim heritage.[22] In response, McCune Smith revised the image to argued that the "spiritual nature" of black people rejected the "cold, evasive Saxon exclusiveness" of cerebral New England religion (exemplified in Unitarianism) for a "warm, spiritual, heart worship" that had acted on liberty long before white abolitionists merely preached it.[23] Blacks' warmer, more active religiosity embraced "a new principle, grander than that announced by the *Mayflower*'s people when they landed on Plymouth Rock. It is the principle of resisting oppression on the spot, against all odds, in contradistinction to the principle of flying from oppression."[24] McCune Smith traced the racial tensions within abolitionism to an autochthonous black American political theology, neither emigrationist nor Garrisonian.

These diverse uses of the two ships reveal the Pilgrim and Puritans' broader ambivalence in antebellum discourses on religion and race. On the one hand, as already noted of Harriet Beecher Stowe and Theodore Parker, Puritan pride often merged with Anglo chauvinism, if not outright Saxonist racism; on the other hand, the Puritans' spiritual legacy was universal in theory and held revolutionary potential for many abolitionists. This ambivalence was even more pronounced for black writers, most of whom as self-professed Americans and Protestants felt a certain connection to this legacy.[25] After black leaders organized in opposition to colonization schemes by the 1820s, nearly all of America's leading black writers had embraced not only some form of Protestantism and its providential vision of history but also a certain sense of their own Americanness. As for white Americans, the Protestant, providential, and American facets of this emergent black identity were closely related, yet complicated by the fact that slavery had played a part in their arrival at each and still plagued the providential history of Protestant America with a color line.

While certain fissures appeared in the black community into the 1850s on the meaning of Protestantism for present black struggle, the war would bring a new unity too. A growing number of black writers experienced Gilroy's observation that "striving to be both European and black requires some specific forms of double consciousness" and causes "a preoccupation with the striking doubleness that results from this unique position—in an expanded West but not completely of it." The question that Gilroy ultimately posed was the same one that gnawed at these thinkers: "Are the inescapable pluralities involved in the movements of black peoples, in Africa and in exile, ever to be synchronised?"[26] While black writers applied the *Mayflower* and the slave ship to increasingly diverse goals, they also reaffirmed the centrality of these two origin stories and ultimately bound them into a tentative synthesis by the time of the Civil War. While these writers used the Pilgrim-Puritan past to spur white audiences with their own values or to justify revolutionary black separation from America, they reaffirmed this central American myth by reimagining it as the product of black roots and the producer of revolutionary black fruits.

"Your Fathers"

Writing in a Newburyport newspaper as early as 1774, a former slave named Caesar Sarter invoked the Puritans in an outsider's jeremiad against the Massachusetts legislature: "Your fore fathers, as I have been often informed, left their native country, together with many dear friends, and came into this country, then a howling wilderness inhabited, only, by savages . . . rather choosing, under the protection of their God, to risk their lives, among those merciless wretches, than submit to tyranny at home." While such deeds affirmed their "exalted sense of the worth of Liberty" and explained the colonists' more recent "manly and resolute struggles" against the crown, their legacy would be tarnished until slavery was abolished. Sarter urged the legislature to again take up abolition, rectifying "the absurdity of your exertions for liberty, while you have slaves in your houses."[27] While Sarter echoed the Puritans' language of a "howling wilderness" filled with "savages," a key difference arose in his use of *your*—"your fore fathers," "your struggles," "your houses"—in place of the jeremiad's typical *our*. Sarter made clear his sense of separation from the Puritans' descendants even as he urged them to live up to their progressive legacies, frequently professed yet rarely honored. Later black writers often appealed to the Puritan past in precisely this way, neither fully embracing the Puritans as their own nor rejecting them, but using them as a rhetorical bridge between Anglo-American identity and African American activism, a strategic means of holding a dominant community accountable to its own better values.

Sometimes this included specific attacks on Congregationalists, as when a journalist for the *Colored American* sniped at a publisher for zealously defending Puritan principles of free speech and "self-government" when it came to minor ecclesiastical matters but ignoring them entirely on the issue of slavery.[28] More often this tactic aimed at all of New England. Writing two years later for Frederick Douglass's *North Star*, "JD" carried readers back to the "hard task of outward severities and inward wrestlings" of the Pilgrims through the present tense. "They are men of sincere, earnest hearts, who, not being permitted to worship God in the way they think right, have fled from their own country to the more liberty-loving shores of a neighboring state," JD wrote: "oh, there is nothing more noble in this our world, than to be engaged in such a conflict!" The author then pivoted to a New England Thanksgiving service in 1847, inside "a large and handsome 'place of worship'" filled with rich carpets, mahogany, and "a well-dressed audience, some of them probably the descendants of the old puritans . . . 'sitting at ease in Zion,' on their soft cushioned seats—their feet resting on ottomans." JD made plain the point: "Oh, how have the descendants of the ancient pilgrim Fathers degenerated! 'Tell it not in Gath!'"[29]

Writing in the *North Star* the next month, "J.H.C." pushed these Puritan origins even further to indict the nation as a whole: "If we look back to the early history of our country, either to that period when the Puritan pilgrims left their island home, and sought a retreat in the wilds of this continent, in quest of civil and religious liberty, or to that period when their descendants declared that 'all men are created free and equal,' . . . we are at a loss to account for the existence of Slavery in a country settled under such circumstances, and taking her station among the nations of the earth, with such principles inscribed upon her banner." Lest Northerners embrace these origins with one arm and hold slavery at a distance with the other, the author emphasized that "slavery is a constitutional, national institution; it is a part of our political system."[30] If America was indeed a nation with Puritan roots, as Bancroft claimed, slavery needed to die.

The tone of these indictments grew more desperate and fierce with the 1850 passage of the Fugitive Slave Act. White abolitionists denounced the once beloved Webster in Miltonic fashion as a fallen angel, but the matter was more personal for black Northerners who now faced the prospect of deportation back into slavery. "Behold what Daniel Webster, Samuel A. Eliot, &c., have done for the descendants of the Puritans," one journalist wrote bitterly in the *North Star*, turning to prophecy rivaling that of any Puritan Jeremiah. "Wait and see, ye prophesiers of smooth things. Pursue your fugitives, ye Pharaohs, even into the midst of the Red Sea. . . . Go up to Ramoth Gilead to battle, ye Ahabs, 'and prosper.' Drink proudly your wine out of the holy vessels, Balshazzar and all ye Nobles of Babylon, till ye behold the handwriting on the wall! But the time cometh when your iniquities shall find you out. Then shall ye know that the Lord God omnipotent reigneth."[31] As in the writing of many Garrisonians, the heat of this invective and the degree to which it could inspire critiques of the nation—even unto praising armed resistance to federal law—hint at the revolutionary potential that black writers would ultimately seize in their unique take on Puritan origins.

Other writers employed the trope of holy New England soil to further dramatize the Fugitive Slave Act as a diabolic invasion encouraged by New England's own representatives. "The Free Soil of the North, consecrated to Freedom by the blood of our fathers," one journalist for *Frederick Douglass' Paper* wrote, "has already been polluted by the footsteps of incarnated devils, in hot pursuit of men, women, and children, who were flying from the hell of slavery. It is to the shame of the sons of the Puritans, that this has been suffered."[32] Samuel Ringold Ward grew so pessimistic over this egregious New England failure to live up to its principles that he wondered whether the failures were themselves the principles, and the principles in fact mere exceptions to a general depravity. "Who would trust a nation who violate their solemn Declaration of Independence, their Bill of Right, their Federal Constitution, their Puritan Faith" so frequently and deeply, he asked, musing that "slaveholding, slave-trading, and slave-breeding are, practically, great American principles."[33]

Another version of Caesar Sarter's "*your* fathers" came in column space that black editors granted to white New England abolitionists who lauded revolutionary Puritan origins. From Emerson's lament in his first major antislavery speech that "the great-hearted Puritans have left no posterity" to Whittier's eulogy for the antislavery John Quincy Adams as "last of the Puritan Tribunes," black papers reprinted speeches from New England's literary and political leaders that gave their readers a sense of both the cultural narratives that mattered to white northerners and the ways in which white allies seized upon the revolutionary potential in these narratives.[34] In the infamous case of Thomas Sims, a fugitive returned to slavery in Boston, Douglass reprinted a speech by Wendell Phillips that sniped bitterly at slavery's defenders with—of all things—the Westminster Confession: "'What is the chief end of man?' The old one of the Westminster Divines, of Selden and Hugh Peters, of Cotton and the Mathers, used to answer, 'To glorify God and enjoy him forever'; that is Kane-treason now. The 'chief end of man'? why, it is to save the Union!"[35] Six months later Douglass reprinted Horace Mann's endorsement of the revolutionary doctrine of "Higher Law" in the House of Representatives, where he lamented that any American could defend slavery "since the May-Flower crossed the ocean with her precious burden." Mann rejected the belief that "that there is no 'Higher Law' than the Constitution" as "nothing less than palpable and flagrant atheism."[36] Similarly, when Douglass covered the Republican Convention two years later, he reprinted Senator Charles Sumner's controversial declaration "I am too familiar with the history of judicial proceedings, to regard them with any superstitious reverence. . . . It was a judicial tribune which condemned Socrates to drink the fatal hemlock, and which nailed the Savior to the cross . . . which persistently enforced the laws of Conformity that our Puritan Fathers persistently refused to obey." In regard to the Fugitive Slave Act, the senator quoted another Puritan writer, John Bunyan: "I cannot obey, but I can suffer."[37]

To contextualize these remarks for their readers, black papers occasionally published historical commentaries on the Puritans, Macaulay's *History of England* being a favorite. Their choice in excerpts is revealing; while Macaulay often mocked Puritan fanaticism, black papers extracted his rarer moments of begrudging praise. Consider, for instance, the resonance that this passage from his *Essay on Milton* would have had for black readers of the *Colored American* when excerpted in 1840. For the Puritan, the difference between the greatest and meanest of mankind seemed to vanish when compared with the boundless interval which separated the whole race from him on whom their own eyes were constantly fixed. They recognized no title to superiority but his favor. . . . They esteemed themselves rich in a more precious treasure, and eloquent in a more sublime language, nobles by the right of an earlier creation, and priests by the imposition of a mightier hand. The very meanest of them was a being to whose fate a mysterious and terrible importance belonged. . . . It was for him that the sun had been darkened, that the rocks had been rent, that the dead had arisen, that all nature had shuddered at the sufferings of her expiring God![38]

Similarly, Douglass's *North Star* excerpted Macaulay's account of Puritans' secret worship under the rule of Bishop Laud, a portrait that echoed accounts of slaves' secret religious services. "Worship was performed sometimes just before break of day and sometimes at dead of night," when ministers were smuggled into congregation in disguise "and many contrivances were used to prevent the voice of the preacher, in his moments of fervour, from being heard beyond the walls. Yet, with all this care, it was often found impossible to elude the vigilance of informers."[39] The next week the *North Star* excerpted Macaulay's praise for John Bunyan's rude yet visionary Puritan plainspeak, another passage likely to inspire black readers who were self-conscious about their lack of access to education. "He knew no language but the English, as it was spoken by the common people. He had studied no great model of composition, with the exception, an important exception undoubtedly, of our noble translation of the Bible," Macaulay noted, and "his spelling was bad. He frequently transgressed the rules of grammar. Yet the native force of genius, and his experimental knowledge of all the religious passions, from despair to ecstasy, amply supplied in him the want of learning. His rude oratory roused and melted hearers who listened without interest to the labored discourses of great logicians and Hebraists."[40]

The point is this: even while black writers and editors felt intense disappointment in New England as the self-proclaimed conscience of America as well as a certain sense of separation from the revolutionary Puritan origin story peddled by blood descendants, they not only took note of this story's influence among their white allies and studied its context but themselves deployed this narrative strategically in their efforts to sway white Americans to their cause. Even the fiercest black critics of white America invoked the Puritans as ammo, and far more embraced this origin story in order to reimagine it as a narrative that justified their own revolutionary impulses.

Fugitive Abolition and Black Pilgrims in Haiti

Despite the disappointment that many black activists felt toward the North into the 1840s and 1850s, they seldom critiqued, mocked, or rejected the narrative of Puritan origins outright. Among major black papers only a handful of such references occur, almost always crowded out by neutral or positive references. In 1838, for an amusing example, the *Colored American* reprinted a piece from Nathaniel P. Rogers's cheeky *Herald of Freedom* that mocked anti-Catholic hysteria. "We really hope the Catholics won't come in here and corrupt the morals and principles of the old Puritans, but she is very hystericky lest they should, [for] she is the last hope of the world. You will see her marked with brightish sort of paint, on the religious maps of the world, to distinguish it from heathen countries. Your anti-abolition divine will point it out, with great complacency, with his rattan, while he lectures on what great things she is doing for the conversion of the world. The rest of the world mainly is painted black."[41] The French Revolution of 1848 was a further opportunity to deflate Protestant-nationalist cant. New England Whigs had long pointed to France as a cautionary tale of a nation that strove for republicanism without the necessary foundation of Protestantism, while abolitionists retorted that revolutionary France had a far better record on slavery. Two pieces in the *North Star* mocked plans to send missionaries from "our 'favored land'" to France—that is, to overlook domestic shortcomings in order to drive out papists and infidels. One critic wrote bluntly that "the French have just conceptions of Human Rights. The Puritans fled from oppression in the Old World, and hung Quakers and witches in the New. The American Colonists threw off the yoke of King George the Third, and imposed one, far more grievous to be borne, upon one-sixth of their own population."[42]

But such remarks are strikingly rare as a whole. Even black nationalists and emigrationists who by the 1850s had lost much of their faith in black people's prospects in America invoked the Pilgrims and Puritans as precedent for leaving the nation behind. As Laurie Maffly-Kipp has noted, James Theodore Holly, the first black bishop in the Protestant Episcopal Church and one of the major proponents of black emigration to Haiti, modeled his calls for emigration on the Pilgrims' separation from England. "Descendants of the Pilgrims!" he wrote to residents of New Haven on the eve of a departure in 1861, "you are invited to rally to the hearty support of this *Mayflower* expedition of sable pioneers in the cause of civil and religious liberty, which it falls to your lot to Hayti in the name of New England."[43] Holly and the other ministers of the venture continued this parallel even in the difficult early months of settlement, likening the settlers' trials to those faced by the early Pilgrims.[44]

Whites opposed to a multiracial republic could use the same argument. In an article from the *Chicago Daily Tribune* reprinted in *Frederick Douglass' Paper,* one writer argued that black Americans "can do great things if they strike out on their own like the Puritans did, rather than remain in a corrupt country." This writer concluded by granting black Protestants the same glorious destiny in Africa as the Puritans won in America. The Puritans "might have remained and vegetated like animals in England, or they might have contended hopelessly for a recognition of their rights, just as the colored people here do," the author wrote, "but they decided differently. To that decision we measurably owe the free Institution we now enjoy. . . . And why may not a similar condition of things result from the colonization of Africa by men who are indoctrinated with Christianity and a love of freedom?"[45] Either duplicitous or fatalistic, the author conceded the great results of the Puritans' love of liberty but foreclosed the possibility of black Americans' achieving similar results in the very nation established by the Puritans, now too corrupt to revive its better origins. In effect, black Americans could be heroic Puritans too—just not in decaying America.

On the other hand, abolitionists directed this same argument toward more revolutionary ends: namely, a reason to break federal law and support fugitive slaves. Samuel J. May, a Unitarian minister descended from Boston merchants and Puritans, directly flouted the Fugitive Slave Act while ministering at the great hub of the Underground Railroad in Syracuse. He raised money for fugitives, aided their escapes to Canada, and even participated in the great "Jerry Rescue" of 1851. Early that year, Senator Daniel Webster had warned abolitionists that fugitives would be arrested even in the midst of abolitionist Syracuse, making clear his intent to enforce the Fugitive Slave Act everywhere; local authorities soon followed suit during the Liberty Party state convention in October by arresting a slave named William Henry, "Jerry." When word spread, May helped organize hundreds of Liberty Party abolitionists alongside Samuel Ringold Ward and Gerrit Smith, storming the town jail and successfully freeing Henry, who made his way to Canada. When twenty-six of the rescuers were brought to court, residents of Buffalo signed a statement of solidarity, published in *Frederick Douglass' Papers* the next month, which situated the rescuers in a Protestant lineage and cast their prosecutors as papal imperialists. "We too have our HAPSBURGHS," they wrote (the Catholic monarchy of the Thirty Years' War), "who would fain make you martyrs to those great truths of which they charge you with being the missionaries; truths which they themselves blasphemously sneer at and deny;—that the HIGHER LAW, the will of Almighty God, written on the enlightened conscience, is SUPREME; that the LOWER LAW, the will of man, when in conflict with the HIGHER, is to be trampled in the dust with the tribunals that administer it." To justify these bold statements, allies declared that such were "truths which English whigs died for, our Puritan ancestors were exiles for, and to establish which our Revolutionary Fathers pledged their lives . . . truths questioned, in those times, only by tories and bigots."[46] Although certain black writers excoriated the Fugitive Slave Act as white America's most egregious betrayal of its supposed Puritan principles, a coalition of white and black abolitionists, including influential leaders like Sumner and Mann, cited these same origins as support for counter-state resistance in the name of "Higher Law."

Reverend May further developed this idea when he visited the Elgin Colony of former fugitive slaves in Buxton, Ontario, the next year, agreeing with Bishop Holly that these brave settlers resembled the Pilgrims far more than his blue-blooded self did. He reflected on the experience in a letter to Reverend William King, the Irish-Presbyterian founder of the settlement (later reprinted in *Frederick Douglass' Papers*).

> There appeared in them some points of striking resemblance to our Pilgrim Fathers of New England. Like them, they had fled from the abodes of civilized men, and sought homes in the wilderness, that they might be free, [and] like those men of old, whom we are wont so highly to revere, they count it all joy to suffer hardships, perils by land and by water, travels by night, a flight in the winter, and a life in the wild; and in an inhospitable climate, if by so suffering they may a cure to themselves and their posterity the boon of freedom. Who will presume to say that as great results will not come out of this expulsion of the colored people from our country as came out of the expulsion of the Jews from Egypt or the Puritans from England?[47]

Passing the Israelites' and Pilgrims' sacred torch on to this band of fugitives, May anticipated what W. E. B. Du Bois asserted in *Black Reconstruction* (1935) and what scholars of slavery and abolition now acknowledge: fugitive slaves were themselves a revolutionary historical force.[48]

Similar rhetoric simmered during the explosive trials of fugitive slaves like Anthony Burns, captured and tried under the Fugitive Slave Act in Boston in 1854. The case prompted an even more publicized replay of the Jerry Rescue as black and white abolitionists stormed the Boston courthouse in an attempted rescue that killed a US deputy marshal in the process. *Freder-*

ick Douglass' Papers immediately relayed the news as it made its way to upstate New York over telegraph. It also reprinted a circular, "To the Yeomanry of New England," that had been sent throughout rural New England by the interracial Boston Vigilance Committee in hopes of "lead[ing] into the city a strong force from the country towns." "Come down, then Sons of the Puritans," it read, "and take such action as your manhood and patriotism may suggest," urging New Englanders to converge upon Boston in protest of Burns's trial. Despite such protests, the court ruled against Burns, and Boston faced martial law as protesters watched city officials carry Burns back to slavery.[49] While McCune Smith distinguished white from black activism by cleaving them into separate religious traditions, black and white abolitionists together invoked these roots as they moved toward increasingly militant action in the decades before the Civil War.

Grafting Protestantism to Ethiopian Roots for Black Fruits

To claim Protestantism for resistance, black writers actively remade these lineages into their own, often by tracing them back to black origins and forward to revolutionary black destinies. Here too Henry Highland Garnet led the way, reviving the two ships to symbolize an impending clash between America's best and worst origins but also to emphasize the entwinement of black and white people throughout sacred history. While antebellum Christians generally accepted the idea that Moses was trained in the Egyptian arts and sciences, Garnet noted in *Past and Present* that both secular and sacred historians described the ancient Egyptians as black. This meant, Garnet argued, that the patriarch of sacred history had in fact received "the materials with which he reared that grand superstructure . . . which has filled the world with wonder and praise" (i.e., Judaism and, ultimately, Protestant Christianity) from a great black civilization.[50] Where figures like Bancroft and Giddings often imagined sacred history as a series of "graftings" and replantings of superior fruits, Garnet went a step further: America's lauded Protestant vine, if followed beyond Judaism, had itself been grafted onto Ethiopian and Egyptian roots.

Moreover, Protestantism's black ancestors had achieved the heights of civilization while "the ancestors of the now proud and boasting Anglo Saxons were among the most degraded of the human family," cavedwellers with a propensity for human sacrifice.[51] Whites who boasted of their superior civilization in fact needed to thank the ancient Ethiopians for raising them out of barbarity on both fronts; mixing Protestant and Ethiopianist history, Garnet flipped the frequent argument that slavery was justified because it civilized and Christianized blacks. Abner Hunt Francis, an agent for the *Colored American* and *North Star*, repeated this argument more plainly the next year, praising the "sterling principles of our Puritan fathers" only to trace these roots back to "the light of science and letters which dawned upon their benighted visions from our Egyptian ancestors." Like Garnet, Francis sharply switched the terms of a common narrative: "Had not that day dawned upon our ancestors . . . what would a horde of naked savages have had today to boast of in their Anglo Saxon or Caucasian origin?"[52]

While Garnet traced America's Puritan values back to black origins, he also followed it forward to a black destiny that would revive these flagging virtues; while he could concede the Puritans' greatness, he also imagined a global abolitionist movement led by black heroes as their modern heirs. In his controversial "Call to Rebellion" at the 1843 National Negro Convention, Garnet revised his earlier appeal to the *Mayflower*. When the first slaves arrived in North America, they did not come "upon the wings of Liberty, to a land of freedom." Stolen from their homes, they were no Pilgrims; in fact, liberty-loving Protestants were the ones who had instituted and sustained slavery, even forbidding slaves to read the Bible for themselves. Himself a devout Presbyterian, Garnet then unfolded a Protestant line of reasoning that terrified the nation when it was first pioneered in David Walker's incendiary *Appeal to the Colored Citizens of the World* (1829) but one that abolitionists would increasingly countenance into the more volatile 1850s: by stamping out the "good seeds of liberty" planted by God in every individual soul, he argued, slavery "commits the highest crime against God and man" in preventing these souls from cultivating their own relationship with and duties to God. As such, it was inherently sinful for slaves to resign themselves to slavery, and "the God of heaven would smile upon every effort which the injured might make to disenthral themselves" of it. This logic led to the revolutionary conclusions that shocked many: "THEREFORE IT IS YOUR SOLEMN AND IMPERATIVE DUTY TO USE EVERY MEANS, BOTH MORAL, INTELLECTUAL, AND PHYSICAL THAT PROMISES SUCCESS." To his Garrisonian critics like (at the time) Douglass, Garnet responded that the spiritual redemption of a society had always required bloodshed in the past. Like other abolitionists, Garnet sanctioned these radical statements by fitting them into a celebrated lineage. Though black revolutionaries like Toussaint Louverture, Denmark Vesey, Nat Turner, Joseph Cinque, and Madison Washington were currently despised as insurrectionists, these "noble men . . . who have fallen in freedom's conflict, their memories will be cherished by the true-hearted and God-fearing in all future generations." Garnet prophesied that these figures would eventually be praised in the same way that Moses and the Puritan revolutionary John Hampden now were: as godly warriors for spiritual liberty.[53]

Garnet extended this lineage in *Past and Present*. In a purposeful juxtaposition, directly after invoking the *Mayflower* and the slave ship, he outlined a global antislavery movement that outpaced the United States' own claims to liberty. He noted that even the pope had recently condemned slavery, joining his voice with Britain, Mexico, Sweden, Denmark, Turkey, and especially revolutionary Haiti and France. Thankfully, America's North was catching up to this global movement, returning to its own local memories of liberty. "In the East the sons of New England are waking up at freedom's call, among the tombs of their fathers," Garnet said, quoting James Russell Lowell: "*Grey Plymouth's Rock hath yet a tongue, and Concord is not dumb.*"[54] Just as Garnet mixed a revolutionary brew of Ethiopian, Protestant, and American origin stories with a global black destiny, he ultimately prophesied a similar intermingling of races in the future. "*This western world is destined to be filled with a mixed race,*" he predicted (emphasis original), for "we speak of prejudice against color, but in fact, nothing of the kind exists. The prejudice is against the condition alone"—that is, slavery. When slavery ends, "so shall this race come forth and re-occupy their station of renown." In the meantime, black and white Americans remained together "on the field where the great battle is to be fought," a spiritual war for the future of Garnet's own chosen nation.

> Some people of color say that they have no home, no country, [but] America is my home, my country, and I have no other. . . . I love whatever of good there may be in her institutions. I hate her sins. I loathe her slavery, and I pray Heaven that ere long she may wash away her guilt in tears of repentance. . . . I love every inch of soil which my feet pressed in my youth, and I mourn because the accursed shade of slavery rests upon it. I love my country's flag, and I hope that soon it will be cleansed of its stains, and be hailed by all nations as the emblem of freedom and independence.[55]

Here again Garnet anticipated Douglass's "What to the Slave," and even more James Baldwin's remark "I love America more than any other country in this world, and, exactly for this reason, I insist on the right to criticize her perpetually." In blending Protestant and black traditions within an outlook that was at once national and cosmopolitan, both followed in Garnet's footsteps.[56] Here as elsewhere, as Carter G. Woodson put it, "Garnet created the idea" that later leaders "tempered and presented to the world in a more palliative and acceptable form."[57]

Black Cromwellians in the Union Army

While black writers drew diverse ideological threads from the entangled origin stories of the *Mayflower* and the slave ship, they achieved a tentative unity of purpose with the outbreak of the Civil War in 1861 and especially in 1863 after the Emancipation Proclamation in their efforts to convince the nation to arm black troops and, after their success, to recruit black troops for the Union. On this front, black nationalists like Martin Delany found common cause with integrationists like William Wells Brown as most major black writers of the period—Delany, Nell, Garnet, Douglass, Brown, and more—joined as recruitment agents for the Union.[58] Emigrationists found a reason to stay and Garrisonians found a reason to fight. Black writers had long sensed that a spiritual war against slavery would come to bloodshed, but with white peers they accepted violence as the price of providence. Further, they urged white peers to see black soldiers as leading protagonists in this drama.

Black writers and papers connected black Union soldiers to a Protestant tradition of Christian heroism and spiritual warfare. An 1851 article reprinted in *Frederick Douglass' Papers*, "The Characteristics of Christian Warriors," took Oliver Cromwell and his New Model Army as its leading example, the fiercest force in history because its was fueled by spiritual conviction rather than mere loyalty to king or lust for power. Cromwell "well understood that none would be such engaged valiant men, of such devoted bravery, as the religious . . . who considered the cause they were engaged in as the cause of God, and therefore as their cause, personally and individually. These men were never beaten." Such Christians were badly needed today, the author wrote, "a regiment of Christ's Invincibles . . . ready to take their scaling ladders, if need be, and go in the face of fire and death to the siege, the assault, the storming of the enemy."[59]

This tendency to focus on Protestantism's militant "warrior" genealogies may be one reason that most of the black writers in this study were men (though pseudonyms in periodicals leave open the possibility of more women writers). Yet even America's "first Black feminist-abolitionist" contributed to this conversation. Raised by a white Hartford minister, Maria Stewart early on found models for a humbler variant of Christian heroism in the Pilgrims and Puritans. After David Walker's *Appeal* sparked what she described as her second conversion, she penned her own jeremiad in *Religion and the Pure Principles of Morality* (1831), one that was "militant and modest" alike.[60] "Pure" appears throughout as her primary matrix for religion, from "pure principles of religion" to "pure piety . . . morals . . .

virtue . . . minds" and "hearts." At its core, Stewart concluded, "religion is pure," and it formed the bedrock of her race heroism, if of a less aggressive variety than Walker's and Garnet's. Stewart rooted her religious heroism first in female industry and found models in New England. Like Garnet, Stewart intertwined Ethiopianism and Puritanism: because Africans were once great, she declared, their descendants were capable of claiming a place within America's heroic history—"Did the pilgrims, when they first landed on these shores, quietly compose themselves, and say, 'the Britons have all the money and all the power, and we must continue their servants forever?' . . . No; they first made powerful efforts to raise themselves, and then God raised up those illustrious patriots, WASHINGTON and LAFAYETTE, to assist and defend them."[61] Stewart's historiography moved her audience from the position of victimhood to that of quintessential American warriors, putting "sword, shield, and helmet on the woman warrior."[62] Stewart minced no words: "WE CLAIM OUR RIGHTS."[63] Her call for black Christian heroes would be amply answered in the war.

Devoting two of his fifty-three biographical sketches to Phillis Wheatley and Charlotte Forten, William Wells Brown focused on men in *The Black Man: His Antecedents, His Genius and His Achievements* (1863) as he retrospectively imagined similar spiritual impulses in more controversial black revolutionaries. Nearly all of Brown's heroes were deeply religious, even the most militant—and often this militancy went hand in hand with their religiosity. Devoting the most pages to the revolutionaries Nat Turner and Touissaint Louverture, Brown emphasized their spiritual character, at times painting them in explicitly Puritanical colors.[64] Louverture, in Brown's telling, "had a deep and pervading sense of religion, and in the camp carried it even as far as Oliver Cromwell."[65] Brown most likely encountered Cromwell through Thomas Carlyle's *On Heroes*, a book that led him to "a high opinion of [Carlyle's] literary abilities" even if the Scottish author's flagrant racism in "On the Negro Question" (1849) and his "one page in favor of reform, and ten against it . . . had created in my mind a dislike for the man."[66] Brown's Louverture parallels Carlyle's Cromwell in several respects. Like Cromwell, Louverture was "a Christian, a statesman, and a general" (in that order). His revolution was essentially religious in nature; he proclaimed to his troops, "You are now to meet and fight enemies who have neither faith, law, nor religion." As with Cromwell, his religious intensity manifested in asceticism, "an austere sobriety which bordered on abstemiousness." And just as Carlyle concluded that Cromwell was greater than Napoleon because his religious conviction overcame his lack of military training, Louverture triumphed similarly; "without being bred to the science of arms," Brown wrote, he "baffled the skill of the most experienced generals that had followed Napoleon."[67] Brown painted a similar portrait of Nat Turner, emphasizing the rebel slave's "belief that his mission was a religious one," guided by visions and "direct communication with God." Brown emphasized the Christian rather than African nature of Turner's religiosity, his speaking with God through Christ and the Holy Spirit; "he had no faith in conjuring, fortune-telling, or dreams, and always spoke with contempt of such things," Brown noted, positioning him as a Christian warrior, likely in order to ward off charges of pagan fanaticism.[68] To stress the purity of Turner's goals, Brown even imagined a speech given on the eve of his attack, as he imagined for Louverture. "We do not go forth for the sake of blood and carnage," Brown's Turner proclaims, but "to carry on the war upon a Christian basis."[69]

While Brown imagined Turner and Louverture as modern Cromwells, other writers worked to fit black Union soldiers into a similar though more explicitly American lineage. The *Christian Recorder*, official periodical of the African Methodist Episcopal Church, not only took up coverage of the Union's black regiments but also featured articles on how black and white Americans should interpret the role of these troops in sacred history. In a preamble and resolution reprinted in the *Christian Recorder*, for instance, "a mass meeting of colored people" in Boston aimed to fill the quota for what would become the historic Fifty-Fourth Massachusetts Infantry Regiment, sketching a history of Puritan resistance to slavery as a reason for black troops to enlist. "Whereas, We recognise in Massachusetts (the old Bay State) the representative of those immutable principles introduced by the Pilgrim Puritans," these black leaders declared, and "whereas, Massachusetts, true to the instinctive principles of those Puritan Fathers, has ever been foremost in maintaining human freedom"—here the leaders included a lengthy list of Massachusetts firsts in the struggle for black freedom—"therefore, Resolved, That we, the colored people of the United States, owe a duty to Massachusetts that cannot better be paid than by giving her every influence in our power in order to make the Fifty-fourth Regiment, Massachusetts Volunteers, a perfect success, a model regiment by the way, speaking trumpet-tongued to her prejudiced sister States, saying, 'Go thou, and do likewise.'"[70] When Colonel Shaw died alongside half of his men in their assault on Fort Wagner, black abolitionists praised Shaw and his troops equally. A mix of Brahmin and black bravery, the Fifty-Fourth brought the *Mayflower* and the slave ship together into an especially effective narrative of holy war.

The *Recorder* was also distributed among black troops after they were allowed to serve in 1862, and it often instructed troops and their families to think of themselves and fellow white soldiers as Christian warriors in a holy cause. Before black enlistment, the *Recorder* reprinted a sermon from the (white) Presybterian Reverend Theodore L. Cuyler in which the preacher comforted the parents of soldiers by highlighting the religiosity of the Union Army. In their camps, Cuyler reflected, there "are probably a larger number of religious books and of religious men than have been found in any equal military gathering since 'Old Noll' [Cromwell] mustered his Puritan regiments at Naseby and Marston Moor." For that reason, he wrote, "Let not your hearts be troubled, neither let them be afraid. Your sons and husbands are fighting the battles of the Lord. If true believers, their lives are hid with Christ in God."[71] A month later the *Recorder* reprinted an article from the *New York Tribune* calling for more military chaplains to preserve "the moral and religious life of the corps." Union soldiers, the author declared, "are fighting this battle as one of law, liberty, and righteousness, and they must fight it as their Puritan forefathers, with Bible and Psalm-book in hand."[72]

Two months later the *Recorder* published a piece by the Reverend Gilbert Haven, an antislavery bishop in the Methodist Episcopal Church and a Massachusetts war chaplain, in which he revived the *Mayflower* and the slave ship. The war would be fierce, Haven warned, because "a feud of nearly two hundred and fifty years' standing is being settled to-day," namely, "Shall the slave power on this continent be supreme, or be utterly blotted out? Two hundred and forty years ago the seed was sown . . . out of which this bloody harvest is being reaped."[73] This trope was over two decades in the making, winding its way among white and black abolitionists of various ideological stripes and to various ends. Reverend Haven, a white New Englander, echoed Robert C. Winthrop's desire to see New England culture triumph over Southern depravity. But in reprinting this piece and spreading it among black readers, the *Recorder* followed in Garnet's footsteps, enlisting black soldiers into the vanguard of sacred history. As William Wells Brown, Benjamin Quarles, and others have amply demonstrated, black soldiers and fugitive slaves assumed this role with distinction, and the Union's "holy cause" would have failed without them.[74] At their most potent, black writers used the Pilgrims and Puritans not merely to claim their own American identity but to hint that they were *more* American than their white peers, fighting their way into the next chapter of the nation's sacred drama.

Paradise Lost?

After the smoke settled, Herman Melville was certain of only one thing: the Civil War was not a Miltonic battle between Heaven and Hell. The North was no righteous Puritan nor the South a reprobate Cavalier, and such millennial battle lines only intensified the bloodshed of America's deadliest conflict to date. While his peers accepted the staggering violence of a half million dead as the price of purification, Melville saw further evidence of idealist naiveté, "optimist-cheer." When Appomattox gave way to the question of reconstruction, he quietly contested Northern exultation in *Battle-Pieces and Aspects of the War* (1866). The collection of poems opened with a brooding meditation on John Brown's executed body, not the neo-Puritan martyr of his peers but a "meteor of war" portending calamity. Against the battle hymns of Howe and Whittier, Melville emphasized the war's common suffering, the ironic and tragic experiences that affected northern and southern soldiers alike. Cumulatively, *Battle-Pieces* imagined the war as America's fall from innocence.

But it also hoped that the war might become a fortunate fall that prevented future holy wars by dousing juvenile faith in American exceptionalism with "nature's dark side," evidence that America was just as susceptible to tragedy as the rest of the postlapsarian world. Robert Milder gives the best reading of *Battle-Pieces*, demonstrating how it shepherds readers away from Miltonic righteousness and toward humane compassion, "a new political faith" rooted in what Melville elsewhere called an "infinite fraternity of feeling" (176–77).[1] Against abolitionists' adamant faith in "Higher Law," Melville's faith in fraternity grew from his uncertainty that the universe was ruled by a God that bent history toward justice. He hoped that an honest reckoning with the possibility that history was not providential nor America its vanguard might unite humanity, on our own but in it together.

"Let us revere that sacred uncertainty which forever impends over men and nations," *Battle-Pieces* concluded, advocating peacetime humility and solidarity in place of abolitionist certitudes gashed with battle lines.[2]

For postbellum national policy, this especially meant mercy toward the defeated South, to "not urge / Submissiveness beyond the verge" lest the country "prolong the evil day." In its two final poems and "Prose Supplement," *Battle-Pieces* coaxed the North toward clemency that honored the valor of Southern soldiers if not the planters that "cajoled" them into an immoral cause. While he rejoiced at the end of slavery's "atheistical iniquity," he also urged his countrymen to "remember that emancipation was accomplished not by deliberate legislation" but "only through agonized violence" that surpassed everyone's expectations. Facing an uncertain universe with magnanimous solidarity "is a brave thought, unmatched in the writing of any of his contemporaries," Milder concludes, "and brave even in the early twenty-first century in light of the neocovenantal righteousness that has again come to guide or verbally gild national policy."[3]

Yes and no. Melville's caution regarding American exceptionalism and his doubts about Providence certainly fare better with modern critics than the strident optimism of his idealist peers, just as his dissent within a wartime chorus of nationalism appears prophetic in retrospect. On the other hand, it is unavoidable to read *Battle-Pieces* through Reconstruction's failure: the revived power of the planter class, the birth of the Klan and Jim Crow, the broken promise of "forty acres and a mule," and the half century of lynch law that tumbled the nation toward its "nadir of race relations," the effects of which still plague us today. On this front, Melville's call for reconciliation and his support for Andrew Johnson fare worse in the judgment of history. As David Blight and Eric Foner have shown, sectional reconciliation in the postbellum decades most often meant a *white* reconciliation that came at the expense of lasting racial progress. Though Confederate ideology lost the military conflict, it made troubling gains in the fight over the memory of the war and the course of the postbellum decades by spreading the myth of the "Lost Cause" and the "Dunning School" of history that interpreted Reconstruction as a disaster, a perspective especially popularized by D. W. Griffith's *The Birth of a Nation* (1915).[4]

Melville's vision for postbellum America was argued in far better faith than Griffith's, but it tended toward the same results. Though he sympathized with the freedpeople and applauded federal efforts to protect its citizenry, he argued that "such kindliness should not be allowed to exclude kindliness to communities who stand nearer to us in nature"—that is, white southerners, his "us" white northerners. "For the future of the freed slaves we may well be concerned," he concluded, "but the future of the whole country, involving the future of the blacks, urges a paramount claim upon our anxiety. Effective benignity, like the Nile, is not narrow in its bounty." Yet postbellum prosperity was not a rising tide that lifted all ships; it was a river dammed toward white mills and fields. The final poem of *Battle-Pieces* imagines Robert E. Lee's chastened plea for fraternity before a vindictive Congress, but the dissolution of Reconstruction came about through the reverse as the vanquished waged a new war against black citizenry.

Daniel Aaron suspected that the Civil War failed to spark a great work of literature, in a word, because of race. "Without the Negro, there would have been no Civil War, yet he figured only peripherally in the War literature," he writes, "remain[ing] even in the midst of his literary well-wishers an object of contempt or dread, or an uncomfortable reminder of abandoned obligations, or a pestiferous shadow, emblematic of guilt and retribution."[5] Melville came the closest to writing the war's masterpiece in *Battle-Pieces*, but his white "us" handicapped him. Only two of the collection's seventy-two poems deal in any way with black Americans; this suggests a hyperreticence on race that hindered Melville's sharp sensitivity to the war's tragic dimensions. This lost opportunity is all the more disappointing because Melville was the likeliest of white writers to do justice to the complexities of race, if *Moby Dick* and *Benito Cereno* are any evidence.[6] Unlike many northerners, he seemed entirely uninterested in the wartime heroism of individuals like Harriet Tubman and Robert Smalls, the half million "contraband" fugitives that seized freedom by fleeing for the Union front, and especially the Union's 166 black regiments who formed an eighth of overall forces (even a quarter of the navy that Melville loved) and served with valor at Milliken's Bend, Fort Wagner, and more. Melville was likewise uninterested in blacks' central role within the tragic elements of the war that so transfixed him, whether in individual battles like the Fort Pillow Massacre and the Battle of the Crater or—most importantly—in the nearly two centuries of slavery that catalyzed the war. In his distaste for battle lines, even Melville avoided the conflict's root cause like a "pestiferous shadow."

One need not choose between a good cause and its concomitant tragedies, its morality and complexity. A truly mature vision of the war as a "fortunate fall" would recognize slavery as the greatest tragedy of all, combining sympathy for the Confederate soldier with regret that his valor was enlisted to guard planter wealth. When Melville's Lee appeals to Congress for reconciliation, he raises a voice "from these charnel-fields, / A plaintive yet unheeded one: / 'Died all in vain?'" A more courageous vision of "nature's dark side" would dare to consider that the answer for the Confederacy is, tragically, yes, and it was a minimization of *this* tragedy that in fact "prolonged the evil day" into Jim Crow and beyond. Even today many feel forced to choose between a tragic and a moral interpretation of the war. Harry Stout and Andrew Delbanco side with Melville's tragedy and his skepticism toward abolitionists' Puritanical crusade, valuing his liberal attention to the ambiguities and ironies of multiple perspectives. Meanwhile John Stauffer and Manisha Sinha side with the radicals, retorting that the abolitionist cause was the more courageous risk than Melville's detached tragedy, while Ta-Nehisi Coates is even more blunt: "The Civil War Isn't Tragic."[7]

It's both. "Yea, and Nay— / Each hath his say; / But God He keeps the middle way," Melville wrote in *Battle-Pieces*, and he nearly reached it. He fell short of perceiving what Raymond Williams called "the whole experience" of a revolution, the inseparability of its suffering and its progress. Himself a committed socialist, Williams admits that radicals downplay the violence and complexity of revolutions as preludes to national (re)birth, abstracting individuals into ideological angels and demons—precisely Melville's complaint against his peers. Yet conversely, others point to this naiveté "either to oppose revolution as such, or to restore the convenient belief that man cannot change his condition."[8] In his frustration with idealists, Melville tended to this extreme, more eager to adopt the perspective of the defeated southerner than that of the slave, readier to explore the war's common suffering than the claims that catalyzed it in the first place. He fumed with Ishmael, "Who aint a slave?" during a war over that very question.

Instead we can "follow the whole action: not only the evil, but the men who have fought against evil; not only the crisis, but the energy released by it, the spirit learned in it."[9] The desire for "the total redemption of humanity" may be naive and hubristic in a reality that resists violently, but this makes redemption more rather than less precious. A revolution like the Civil War, Williams concludes, is the "inevitable working through of a deep and tragic disorder," its tragedy and morality inseparable. One can face the disorder honestly, as Melville insisted, but also work against it, for "what we learn in suffering is again revolution, because we acknowledge others as men."[10] Clemency for the defeated South could be sympathetic to its suffering and respectful to its valor yet still contingent upon its willingness to recognize black citizenship precisely because, in the words of Lincoln, "As I would not be a slave, so I would not be a master."

The year after the publication of *Battle-Pieces*, a (still) unknown black lay preacher named Lorenzo Dow Blackson imagined a new Miltonic holy war for reconstruction in his strange *The Rise and Progress of the Kingdoms of Light and Darkness* (1867). Explicitly modeled on *Paradise Lost* and *Pilgrim's*

Progress, the work retold all of human history as an ancient war between Kings "Alpha" and "Abadon" (God and Satan) that had erupted in the Reformation, the American Revolution, and most recently in the Civil War. Blackson's providential history culminated in his call for his heavenly regiment to maintain arms against "prejudice to color, which did not die with slavery, but is still rampant in the land, stalking abroad" (178–79). As Melville predicted, here was the alternative to his tragic vision: another millennium, another holy war, another "last great battle that is to be fought." Blackson, who may have served in the war, lamented its "vast waste of blood and treasure" that "fill[ed] the land with widows and orphans," but as the son of former slaves, he also emphasized emancipation as the war's great achievement and white supremacy as a lasting threat to its gains. In his call to maintain arms, Blackson echoed his abolitionist heroes. "Power concedes nothing without a demand. It never did and it never will," Douglass wrote, for injustices grow "till they are resisted with either words or blows." "Never look for an age when the people can be quiet and safe," Wendell Phillips similarly declared, for "republics exist only on the tenure of being constantly agitated." Americans ought to "live like our Puritan fathers . . . with their musket-lock on the one side and a drawn sword on the other," for "there is no Canaan in politics. . . . Eternal vigilance is the price of liberty."[11]

Melville had enough of Puritan swords and rightly highlighted martial rhetoric's propensity to erupt into real warfare, yet reformers' imaginative battle lines remain not only inevitable but necessary. The abolitionists' accomplishments and flaws have been debated since the war, but Eric Foner's account remains the most persuasive. "Abolitionists pioneered the practice of radical agitation in a democracy," he writes, echoing Phillips, and "by changing public discourse, by redefining the politically 'possible,' the abolitionist movement affected far more Americans than actually joined its ranks" as "their agitation helped to establish the context within which politicians like Lincoln operated."[12] That is, abolitionists' imaginative battle lines forced a clearer terms of debate—indeed forced the nation *to* debate—and in the process redefined *possible*. "Utopian dreams of social justice," William James wrote, "are, in spite of their impracticability and non-adaptation to present environmental conditions, analogous to the saint's belief in an existent kingdom of heaven. They help to break the edge of the general reign of hardness, and are slow leavens of a better order." Here as in the antislavery fight these "creative energies" were destructive and reconstructive alike, "animaters of potentialities of goodness which but for them would lie forever dormant."[13]

The more tragic reality of Reconstruction may be that the nation agreed with Melville more than he realized, more eager in their war weariness to achieve sectional reconciliation than lasting racial progress. A new generation of writers from Mark Twain and Ambrose Bierce to Stephen Crane would remember the war as "a tragic farce, a sick joke that belied the lofty rhetoric of writers and politicians from the previous generation."[14] Perhaps this was inevitable after a conflict of such magnitude. "Red republicanism, in the father, is a spasm of nature to engender an intolerable tyrant in the next age," Emerson concluded.[15]

Deeper than the Puritanical holy warriors and the detached tragic heroes are the invisible people working "underground" to make individuals of themselves within this "deep and tragic disorder." Throughout *Invisible Man*, Ellison's narrator wrestles with a riddle left by his dying grandfather. "Our life is a war, and I have been a traitor all my born days, a spy in the enemy's country ever since I gave up my gun in Reconstruction. . . . Live with your head in the lion's mouth. I want you to overcome 'em with yeses, undermine 'em with grins, agree 'em to death and destruction, let 'em swoller you till they vomit or bust wide open." The narrator tries various ideologies—Bookerite vocation, (early) Du Boisian cultivation, Marxism, black nationalism—but none fit this cryptic advice. Instead he goes underground. "They were all up there somewhere, making a mess of the world. Well, let them. I was through and, in spite of the dream, I was whole."

This wholeness is not asocial escapism but a new declaration of independence at once American, black, and human. In his epilogue, Ellison's narrator considers three final interpretations of Grandfather's riddle in his underground isolation, passing dialectically to a tentative resolution. First, he wonders if his grandfather meant "we were to affirm the principle on which the country was built and not the men" who failed to live up to it, "to affirm the principle, which they themselves had dreamed into being out of the chaos." From the ideal of American democracy, he counters himself with the reality of black oppression: perhaps Grandfather's riddle meant "that we had to take responsibility for all of it"—the promise and the failure that Williams called "the whole action"—because black Americans understood more than any the deepest failures and promises of America's democratic ideals. If so, the narrator finally considers that Grandfather would want him to "affirm the principle because we, through no fault of our own, were linked to all the others," to the oppressors as much as the oppressed precisely because the oppressed were better able to see their fundamental equality. Thus to live "in the lion's mouth" and to "agree 'em to death" until they "bust wide open" was to embrace one's Americanness, blackness, and humanity as synonyms in the midst of a world intent on tearing them apart.[16]

Invisible Man was Ellison's own attempt to answer this riddle, an "underground" effort to live as a whole human being within lionlike violence. A disciple of both Emerson and Melville, Ellison achieved a unique combination of "optimist-cheer" and detached tragedy, neither a blithe denial of tragic disorder nor a fixation on it, but a "working through it," as Williams would say. "In going underground, I whipped it all except the mind, the mind. And the mind that has conceived a plan of living must never lose sight of the chaos against which that pattern was conceived. That goes for societies as well as for individuals. Thus, having tried to give pattern to the chaos which lives within the pattern of your certainties, I must come out, I must emerge." Chaos and pattern, mind and emergence, thought and action. Tragic conscience makes no coward of the invisible man but prepares him to climb up from the ground and confront the frightening fact that "on the lower frequencies, I speak for you." Emerson concluded early on that "to believe your own thought, to believe that what is true for you in your private heart is true for all men,—that is genius." This self-reliance led him to empyrean heights of holy war and Melville to the maddening depths of tragedy. Ellison kept the middle way, his own.

ACKNOWLEDGMENTS

My gratitude goes first to my scholarly mentors. Leigh Schmidt advised with wit and charm while Rafia Zafar enlightened and encouraged me in equal parts. Abram Van Engen went far beyond the call of advising in his generosity of intellectual and professional guidance. Robert Milder remains my Emersonian mentor, urging me toward still higher visions. My sincere thanks, too, to Washington University in St. Louis for seven years of varied support and funding. I remain indebted to this collective generosity.

I completed this manuscript during an influential year as a Volkswagen postdoctoral research fellow at Universität Heidelberg's Center for American Studies, where I worked with Jan Stievermann, a superb scholar and mentor. My thanks to him for a deeply rewarding collaboration. *Vielen dank*, too, to Günter Leypoldt, Manfred Berg, Ryan Hoselton, James Strasburg, Claudia Jetter, Benjamin Pietrenka, David Reißmann, and Paul Schweitzer-Martin for many fruitful conversations. I am thankful for the institutional and financial support of the Heidelberg Center for American Studies, for the Volkswagen Stiftung and its director Wilhelm Krull, and for William F. Tate and Paul Michael Lützeler, who oversaw the Stiftung at Washington University. It was strange to watch 2017–18 unfold in the US. from across the Atlantic yet encouraging to live among an international community eager to unfold its manifold meanings. Hiking up the Gaisberg and biking down the Plöck, I felt Hegel, Weber, and Gadamer hovering in the Neckartal.

Various other individuals read or heard portions of this work in conferences and workshops, offering useful feedback on the way. Special thanks to Laura Dassow Walls, Christopher Cameron, John Stauffer, and Andrew Delbanco for reading early work. On the project's digital component,

Stephen Pentecost and Doug Knox of Washington University's Humanities Digital Workshop graciously answered dozens of Python-related queries, while Anupam Basu advised on stats. Hannah Wakefield and Jonathan MacGregor were friends and fellow travelers at Wash U and beyond. An ALA symposium in 2015, God and the American Writer, at San Antonio brought me into the welcomed company of Jennifer Gurley and Peter Balaam. I organized a panel for the Sacred Literature, Secular Religion conference at Le Moyne College in 2015 to garner the insights of Neal Dolan and Len Gougeon, who obliged with grace. A Mellon Seminar in 2015, "Troubling History," with Steven Zwicker and Derek Hirst improved both the early modern and the theoretical components of this book. I benefited from a talk in 2016 at the Massachusetts Historical Society led by Kate Viens and Conrad Wright. Likewise, an international conference called Transcendentalist Intersections at Universität Heidelberg's Center for American Studies yielded useful insights from Paul Kerry, Tae Sung, Phyllis Cole, Dan Malachuk, Benjamin Park, Walter Grünzweig, and more. My thanks to all of you for your collegiality and camaraderie.

Much of the book's archival research was the result of a generous grant from the New England Regional Fellowship Consortium. I want to thank this excellent program and the many institutions and archivists that aided my work. Special thanks to Peter Accardo at Harvard's Houghton Library for his help in deciphering the scribblers of antebellum New England; to Margaret Bendroth at the Congregational Library & Archives for her energizing curiosity; to Beth Prindle and Kimberly Reynolds at Boston Public Library's Rare Books Department; to Tim Salls, Lynn Betlock, and Christopher Child at the New England Historic Genealogical Society; to Marilyn Dunn of the Schlesinger Library at Harvard's Radcliffe Institute for Advanced Study; and finally to Kate Viens, Conrad Wright, and the wonderful staff at the Massachusetts Historical Society. These archives are an embarrassment of riches in texts and people alike, so a collective thank you to all involved, named and unnamed.

I am especially grateful to University of Chicago Press for taking a chance on a young scholar's first book. It was truly a pleasure to work with Timothy Mennel, Susannah Marie Engstrom, and the rest of the Chicago team. My thanks, too, to Edward Gray, Stephen Mihm, and Mark Peterson as series editors for the American Beginnings, 1500–1900 series and to the two anonymous readers who took the time to read the work with care and insight.

Early versions of some chapters first appeared elsewhere as articles. A portion of chapter 1 appeared in the *New England Quarterly* as "Swept into

Puritanism," while condensed versions of chapters 3 and 6 appeared respectively in *Journal of American Studies* and *MELUS* as "A Paper Puritan of Puritans" and "The Mayflower and the Slave Ship."

To conclude at the start: Mom and Dad, thank you for your tenacious faith; Erin, your grace keeps me going. My love to you.

St. Louis—Heidelberg

NOTES

INTRODUCTION

1. I refer to the Pilgrims and Puritans jointly as "Puritans," adopting the antebellum tendency to group them together for the sake of shorthand. Perhaps more surprising, Hawthorne does not feature in this study. His views of Puritanism and abolition are already amply documented, and they remain outliers among those of his literary peers.

2. Everett, "The Pilgrim Fathers," in *Orations and Speeches on Various Occasions*, 2:484–89; "sacred fire of liberty" quoted from Henry Hallam's history of England.

3. The most recent and important example is Abram Van Engen's *City on a Hill*, which deftly tracks how a narrative of America's exceptional Pilgrim/Puritan origins coalesced into the start of the nineteenth century. Additionally, Lawrence Buell's account of the Puritans as a "literary construct" in *New England Literary Culture* remains authoritative, as does Jonathan Seelye's *Memory's Nation* and Joseph Conforti's *Imagining New England*. For the Puritans' legacy among their most direct institutional descendants, the Congregationalists, see Bendroth, *The Last Puritans*; more focused reception histories of particular Puritan authors include Stavely, *Puritan Legacies*; Felker, *Reinventing Cotton Mather*; and Baker, *America's Gothic Fiction*. I remain indebted to each of these works, but in general I aim to emphasize the *potential* of a constructed past as much its inaccuracies and pitfalls.

4. Orestes Brownson, "Miracles," qtd. in Miller, *The Transcendentalists*, 208; William Lloyd Garrison, qtd. in Mayer, *All on Fire*, 119–20.

5. Mason, *Apostle of Union: A Political Biography of Edward Everett*.

6. Everett, *Orations and Speeches on Various Occasions*, 486, 491.

7. Littell and Littell, *Littell's Living Age*, 3:270. *Liberator*, January 2, 1846.

8. The *Liberator* made some reference to Milton every third issue, on average.

9. Henry Vane the Younger served a brief term as governor of the Massachusetts Bay Colony before returning in 1637 to England, where he worked as a leading parliamentarian and ally of Cromwell; despite dismissing himself from his governmental post after Cromwell dissolved Parliament, he was later convicted of treason and beheaded in 1662. Algernon Sidney was a leading republican theorist and commissioner for the trial of King Charles I who—despite his opposition to Charles's execution—was also convicted of treason and beheaded in 1683; Sydney Ahlstrom calls Sidney "Puritanism's greatest political philosopher." *A Religious History*, 129.

10. Reynolds, *John Brown, Abolitionist*, 230. Phillips, "The Puritan Principle and John Brown," delivered in Music Hall to the Twenty-Eight Congregational Society, 18 December 18, 1859. Phillips and Pease, *Speeches, Lectures, and Letters*, 2:300–305. Brown and his defenders are explored at greater length in chapter 1.

11. *The Unwritten War; American Writers and the Civil War*, supplement 1, 343.

12. *Eight Years in Congress, from 1857–1865. Memoir and Speeches*, 282.

13. Jefferson Davis, "Speech at Jackson, December 26," in *The Papers of Jefferson Davis*, vol. 8, *1856–1860*, 567.

14. Adalbert Volck, "Worship of the North," Gilder Lehman Institute for American History, Collection GLC00493.01.

15. Adams, *The Education of Henry Adams*, 4, 20.

16. Bercovitch, *The Rites of Assent*, 14, 355–56.

17. Pease, *The New American Exceptionalism*, 77–78. Among the most prominent critiques of the Millerite school include Amy Kaplan's argument for the "absence of empire" in Miller's work or Donald Pease argument that the early "Myth and Symbol" school of American studies, informed by Miller, "corroborated American exceptionalism" and "legitimized hegemonic understanding of American history"; Kaplan and Pease, *Cultures of United States Imperialism*, 3–40. I agree here with Leo Marx in "Believing in America" that such characterizations are polemical straw men given the pervasive leftism and New Deal liberalism among the founders, characterized by an ambivalent "doubleness" and a "*provisional* belief in the idea of America" (emphasis mine). For a more careful study of Miller's mixed feelings toward America, I appreciate Fuller, "Errand into the Wilderness."

18. In her 2016 history of abolition, Manisha Sinha confirms a moment in history that abolitionists like Wendell Phillips themselves often cited: in 1645 two Africans were released from bondage by Boston courts when it was sufficiently proved they had been taken by "man stealing." *The Slave's Cause*, 67. For other histories of slavery in colonial New England, three excellent studies (all appearing in 1998) include Horton and Horton, *In Hope of Liberty*; Melish, *Disowning Slavery*; and Fitts, *Inventing New England's Slave Paradise*. The most recent and, to my mind, most valuable study of slavery in New England is Wendy Warren's *New England Bound*, but here too I wonder about its broader framing as a skeptical effort that "punctures the myth of a shining 'City on a Hill.'"

19. Wood, "Struggle Over the Puritans," *The New York Review of Books*, November 9, 1989

20. Kammen, *Mystic Chords*, 39, 31.

21. *Ursprung ist das Ziel* comes from Benjamin's "Theses on the Philosophy of History," in *Illuminations*, 261; John David Pizer offers a helpful explanation of the passage in *Toward a Theory of Radical Origin*, 59–63. "Politics of memory" is the more hopeful half of memory studies, those who see nostalgia, origins, and tradition as potential spaces for reevaluating culture in fundamental ways. One can trace this tradition from Benjamin and Gramsci to Foucault, Jameson, Eagleton, the Birmingham Popular Memory Group, John Bodnar, Raymond Williams, and others. Jameson, for instance, reflects that "there is no reason why a nostalgia conscious of itself, a lucid and remorseless dissatisfaction with the present on the grounds of some remembered plenitude, cannot furnish as adequate a revolutionary stimulus as any other." "Walter Benjamin, or Nostalgia," in *The Salmagundi Reader*, 575. See also Eagleton, "Capitalism, Modernism and Postmodernism." Deleuze voiced a similar sentiment in declaring that a healthy literature "consists in inventing a people who

are missing," imagining "the origin and collective destination of a people to come still ensconced in its betrayals and repudiations." American literature especially has an "exceptional power to produce writers who can recount their own memories, but as those of a universal people . . . always in becoming, always incomplete." *Essays Critical and Clinical*, 4.

22. Bercovitch himself noted this "problem of ideology," but his proposed solution to simply accept and work within our own ideological presumptions still operated on the belief that "ideology is basically conservative," a consensus; *The Rites of Assent*, 355.

23. Van Dijk, "Ideology and Discourse," in *The Oxford Handbook of Political Ideologies*, 180. He elaborates in his book-length study *Ideology*.

24. Phillips, "Under the Flag," in *Speeches, Lectures, and Letters*, 1:413, 408, 419.

25. Buell, "The Politics of Historiography," in *New England Literary Culture from Revolution through Renaissance*, 214–38. Here as in innumerable other respects I am deeply indebted to Buell's work, though I emphasize how the Puritans acquired a positive political resonance into the 1840s and 1850s, especially for writers impatient with Unitarian equipose on slavery and elsewhere. "Religion pure and undefiled" comes from James 1:27, a favored verse of scripture among abolitionists.

26. On the one hand, this reclamation of a fiery Puritan legacy of righteous hatred counteracts popular images of the Puritans (then and now) as emotional stoics; on the other hand, it reaffirms the popular image of Puritans as unsentimental in their severity, descended from Ann Douglas but most recently challenged by Abram Van Engen's *Sympathetic Puritans*, which traces how a Calvinist theology of "fellow feeling" and mutual affections left a lasting impact on sentimentalism.

27. Adams, *The Education of Henry Adams*, 4.

28. "Self-Reliance," in *Emerson's Prose and Poetry*

29. Phillips and Pease, *Speeches, Lectures, and Letters*, 1:396–409.

30. James, *The Varieties of Religious Experience*, 367, 360. Recent studies of abolition that have followed this Jamesian line include Stauffer, *The Black Hearts of Men*; Petrulionis, *To Set This World Right*; Gougeon, *Virtue's Hero*; and Sinha, *The Slave's Cause*.

31. Adams, *The Education of Henry Adams*, 5.

32. Santayana and Wilson, *The Genteel Tradition*, 41, 47.

33. Parrington, *Main Currents in American Thought*, 6; Brooks, *The Flowering of New England, 1815–1865*, 388–89. More recently the link between Puritan and abolitionist is implied by Andrew Delbanco in Delbanco et al., *The Abolitionist Imagination*, and explicitly declared by David Reynolds in *John Brown, Abolitionist*, 14–28, and *Mightier Than the Sword*, 6.

34. Mencken, *A Book of Prefaces*, 212–13, 229–30.

35. Everett, *Orations and Speeches on Various Occasions*, 491.

36. Phillips, "Speech at the Dinner of the Pilgrim Society, in Plymouth, December 22, 1855," in *Speeches, Lectures, and Letters*, 1:230. I analyze this pervasive language of spirit in chapter 3. Paul Ricoeur, "The Conflict of Interpretations," in *Freud and Philosophy*, 27.

37. Everett, *Orations and Speeches on Various Occasions*, 492.

38. It should also be noted that many abolitionists—Child foremost—were also outspoken critics of US policy on Native Americans, more aware than most of the imperial risks in appealing to Puritan history.

39. Margot Minardi has done similar work on nineteenth-century Massachusetts's memories of the revolution and emancipation in New England. Like Minardi's, my

primary point is that these memorial and historiographical efforts influenced action against slavery. *Making Slavery History.*

40. Wai Chi Dimock's theory of resonance especially clarifies what critics like Gordon Wood mean when they speak of the Puritans' continued "resonance" in the present. What Dimock calls textual "resonance"—the ways in which texts retain, change, and accrue meaning across time as they are encountered in new contexts—emphasizes literary history as "a democratic institution" by highlighting how "its very words become unfixed, unmoored, and thus democratically claimable" across time, allowing literary historians to determine central threads of "temporal interdependency without telos." For present purposes, I consider this to be a fruitful synthesis beyond the Puritan origins thesis and its critique-driven antithesis. Neither a master narrative nor a babel of deconstruction, Dimock's "diachronic historicism" illuminates why certain texts and themes remain persistent and why they acquire new meanings in new eras. This approach frames the question of the Puritans' legacies differently: instead of solely defending or deconstructing a Puritan origin story, it asks why certain legacies of the Puritans have waxed or waned throughout American history. "A Theory of Resonance."

41. Milder, "From Emerson to Edwards."

42. "Connected criticism" is Michael Walzer's idea, from *Interpretation and Social Criticism* and *The Company of Critics.*

43. For good overviews of memory studies in its present form, see Olick, Vinitzky-Seroussi, and Levy, *The Collective Memory Reader*; Tota and Hagen, *Routledge International Handbook of Memory Studies*; and Kattago, *The Ashgate Research Companion to Memory Studies.* A growing number of scholars emphasize the role of memory in abolitionism and Reconstruction: see chapter 1 of McInerney, *The Fortunate Heirs of Freedom Abolition and Republican Thought*; Young, *The Shoemaker and the Tea Party*; and Blight, *Race and Reunion.*

44. Wood, "Struggle over the Puritans."

45. As Carlyle spent most of his final days railing against the mediocre chaos of republics and the folly of emancipation, it is high irony that his works would inspire black and white abolitionists insistent on the potential of democracy, but as Jon Roper notes, "Carlyle can be quarried by ideologues of all persuasions." Roper, *Democracy and Its Critics*, 174. Roper further notes that "the attraction of the work for Emerson and American transcendentalists lay in his rejection of the ethos of nascent industrialism, materialism and laissez-faire economics. . . . [He] saw the real greatness of a nation in the intensity and depth of its moral life and its intellectual achievements and not in its political aspirations."

46. Whittier, "A Summons," in *Anti-Slavery Poems: Songs of Labor and Reform*, 41.

47. Butler, *Awash in a Sea of Faith.*

48. Douglas, *The Feminization of American Culture.*

49. James, *The Secret of Swedenborg*, 221.

50. Stowe, "New England Ministers," *Atlantic*, 1858.

51. Carlyle, *Heroes, Hero Worship and the Heroic in History*, 124–26.

52. Here I am indebted to James Brewer Stewart's reading of the "transformed state of mind" that abolition offered adherents in *Holy Warriors*, 36.

53. I am most concerned with abolition's imaginative and literary qualities, especially its "discourse of martyrdom and Holy War" as a neglected thread in American literary history. Wood, *The Poetry of Slavery*, xxx. I draw from the growing "New Formalist" movement that seeks to explore the connections between the political and aes-

thetic rather than their separation. Suvir Kaul and Marcus Wood have been models in their careful attention to the formal qualities of abolitionist literature in *Poems of Nation, Anthems of Empire*, 230–68, and *The Poetry of Slavery*, xiv. (Both generally focus on the British movement, which possessed an imaginative landscape distinct from that of its American counterpart.)

54. Cox, *Eight Years in Congress, from 1857–1865*, 288.
55. Cox, *Puritanism in Politics*, 10.
56. Taylor, *A Secular Age*. After submitting a portion of this work to a journal, I received reader reports that aptly captured this split opinion: reviewer 1 concluded that abolitionism was obviously a religious movement, reviewer 2 that it was obviously a force for secularization. Taylor is especially helpful in pushing us beyond this either-or.
57. Jeffrey, *The Great Silent Army of Abolitionism*.
58. Among the most recent noteworthy histories of slavery that espouse this emphasis are Berlin, *Generations of Captivity*. and *Long Emancipation*; Hahn, *A Nation under Our Feet* and *The Political Worlds of Slavery and Freedom*; Johnson, *River of Dark Dreams*; Baptist, *The Half Has Never Been Told*.
59. Wright, *Quarterly Anti-Slavery Magazine*, 311.
60. My goal here is to apply Gilroy's call for "the theorisation of creolisation, métissage, mestizaje, and hybridity" to the complex realm of interracial organizing in American abolition. *The Black Atlantic*, 2.
61. Gilbert Haven, "The Pulpit and the Press on the War," *Christian Recorder*, August 24, 1861. All further references to the *CR* were accessed through *Accessible Archives*' African American Newspapers database at https://www.accessible-archives.com/collections/african-american-newspapers/the-christian-recorder/.
62. Foner, *The Fiery Trial*, 20, xix. Kraditor, *Means and Ends*, 276.
63. Edmund Morgan, *American Slavery, American Freedom*. This is a final reason for my focus on antebellum writers, radicals, Garrisonians, and Transcendentalists despite the recent direction of abolitionist studies to highlight the movement's pre-Garrisonian longue durée, its international character, and especially its African American vanguard of free blacks and the slaves themselves. The writers featured here were a numerically minor strain of the movement as a whole, but they punched above their weight in shaping how the conflict was imagined, the style and terms in which it was debated, the "structures of feeling" in which it was handled. Critics frequently and inaccurately held up the most radical examples of Garrisonian incendiarism, disunionism, and "harsh language" as damning representatives of the abolitionist movement as a whole, for instance, while these writers conversely used this same harsh language to inspire and discipline adherents or to urge complacent bystanders to take sides in a sacred battle.
64. Raymond Williams, *Modern Tragedy*, 84.
65. Theodore Parker, *Collected Works*, 4:222.

CHAPTER ONE

1. For a comprehensive account of Brown's life, see Reynolds, *John Brown, Abolitionist*.
2. Theodore Parker to Francis Jackson, December 24, 1859, in Redpath and Alcott, *Echoes of Harper's Ferry*, 91; Frederick Douglass, "John Brown and the Slaveholders' Insurrection: An Address Delivered in Edinburgh, Scotland, on 30 January 1860," in *The Frederick Douglass Papers*, series 1, 3:312; Henry David Thoreau, "A Plea for Captain John Brown," in *Reform Papers*; Wendell Phillips, "Harper's Ferry," delivered in

Brooklyn, November 1, 1859, in *Speeches, Lectures, and Letters*, 1:280; Ralph Waldo Emerson, "Address at the John Brown Relief Meeting," delivered in Boston, November 18, 1859, in *The Collected Works of Ralph Waldo Emerson*, vol. 10.

3. On the reaction of the press and writers to Brown in the immediate aftermath of Harper's Ferry and Brown's longer legacy, see Russo and Finkelman, *Terrible Swift Sword*. and Beck, *Creating the John Brown Legend*.

4. Reynolds, *John Brown, Abolitionist*, 221, 224, 227.

5. Gunpowder, that is. "Trust in God and keep your powder dry" is a saying attributed to Oliver Cromwell which first appeared in William Blacker's 1834 poem "Oliver's Advice," a reimagination of Cromwell's address to his soldiers during the invasion of Ireland.

6. Douglass, *Life and Times of Frederick Douglass* (book 1), in *The Frederick Douglass Papers*, series 2, 3:353; Emerson, "Address at the John Brown Relief Meeting," in *The Collected Works of Ralph Waldo Emerson*, vol. 10; Parker to Francis Jackson, December 24, 1859, in Redpath and Alcott, *Echoes of Harper's Ferry*, 91, reprinted in the *Liberator*. February 3, 1860, 4; Phillips, "Harper's Ferry," in *Speeches, Lectures, and Letters*, 1:276; Thoreau, "A Plea for Captain John Brown," in *Reform Papers*.

7. Phillips, "The Puritan Principle and John Brown," delivered in Music Hall before the Twenty-Eight Congregational Society, December 18, 1859, in *Speeches, Lectures, and Letters*, 2:300–305.

8. While recent studies have emphasized how New England religious and political radicalism overlapped in shared social networks, it also grew from a shared historical vision. See Gougeon and Myerson, *Emerson's Antislavery Writings*; Von Frank, *The Trials of Anthony Burns*; Petrulionis, *To Set This World Right*; and Gougeon, *Virtue's Hero*. Young and Cherry demonstrate in "The Secularization of Confessional Protests" how abolitionism often drew activists away from religious orthodoxy. I build upon Gougeon's similar comparative study of Emerson and Douglass in "Militant Abolitionism."

9. See Carlyle's "Occasional Discourse on the Negro Question" (1849) and "Latter-Day Pamphlets" (1850).

10. Leypoldt and Engler, *American Cultural Icons*.

11. Carlyle, "Signs of the Times," *Edinburgh Review*, reprinted in *The Collected Works of Thomas Carlyle*, vol. 3.

12. On the reception of *Sartor* in the States, see Vance, "Carlyle in America before *Sartor Resartus*," and Jackson's *The Social Construction of Thomas Carlyle's New England Reputation, 1834–36* and "The Reader Retailored." Jackson argues that Carlyle especially appealed to doubting Calvinists for providing the emotional framework of Calvinist conversion without the creedal baggage. The same can be said for liberal readers who had already abandoned Calvinism but yearned for its emotional equivalent.

13. Carlyle, *Sartor Resartus*, 137.

14. Carlyle, *On Heroes, Hero Worship & the Heroic in History*, 106.

15. Milder, "A Radical Emerson?"; Porte and Morris, *The Cambridge Companion to Ralph Waldo Emerson*. For a helpful overview of scholarship on Emerson's political views as well as more general "Emersonian strategies" on political questions "from Emerson himself to George Kateb today," see Patell, "Emersonian Strategies."

16. Taylor, *A Secular Age*, 60–63.

17. Emerson, "New England Reformers, A Lecture read before the Society in Amory Hall, on Sunday, 3 March, 1844," in *The Collected Works of Ralph Waldo Emerson*, 3:150.

18. Joe Fulton has noted that Emerson's vision of aesthetic renaissance was inextricable from his desire for ongoing religious reformation; this historical dynamic was political as much as religious and aesthetic, three fruits of the same spiritual transformation. "Reason for a Renaissance."

19. Emerson, "The Transcendentalist, a Lecture read at the Masonic Temple, Boston, January, 1842," *The Collected Works of Ralph Waldo Emerson*, 1:206.

20. The lecture was later revised into essay form in "Milton," in Rice et al., *Essays from the "North American Review*," 112–15.

21. Emerson, *The Early Lectures of Ralph Waldo Emerson*, 1:167, 181.

22. Emerson, *The Early Lectures of Ralph Waldo Emerson*, 1:330–47.

23. Phillips, *Speeches, Lectures, and Letters*, 1:3–8.

24. When Phillips wrote to English abolitionist George Thompson shortly after, he similarly rejoiced that British abolitionism still thrived "in the land of Vane and Milton, of Pym and Hamden," all prominent Puritan sympathizers in the English Civil War. Phillips, *Speeches, Lectures, and Letters*, 2:9. Phillips later deemed Vane to be Boston's "noblest human being. . . . Milton pales before him."

25. Emerson, *The Journals and Miscellaneous Notebooks of Ralph Waldo Emerson*, 13:281.

26. Carlyle was specifically thinking of efforts like Brook Farm and Bronson Alcott's Fruitlands. During Carlyle's writing of *Past and Present*, Alcott was in England, where he circulated copies of Emerson's "Man the Reformer." Carlyle, *Past and Present*, 290, 512–13.

27. Bancroft, *A History of the United States, from the Discovery of the American Continent*, 817–18.

28. Parker, *Collected Works of Theodore Parker*, 4:267.

29. Salem Transcendentalist Thomas Treadwell Stone explicitly theorized the abolitionist movement as a "second Reformation." Just as the first Reformation defeated the Roman Church's "assumption of divine authority," Stone imagined the abolitionist movement as a Second Reformation that "shall expose the falseness of the same claim in behalf of political institutions. Grant them of divine origin or ordinance; yet never, certainly, more divine than the individual man." "The Second Reformation," *Liberty Bell*, 1851.

30. Bartlett, *Wendell and Ann Phillips*, 13. See Weil, "John Farmer and the Making of American Genealogy," on the origins of the New England Historic Genealogical Society and antebellum efforts to reconcile a burgeoning interest in genealogy with a dedication to republicanism.

31. Bartlett, *Wendell and Ann Phillips*, 15. During a disappointing trip to England in 1841, Phillips failed to win much British support for the antislavery cause but succeeded in exploring England's archives, where he hired genealogists to trace his roots beyond colonial New England. Phillips also discovered that his wife Ann's first North American ancestor was an associate of Roger Williams. Ann and Wendell had married well, both dissenting descendants of dissenting Dissenters.

32. Bartlett, *Wendell and Ann Phillips*, 18.

33. Richardson, *Emerson*, 25.

34. Cole, *Mary Moody Emerson and the Origins of Transcendentalism*, 17, 79; Emerson, *Emerson in His Journals*, 253.

35. Emerson, *Emerson in His Journals*, 253.

36. Cole, *Mary Moody Emerson and the Origins of Transcendentalism*, 17. See also Buell, "Religion on the American Mind," for a summary of recent works that all assume a "lived religion" approach to religion in literature.

37. Ripley was no Puritan theologically, but a moderate who in fact managed the town's smooth transition from Calvinism to Unitarianism.
38. Emerson, *Emerson in His Journals*, 260.
39. Emerson, *The Later Lectures of Ralph Waldo Emerson, 1843–1871*, 1:4.
40. Emerson, *The Later Lectures of Ralph Waldo Emerson, 1843–1871*, 1:7–14.
41. "In the United States I found very few men who displayed any of that manly candor and that masculine independence of opinion," de Tocqueville wrote, "which constitutes the leading feature in distinguished characters." (With many of his American readers, de Tocqueville relied on categories of republican manhood and emergent Victorian norms in gendering independence as "manly.")
42. Buell, *Emerson*, 269–70.
43. Emerson, *Emerson's Antislavery Writings*, 24–28.
44. Emerson, *Emerson's Antislavery Writings*, 40–43.
45. Here I build on Robert Milder's argument that Emerson's early anticapitalism cooled into the late 1840s becaues he felt that the socialist movement was spiritually premature. I argue that Emerson's growing embrace of abolitionism at this very moment in fact stems from the same desire, a way to preserve his sense of politically potent spiritual transformation. In this respect, Emerson's radicalism doesn't decline with old age and spiritual disillusionment but changes its political program as history grew more apocalyptic over slavery than capitalism. See Porte and Morris, *The Cambridge Companion to Ralph Waldo Emerson*, 49–75.
46. Douglass, *The Frederick Douglass Papers*, series 2, 1:11–12.
47. Parker, *Collected Works of Theodore Parker*, 4:5, 16–19.
48. Parker, *Collected Works of Theodore Parker*, 4:37–40.
49. Parker, *Collected Works of Theodore Parker*, 4:70–74.
50. Teed, "The Politics of Sectional Memory," 311. Parker again sniped puritanically at Winthrop with the death of John Quincy Adams in 1848. In his eulogy for the former president and his fellow Massachusetts representative, Winthrop praised Adams without making any mention of his antislavery work in Congress nor his strong criticism of the Mexican War. In Parker's eulogy for the *MQR*, by contrast, Adams emerged as a Puritanical revolutionary, loyal only to higher law: "that New England knee bent only before his God." Teed, "The Politics of Sectional Memory," 318–20.
51. Teed, "The Politics of Sectional Memory," 322–24. For Teed this is "startling evidence of Parker's inability to fully transcend conservative visions of regional history," seen especially in his unwillingness to discuss New England's participation in slavery, a willful amnesia that Joanne Pope Melish has explored as the "linchpin of a burgeoning antebellum New England nationalism." See Melish, *Disowning Slavery*. If Parker, like most white New Englanders, deemphasized his region's own involvement with slavery, he elsewhere found much to critique in the Puritans. Since his *Discourse on Matters Pertaining to Religion* (1842), Parker was forthright in his critiques of Calvinist theology and Puritan intolerance, and he opposed nostalgia as a barrier to recognizing what parts of the Puritans' legacies were flawed and "transient" versus those that were progressive and "permanant." In the *MQR* Parker defended Richard Hildreth's antislavery *History of the United States* (1849) and its critical portrait of the Puritans from conservative reviewers like Francis Bowen.
52. Parker, Cabot, and Emerson, *The Massachusetts Quarterly Review*. 2:15.
53. Peterson, *The Great Triumvirate*, 466.
54. Peterson, *The Great Triumvirate*, 466.
55. Emerson, *Emerson's Antislavery Writings*, 67, 78.

56. Emerson, *Emerson's Antislavery Writings*, 83.
57. Cole, *Mary Moody Emerson and the Origins of Transcendentalism*, 281.
58. It should be noted that Seward was less transcendental-idealist than his "higher law" language suggests—an instance of potent phrasemaking outrunning one's platform. My thanks to University of Chicago Press's anonymous reader for making this excellent observation.
59. Parker, *Collected Works of Theodore Parker*, 4:222.
60. Parker, *Collected Works of Theodore Parker*, 5:105.
61. Parker, *Collected Works of Theodore Parker*, 5:130–31.
62. Martyn, *Wendell Phillips*, 124.
63. Phillips, *Speeches, Lectures, and Letters*, 2:49–54.
64. Phillips, *Speeches, Lectures, and Letters*, 1:121–146.
65. Parker, *Collected Works of Theodore Parker*, 5:245–46.
66. Parker, *Collected Works of Theodore Parker*, 5:252–53, 259–262.
67. Here I build on John Seelye's work that reveals how abolitionists succeeded in repoliticizing these celebrations by the 1850s. See especially Seelye, *Memory's Nation*, 270.
68. Phillips, *Speeches, Lectures, and Letters*, 1:230–31.
69. Phillips, *Speeches, Lectures, and Letters*, 1:236.
70. Weiss, Parker, and Oliver Wendell Holmes Collection (Library of Congress), *Life and Correspondence of Theodore Parker*, 172.
71. Emerson, *The Collected Works of Ralph Waldo Emerson*, 11:289.
72. Phillips, *Speeches, Lectures, and Letters*, 2:436.
73. *Liberator*, October 19, 1860.
74. Phillips, "Under the Flag," in *Speeches, Lectures, and Letters*, 1:413, 408, 419.
75. Phillips, "Under the Flag," in *Speeches, Lectures, and Letters*, 1:479.
76. Buell, *Emerson*, 267–70. Peter S. Field has similarly concluded that "on the verge of a second American revolution, Emerson's imagination largely failed him" as he became convinced that American greatness was largely "the product of its Saxon heritage and history." Field, *Ralph Waldo Emerson*, 198.
77. Buell, *Emerson*, 269.
78. Emerson, *The Journals and Miscellaneous Notebooks of Ralph Waldo Emerson*, 1968, 9:125.
79. Emerson, *Emerson's Antislavery Writings*, 30–32.
80. At a New Year's celebration of the Proclamation, Emerson grafted the event into his vision of history with his "Boston Hymn," opening with the Pilgrims departing for the New World as they chased an angel named Freedom. The poem tracked the growth of New England but then turned unexpectedly toward the (still) radical idea of reparations. "Pay ransom to the owner, / And fill the bag to the brim," Emerson's God decrees. "Who is the owner? The slave is owner, / And ever was. Pay him." If this financial reckoning was refused, the Lord prophesied a harsher future reckoning: "laying hands on another / To coin his labor and sweat, / He goes in pawn to his victim / For eternal years in debt."
81. Hargrove, *Black Union Soldiers in the Civil War*, 77–80.
82. Hargrove, *Black Union Soldiers in the Civil War*, 159.
83. Emerson, *The Collected Works of Ralph Waldo Emerson*, vol. 9.
84. Emerson, *Emerson's Antislavery Writings*, 146.

CHAPTER TWO

1. James, *The Bostonians*, 91.
2. James, *The Bostonians*, 41.

3. James, *The Bostonians*, 14, 156.
4. James, *The Bostonians*, 45.
5. Jeffrey, *The Great Silent Army of Abolitionism*.
6. Puritan, *The Abrogation of the Seventh Commandment*, 3–6, 17.
7. Puritan, *The Abrogation of the Seventh Commandment*, 17, 19.
8. Welter, "The Cult of True Womanhood." This chapter is deeply indebted to those scholars who first emphasized the centrality of women to the abolitionist movement and their anticipations of the suffragist movement, in particular Kraditor, *Means and Ends in American Abolitionist*, and, more recently, Yellin, *Women and Sisters*.
9. Deborah A. Logan, introduction to Maria Weston Chapman, *Memorials of Harriet Martineau*, 4–5.
10. Barker-Benfield, *Portraits of American Women*, 147–67.
11. Taylor, *Women of the Anti-Slavery Movement*, 2.
12. As Yellin and Van Horne note, the "Female Association for Promoting the Manufacture and Use of Free Cotton" and the "Colored Female Free Produce Society" had been established in Philadelphia in 1829, but the BFAS was the first society dedicated explicitly to an antislavery platform. *The Abolitionist Sisterhood*, xv.
13. Anti-Slavery Meeting, *The Boston Mob of "Gentlemen of Property and Standing,"* 14.
14. Boston Female Antislavery Society and Society for the Collegiate Instruction of Women (U.S.), *Report of the Boston Female Anti-Slavery Society*, 28, also reprinted the day after the mob in the *Boston Commercial Gazette*.
15. The anecdote is recounted in Chapman, *Right and Wrong in Massachusetts*, 33, and Garrison and Garrison, *William Lloyd Garrison, 1805–1879*, 15, among other sources.
16. Garrison and Garrison, *William Lloyd Garrison, 1805–1879*, 16.
17. Boston Female Anti-Slavery Society, "Annual Report of the Boston Female Anti-Slavery Society," 24–26.
18. Boston Female Anti-Slavery Society, "Annual Report of the Boston Female Anti-Slavery Society," 40–52.
19. Boston Female Anti-Slavery Society, "Annual Report of the Boston Female Anti-Slavery Society," 50.
20. Boston Female Anti-Slavery Society, "Annual Report of the Boston Female Anti-Slavery Society," 52.
21. Ruth Bogin and Jean Fagan Yellin especially highlight this tension. "The culture of female antislavery involved women who rejected traditional gender patterns and women who accepted them," Yellin and Bogin note, above all emphasizing the variety of ways in which female abolitionists both reproduced and subverted antebellum gender norms. In Yellin and Van Horne, *The Abolitionist Sisterhood*, 3.
22. For the fullest study of female abolitionists from British dissenting and American Puritan tradition, see Clapp and Jeffrey, *Women, Dissent and Anti-Slavery in Britain and America, 1790–1865*; see especially Julie Roy Jeffrey's contribution therein, "Women Abolitionists and the Dissenting Tradition," 132–54, from which the Neall quote comes on p. 150.
23. Boston Female Anti-Slavery Society, *Annual Report of the Boston Female Anti-Slavery Society in 1837, with a Sketch of the Obstacles Thrown in the Way of Emancipation by Certain Clerical Abolitionists and Advocates for the Subjection of Woman*, 94, 32.
24. See Chambers, *The Weston Sisters*, for one of the most recent and useful studies of the Weston sisters. Notes 1–3 on pp. 195–96 in particular offer a helpful overview of the scholarly debate on the nature of the BFAS's internal tensions.

25. *Songs of the Free, and Hymns of Christian Freedom*, 9–10. Garrison had put out his own hymnbook two years prior; see *A Selection of Anti-Slavery Hymns*.

26. *Songs of the Free, and Hymns of Christian Freedom*, 170, vii.

27. Chapman, *Songs of the Free*, 52–53, 100. The Garrisonian fixation on martyrdom took a specifically Protestant form whose genealogy can be traced to John Foxe's *Book of Martyrs*, which remained popular in antebellum America. For an excellent study of Foxe's American reception—including its influence on abolitionists and Theodore Parker in particular—see Heike Jablonski's *John Foxe in America*.

28. Wood, *The Poetry of Slavery*, xxix. Wood elaborates that these hymns appeal not to eighteenth-century radicals like Paine and Godwin "but to seventeenth-century religious disputation, particularly in terms of the way the conventions of martyrology are employed. Forgotten scaffold oratory in the form of the last speeches of Protestant martyrs, even martyrs as obscure as Henry Vane and Marion Harvey, is quoted as a commentary upon abolition verse" (xxx).

29. Thompson, *American Literary Annuals and Gift Books, 1825–1865*.

30. *Liberator* 18, no. 50 (December 15, 1848).

31. Chapman, *The Liberty Bell*, 1856, 100–103.

32. For a full list of contributors by year, see Glynis Carr's immensely helpful "Index to *The Liberty Bell*."

33. Maria Weston Chapman, "Sonnet Suggested by the Inscription on the Philadelphia Liberty Bell," *Liberty Bbell*, 1839, v–vi; Lydia Maria Child, "Lines to Those Men and Women, Who Were Avowed Abolitionists in 1831, '32, '33, '34, and '35," *Liberty Bell*, 1839, 5–9; Caroline Weston, "The Church and the World," *Liberty Bell*, 1839, 44–50.

34. William Howitt, "Onward! Right Onward!," *Liberty Bell*, 1846, 7–11; Abby Kelly, "What is Real Anti-Slavery Work?," *Liberty Bell*, 1845, 202–8.

35. John Pierpont, "The Liberty Bell," *Liberty Bell*, 1842, p. 1–5; William Lloyd Garrison, "The Cause of Emancipation," *Liberty Bell*, 1839, 92–101.

36. Ann Greene Chapman, "The Armor and the Prize," *Liberty Bell*, 1845, 77–78; Anne Warren Weston, *Liberty Bell*, 91–99.

37. All published in the *Liberty Bell*: James Russell Lowell, "Sonnets," 1842, 37–38; Eliza Follen, "Song, for the Friends of Freedom," 1846, p. 65–67; John Pierpont, "Plymouth Rock," 1841, v; Maria Weston Chapman, "Boston," 1842, 44–45; John Bowring, 1845, 9–10; Frederika Bremer, "Letter on Slavery," 1845, 72–76; Wendell Phillips, "A Fragment," 1843, 49–51.

38. Chapman et al., *Liberty Bell*, 29–44, 1848.

39. Howe, *Reminiscences*, 59, 146, 302.

40. Showalter, *The Civil Wars of Julia Ward Howe*, 17–18.

41. Showalter, *The Civil Wars of Julia Ward Howe*, 150–52. Brown was in turn taken with Julia, whom he described as "a defiant little woman, all flash and fire" like Chapman. Howe's husband Samuel Gridley Howe similarly praised Brown as "of the Puritan order militant" and supported his raid on Harper's Ferry as a member of the "Secret Six."

42. Showalter, *The Civil Wars of Julia Ward Howe*, xiv.

43. See also Stauffer and Soskis, *The Battle Hymn of the Republic*, for a cultural history of the song itself.

44. Child, *A Lydia Maria Child Reader*, 5.

45. Lydia Maria Child, December 17, 1870, in *A Lydia Maria Child Reader*, 415.

46. Karcher, *The First Woman in the Republic*, 82.

47. Karcher, *The First Woman in the Republic*, 451.
48. Karcher, *The First Woman in the Republic*, 31, 23. Invoking her brother's freedom while writing in his old room, she drew a story from an anonymous Puritan manuscript and assumed the voice of a young male narrator. She was inspired by the real call from Unitarian minister John G. Palfrey in the *North American Review* to utilize New England's history for American literature. On Palfrey's call, see Buell, *New England Literary Culture from Revolution through Renaissance*, 227–28. Shortly after, Child elaborated her critique of Puritan imperialism in *First Settlers of New England: Or, Conquest of the Pequods, Narragansets and Pokanokets. As Related by a Mother to her Children, By a Lady of Massachusetts* (1829), an unflinching study of colonial Puritans' harsh policy toward natives as a lesson to Jacksonians who continued this legacy against the Cherokee.
49. Karcher, *The First Woman in the Republic*, 175. Child may have met Garrison as early as 1827, when he worked in the office of her husband's *Massachusetts Whig Journal*, and she received his high praise in 1829 when Garrison reprinted one of her pieces and hailed her as "the first woman in the republic" (xx). She certainly met Garrison in 1830.
50. Child, *Lydia Maria Child*, 25.
51. Karcher, *The First Woman in the Republic*, 199.
52. Karcher, *The First Woman in the Republic*, 136–47, 183, 186. Karcher insightfully notes that the *Appeal*'s "chief originality . . . lies in its thorough dismantling of racist ideology and its respectful and detailed treatment of African cultures. Indeed, the historian Sterling Stuckey credits Child with displaying a fund of knowledge about Africa matched only by Martin Delany among her African American contemporaries and by Mary Lowell Putnam and Herman Melville among whites."
53. "A man has at least as good a right to choose his wife, as he has to choose his religion." Child, *An Appeal in Favor of That Class of Americans Called Africans*, 209.
54. Karcher, *The First Woman in the Republic*, 183.
55. As Karcher notes, Child sent Channing a copy of her abolitionist *Appeal*, and it made such an impact that Channing went to Child's home to personally thank her for arousing his conscience. Two years later he would write his influential *Slavery* (1835). *The First Woman in the Republic*, 136–37, 203. In the years following the *Appeal*, Child dove into the cause by supplementing her writing with organizing, joining the BFAS in 1834. (She would later represent the group at the first Anti-Slavery Convention of American Women.)
56. Letter to Lydia B. Child, South Natick, April 2, 1837, Schlesinger Library, Harvard University. Child made the same point regarding Northampton two years later. "The human soul is stagnant there," she lamented, pining for an escape from "narrowness, sectarianism, and the dead formalities both of religion and gentility" (June 9, 1839). Karcher, *The First Woman in the Republic*.
57. Tarr, "Emerson's Transcendentalism in L. M. Child's Letter to Carlyle," 113. Child's brother the Reverend Convers Francis first read *Sartor* in 1835 and wrote to Ralph Waldo Emerson enthusiastically about the new author. Child quoted *Sartor Resartus*—"the old skin never falls off till a new one has formed under it"—in an argument for female suffrage (noting that it was once thought unladylike to write books but now was common) in "Concerning Women," *Women's Journal*, 1869. She included quotes from Carlyle in her *Aspirations of the World* (1878), her "eclectic bible" that compiled the best grains of wisdom from all world religions.

58. Jackson, "The Reader Retailored," 160–61.
59. Letter to Louisa Loring, South Natick, July 19, 1836, Loring Papers, Schlesinger Library, Harvard University. Child later sniped at the Unitarians in the growing split over Transcendentalism. Reflecting on Emerson's exile from the clergy in 1839, Child again wrote to Louisa. "How absurdly the Unitarians are behaving," she noted, for "the Calvinists, in their turn, could not abide the reformers of the reformed Reformation; and now the Unitarians are expressing the same holy horror of a man who presumes to innovate upon *them*." Letter to Louisa Loring, Northampton, January 12, 1839, Loring Papers, Schlesinger Library, Harvard University.
60. Letter to Louisa Loring, Northampton, January 12, 1839, Loring Papers, Schlesinger Library, Harvard University. Child referenced the Unitarian leader Andrews Norton.
61. Letter to Louisa Loring, Northampton, June 28, 1840, Loring Papers, Schlesinger Library, Harvard University. As Emerson had done in 1867, Child would find an organizational alternative to "decencies forever" when she joined the quite decent Free Religious Association in 1876.
62. Daniel Walker Howe, *The Unitarian Conscience*, p. 138. Before Howe, William R. Hutchinson argued that "the Transcendental protest cannot be understood unless it is seen that the younger radicals were contending from the start against a system whose vital assumptions were far from negative, and whose very denials were built upon the biblical faith of earlier Puritanism." *Transcendentalist Ministers*, 3.
63. Child, *Selected Letters*, 360.
64. Lydia Maria Child, letter to Ellis Gray Loring, New York, May 27, 1841, Ellis Gray Loring Papers (A115), Schlesinger Library, Harvard University.
65. In a letter to James Russell Lowell, someone who managed to sustain a high reputation as both a political and a literary writer, Child again tried to balance these callings. "If anti-slavery made me take one particle less of interest in the sad music of the moon," she maintained, "I would abjure it tomorrow, even at the risk of the Calvinistic hell for my disobedience to conscience." December 13, 1841, Houghton Library, Harvard University.
66. The only extended study of Child's "The Kansas Emigrants" I could find was in Kellow, "For the Sake of Suffering Kansas." It is mentioned in but (to my mind inexplicably) excluded from Karcher's *A Lydia Maria Child Reader*.
67. Child, *Autumnal Leaves*, 302.
68. Child, *Autumnal Leaves*, 304–5.
69. Child, *Autumnal Leaves*, 305.
70. Child, *Autumnal Leaves*, 329. Alice dreams of a beautiful home on nearby Mount Oread. Here too Child quietly invokes a New English and feminist vision for the West: the mountain had just been named for the Oread Institute of Worcester, Massachusetts, a woman's college founded seven years prior by Eli Thayer, the same man who spearheaded the Massachusetts Emigrant Aid Company that began to send New England settlers to Kansas in 1854. This hill is today the home of the University of Kansas, established by Free Staters.
71. Child, *Autumnal Leaves*, 343–44.
72. Child, *Autumnal Leaves*, 351–52.
73. Child, *Autumnal Leaves*, 355–56.
74. Child, *Autumnal Leaves*, 358.
75. Child, *Autumnal Leaves*, 361.

76. Karcher, *The First Woman in the Republic*, 392.
77. Shortly after, she urged John Greenleaf Whittier to mythologize the event in the same manner as Emerson's "Concord Hymn."
78. *Liberator*, December 23, 1859.
79. Child, *Letters of Lydia Maria Child*, 104.
80. Child, *Letters of Lydia Maria Child*, 105–7.
81. Child, *Letters of Lydia Maria Child*, 118.
82. "Lydia Maria Child's Reply to Gov. Wise," *New York Weekly Tribune*, November 26, 1859, 4; Child, *Letters of Lydia Maria Child*, 114–15.
83. Child, *Letters of Lydia Maria Child*, 136.
84. Child, *Letters of Lydia Maria Child*, 136–37.
85. Child, *A Lydia Maria Child Reader*, 17.
86. Child, letter to Anna Loring, Wayland, February 21, 1864, Loring Papers, Schlesinger Library, Harvard University.
87. Child, *A Lydia Maria Child Reader*, 255.
88. Child, *A Lydia Maria Child Reader*, 256.
89. Child, *A Lydia Maria Child Reader*, 260. Child ended, interestingly, by quoting from "Go Down Moses," recently transcribed and sent to her by the Reverend Lewis C. Lockwood while he worked at Fort Monroe. She called it "The Song of the Contrabands" in a letter to Mary Stearns, December 15, 1861; *A Lydia Maria Child Reader*, 261.
90. Her persistent goal was "to help in the breaking down of classes, and to make *all* men feel as if they were brethren." Child, letter to Lucy Osgood, February 4, 1869, found in Child, *A Lydia Maria Child Reader*, 5.
91. Child, "The Black Saxons," *Liberty Bell*, 1841, 19–44.
92. Meltzer, *Tongue of Flame*, 159; Child, letters to John Greenleaf Whittier, Wayland, Massachusetts, January 21, 1862, and September 22, 1861, Child Papers, Library of Congress.
93. "A Tribute to Col. Robert G. Shaw," *New York Evening Post*, August 15, 1863; Child, *A Lydia Maria Child Reader*, 267–68.
94. Child, *The Freedmen's Book*. As elsewhere, Child counterbalanced her admiration for Toussaint's heroism and military valor with an emphasis on his distaste for cruelty ("the business of his life to conquer freedom for his race; but never in a bloodthirsty spirit . . . His motto was, 'No Retaliation,'—a noble, Christian motto") and his domestic commitments ("no trait in the character of Toussaint Breda was stronger than his domestic affections").
95. Child, *A Lydia Maria Child Reader*, 281–82; Foner, *Reconstruction America's Unfinished Revolution, 1863–1877*.
96. Child, *A Lydia Maria Child Reader*, 282.
97. Child, *A Lydia Maria Child Reader*, 283.
98. Child, *A Lydia Maria Child Reader*, 282.
99. Child, *A Lydia Maria Child Reader*, 281.
100. Child, *A Lydia Maria Child Reader*, 292.

CHAPTER THREE

1. "To Mssrs. J. Telemachus Hilton, Robert Wood, and J. H. How, *Committee*, Boston, August 13, 1831," in Garrison, *The Letters of William Lloyd Garrison, 1822–1835*, 1:126; published in *Liberator*, August 27, 1831.
2. Milton, *Paradise Lost*, 4.34–44.

3. This data comes from the Viral Texts project of the NUlab at Northeastern headed by Ryan Cordell and David Smith, whose database draws text from the "Chronicling America" digital archive of US periodicals to "cluster" reprints of articles. A search for "puritan/-s/-ism/-anical" turns up 1328 total references from 536 clusters of original references in 991 nonabolitionist papers in 1837–65 from OH, TN, VT, LA, MO, SC, IN, VA, KY, and NY. My subsequent digital analysis of the *Liberator* have been enabled by Slavery Anti-Slavery: A Transnational Archive by Gale Digital Collections, who were kind enough to share their data. As the word count remains constant, references first rise with the murder of abolitionist printer Elijah Lovejoy in 1838 and especially with the outbreak of the Mexican War, spiking in 1848 amidst the *Liberator's* coverage of the European revolutions and rising steadily in the volatile 1850s. A final jump occurs in 1859 with Harper's Ferry and once more with the outbreak of the Civil War. Occasionally the reference was to the *New England Puritan*, a journal of conservative Congregationalism with which the *Liberator* had a standing feud, or to the history of Puritan persecution of Quakers and Native Americans to deflate New England chauvinists who celebrated a legacy of liberty yet maintained neutrality on slavery.

4. Eden B. Fost, "Sermon," *Liberator*, October 17, 1856; "The Object of the Rebel War," *Liberator*, issue 1, December 16, 1864. Reprinted extract from Reverend Amory Dwight Mayo's "The Progress of Liberty in the United States," *Continental Monthly*, November 1864.

5. See, for instance, Lowell and Higginson in Garrison, *Selections from the Writings and Speeches of William Lloyd Garrison*, ix, xii.

6. Garrison, *Selections from the Writings and Speeches of William Lloyd Garrison*, 239–43, 380.

7. *Liberator*, January 23, 1846, 1.

8. Trish Loughran qualifies the common emphasis on the late eighteenth century as the locus classicus for the emergence of a national consciousness via print; instead she argues that the material infrastructure and technology necessary for a truly national print culture didn't emerge until the 1830s. *The Republic in Print*.

9. Hall, *Cultures of Print*, 76. For an excellent study of this "print explosion," see especially Cohen, *The Fabrication of American Literature*, 5.

10. Among recent work on antebellum American printing, I have found the following excellent studies to be the most useful, though the place of religion and secularization remains only a minor theme in each: Cohen, *The Fabrication of American Literature*; Cohen and Stein, *Early African American Print Culture*; McGill, *American Literature and the Culture of Reprinting, 1834–1853*; Hruschka, *How Books Came to America*; and Smith, *An Empire of Print*. Charvat, *Literary Publishing in America, 1790–1850*, remains a classic in its study of how the evolving publishing industry affected American authors.

11. Nord, *Faith in Reading*.

12. I have drawn the ubiquitous Luther quote from M. H. Black, "The Printed Bible," in *The Cambridge History of the Bible*, ed. Greenslade, 3:432; Nord, *Faith in Reading*, 14. Recent studies in American print culture and the history of the book have reaffirmed Nord's insight, tethering Perry Miller's intellectual history of the "New England mind" to a remarkable circulation of texts and economies of publication that clarify the overlap between Puritan spirituality and print materiality. See Hall, *Worlds of Wonder, Days of Judgment*; Hall, *Cultures of Print*; Green, *Print and Protestantism in Early Modern England*; Casper, *Perspectives on American Book History*; Brown, *The Pil-*

grim and the Bee; Monaghan, *Learning to Read and Write in Colonial America*; and Cohen, *The Networked Wilderness*. The latter remarks that "the region of New England has been fertile ground for the study of what has been called 'print culture'" for this reason. Most of these studies, like scholarship on antebellum print, tend to examine the cultural aspect of print culture synchronically, focusing on its defining features at a particular time (for a representative spectrum of recent approaches to print culture in early America, see Gross and Kelley, *A History of the Book in America*, which employs a focus on ideologies, institutions, education, gender, genre, and publics); this study employs a more diachronic approach by examining how later print cultures can self-consciously reclaim and revise early print cultures.

13. Child, *A Lydia Maria Child Reader*, 288–90; Karcher, *The First Woman in the Republic*, 599.
14. Mayer, *All on Fire*, 70.
15. *Journal of the Times*, Bennington, VT, March 27, 1829, qtd. in Garrison and Garrison, *William Lloyd Garrison, 1805–1879*, 122.
16. On the influence of Lundy and especially Walker's immediatism on Garrison, see Sinha, *The Slave's Cause*, chaps. 7–8, pp. 195–265.
17. October 15, 1830.
18. Qtd. in Mayer, *All on Fire*, 104–5.
19. Qtd. in Mayer, *All on Fire*, 118.
20. Qtd. in Mayer, *All on Fire*, 129.
21. *Liberator*, January 1, 1831.
22. *Liberator*, July 26, 1834, 2.
23. Garrison, "Triumph of Mobocracy in Boston," *Liberator*, November 7, 1835, 178–79. The article appeared again on December 12, 19, and 26, then once more on 9 January 1836; it appeared again much later in the October 26, 1860, issue.
24. Mayer, *All on Fire*, 213–14.
25. Anglen, *The New England Milton*, 97.
26. "Severity of the Abolitionists," *Liberator*, January 9, 1836.
27. Qtd. in Mayer, *All on Fire*, 226, 229; *Liberator*, July 23 and August 6, 1836.
28. Phillips, *Liberator*, April 14, 1837, 2–3; Russell, *Liberator*, August 4, 1837, 1. Russell would later become a founding member of the Boston Vigilance Committee.
29. Qtd. in Mayer, *All on Fire*, 238.
30. *Liberator*, January 12, 1838, 1.
31. For the sake of concision, I omit an exhaustive examination of further examples of explicit connections between Puritan heritage and a free press, but they can be found in the following issues of the *Liberator*: May 18 and December 28, 1838; August 5, 1842; January 23 and March 6, 1846; August 13, 1847; April 6, 1849; June 14 and August 2 1850; January 17, 1851; May 26, 1854; July 12, 1861.
32. *Liberator*, January 19, 1844; April 15, 22, & 29 1859; reprinted as "No Compromise with Slavery," in *Selections from the Writings and Speeches of William Lloyd Garrison*, 139.
33. Child, *A Lydia Maria Child Reader*, 289.
34. Qtd. in Nord, *Faith in Reading*, 122.
35. Qtd. in Nord, *Faith in Reading*, 123.
36. Channing, *Slavery*, 134.
37. Channing, *Slavery*, 136–37.
38. Channing, *Slavery*, 146, 134.
39. *Liberator*, January 9, 1836, 1.

40. Many of the traits by which one scholar distinguishes *The Communist Manifesto* can likewise be applied to the Garrisonian ouvre: "vigorous, varied, and highly concrete, alive with imagery and flashing with figures of speech. In the freshness of its diction and the boldness of its tropes, it may be said to be romantic." Siegel, "The Style of the Communist Manifesto," 223. This is especially true of Garrisonians' frequent recurrence to the language of heat and eruption. "I use strong language, and will make no apology for it," Garrison seethed, defending "the language of hot displeasure, and caustic irony, and righteous denunciation. Every word will burn like molten lead, and every sentence glow like flaming fire." *An Address Delivered in Marlboro' Chapel, Boston.*

41. Mailloux, "Enactment History, Jesuit Practices, and Rhetorical Hermeneutics"; Ballif, *Theorizing Histories of Rhetoric*, 34.

42. Phillips, *Speeches, Lectures, and Letters*, 2:38–40.

43. *Liberator*, April 25, 1835.

44. Phillips, "Public Opinion," in *Speeches, Lectures, and Letters*, 1:43.

45. This sampling come from the following issues of the *Liberator*: "gospel," May 19, 1837; "calculating politicians," May 26, 1837; "Constitution," May 19, 1837.

46. Digital copies of these texts come from the Gale Slavery and Anti-Slavery Transnational Archive and Chronicling America; in the latter, digital texts and xmls need cleaning, and all results are thus preliminary and subject to further refinement. The data follows: I compiled word counts of "spirit" over total word counts for full digital runs of six Southern newspapers included in the Gale Slavery and Anti-Slavery Archive and compared them to the same length of run from the *Liberator*. The data follows as *Liberator*: 11,397 / 57,081,176 = .0200% v. Southern papers: 3,046 / 90,598,684 = .0034%, or 5.9× as frequently. Tracking the word "spirit" from 1856 to 1859 for the *Congregationalist* and 1849 to 1850 for the *Emancipator & Republican* (the years in which full runs of digital issues exist, both from Chronicling America) results in the following word counts over total word count. *Congregationalist*: 2,064 / 9,282,000 = .02% v. *Liberator*: 1,955 / 6,825,000 = .03%, or 1.5× as often; *Emancipator & Republican*: 583 / 4,680,000 = .01% v. *Liberator*: 1,128 / 3432000 = .03% .033, or 2.7× as often.

47. A comprehensive count of all "spirit of" phrases in the *Liberator* runs as follows: slavery 427, liberty 325, the age/times 265, Christ 260, Christian/-ity, 236, freedom 228, the gospel 215, God 170, the national government 165, love 133, the Constitution 112, the Lord 98, truth 92, abolition/-ism 88, war 79, Jesus 78; peace 74; revenge 59; humanity 58; compromise 56; violence 52; reform 52; kindness 47; America 45; the people 42; the Pilgrims / Luther / the Puritans / Protestantism / Reformation / the Mayflower 41; 1776 / 76 / the revolution / the patriots / Bunker 39; justice 39; sectarian 36; the clergy 35; our institutions 32; persecution 32; the law 30 ("letter of the law" is 37); hatred 30; mobocracy 28; philanthropy 27; hostility 26; resistance 24; prophecy 23; party 23; the scripture / Bible 22; our fathers 21; Fanaticism 21; Democracy 7; The Church 5.

48. Emphasis original. Benjamin Rush to John Adams, October 27, 1778, National Archives, Founders Online, https://founders.archives.gov/documents/Adams/06-07 -02-0110.

49. Emerson, *Emerson's Antislavery Writings*, 83.

50. Chapman, *Right and Wrong in Massachusetts*, 164.

51. Gouldner, *The Dialectic of Ideology and Technology*, 84.

52. *Selections from the Writings and Speeches of William Lloyd Garrison*, 122.

53. Milton, "Eikonoklastes."
54. Stephen Zwicker, "Passions and Occasions"; Boesky and Crane, *Form and Reform in Renaissance England*, 288–305.
55. *The Varieties of Religious Experience*, 365–66.
56. *Liberator*, November 27, 1840, 2.
57. Boyle and Garrison, *A Letter to Wm. Lloyd Garrison Respecting the Clerical Appeal*, 13, 9.
58. Boyle and Garrison, *A Letter to Wm. Lloyd Garrison Respecting the Clerical Appeal*, v–xi.
59. Boyle and Garrison, *A Letter to Wm. Lloyd Garrison Respecting the Clerical Appeal*, 30, 35.
60. For an example of a Garrisonian who accepted the charge of Jacobinism, see ibid., 9.
61. Carlyle, *Heroes, Hero Worship and the Heroic in History*; James, *The Varieties of Religious Experience*, 349.
62. Bercovitch, "The Problem of Ideology in American Literary History," 635.
63. On these two meanings of ideology, see Williams, *Keywords*, 107–11; Michael Walzer's looser definition of ideologies as radical movements motivated by "introspective discipline and self-control," for instance, highlighted the radical elements in "Calvinism as an ideology" and the parallels between Cromwellian, Jacobin, and Bolshevik revolution. Walzer, *The Revolution of the Saints*, 1–25
64. Further, this culture also influenced major writers toward countercultural dissent, as with Emerson's path toward Wendell Phillips and his eventual praise of John Brown as a new Christ. And as evidenced by the lives of Garrison and Lovejoy, antislavery editors and journalists took real risks in their desire to challenge the nation and honor the dissenting legacies of Puritan forebears.
65. Cox, *Puritanism in Politics*, 5.
66. Milton, *Paradise Lost*, 4.99.
67. Medico, *A Review of Garrisonian Fanaticism and Its Influence*, 22–23.
68. Adams, *The Education of Henry Adams*, 4–5.
69. Medico, *A Review of Garrisonian Fanaticism and Its Influence*, 11–12.
70. Medico, *A Review of Garrisonian Fanaticism and Its Influence*, 22.
71. James, *The Varieties of Religious Experience*, 360.
72. Garrison, *Selections from the Writings and Speeches of William Lloyd Garrison*, 251–54.
73. Garrison, *Selections from the Writings and Speeches of William Lloyd Garrison*, 259–60.
74. Chapman, *Right and Wrong in Massachusetts*, 159–61.
75. Maria Weston Chapman to James Russell Lowell, James Russell Lowell Papers, MS Am 765, Containers 219–221, Houghton Library, Harvard University.

CHAPTER FOUR

1. William Lowell Putnam and James Jackson Lowell. The war would soon claim a family friend, Robert Gould Shaw, and a third nephew, Charles Russell Lowell Jr., none of these men yet thirty years old.
2. Menand, *The Metaphysical Club*.
3. "New England! I love to tread thy soil,—tred by the few noble spirits,—Garrison, Phillips," Lowell ("one of the great Poets of Humanity"), and especially "my beloved Whittier," the "true poet of humanity." Forten, *The Journals of Charlotte Forten Grimké*, 120–30.
4. Elliott, *The Cambridge Introduction to Early American Literature*, 73. Baxter was no Cromwellian; if he sympathized with the spiritual aims of the Nonconformists, he

feared their antimonarchical impulses and ministered to the army partially in hopes of tempering its radicalism.

5. Baxter, *The Saints Everlasting Rest*, 786, 788.

6. *Indiana Herald* (Huntington), November 15, 1876. In this respect I aim to show another side to Whittier beyond the one who "led the way from the shadows of Calvinist theology into 'the sunlight of spirituality.'" Schmidt, *Restless Souls*, 80–81.

7. Forten, *The Journals of Charlotte Forten Grimké*, July 22, 1856, 160–61. In her first year, Forten heard Garrison, Phillips, Stephen Foster, Abby Kelley, Charles Lenox Remond, Octavius Frothingham, and William Wells Brown alone. Forten was enthralled by Henry Ward Beecher's frank call to disobey unjust laws on slavery and thrilled to meet Lydia Maria Child and Maria Weston Chapman at the Boston Anti-Slavery Bazaar on Christmas Day 1856. She honored Garrison as "the very highest Christian spirit" but rejected his pacifism, "for I believe in resistance to tyrants, and would fight for liberty until death.".

8. Forten, *The Journals of Charlotte Forten Grimké*, 92; Axelrod, Roman, and Travisano, *The New Anthology of American Poetry*, 260. As Dickson Bruce Jr. notes, Forten's career especially illustrates the degree of collaboration between black and white writers in the Garrisonian wing of abolition. Bruce, *The Origins of African American Literature, 1680–1865*, 190–200. *Liberator*, March 16, 155, 4. Carla L. Peterson has an especially sharp reading of what she calls Forten's project to "a narration of the 'social body'" of white and black abolitionists whom she sought to join. *Doers of the Word*, 176–95.

9. Just two months prior, for instance, Forten heard Josiah Quincy trace the widening gulf between North and South to opposed colonial origins, while the next week she attended the abolitionist Thomas Wentworth Higginson's lecture "The Puritan Clergyman," praising its "respect to their stern virtues" and wishing that her mentor had heard it, given her "most enthusiastic love for the old Puritan fathers." Forten, *The Journals of Charlotte Forten Grimké*, 110–13. And Whittier himself had written an extensive reflection on Baxter a few years prior in his *Old Portraits and Modern Sketches* (1850), a collection of vignettes that linked seventeenth-century Puritans and Quakers to modern abolition. Forten may well have read the work, and the book that she did read further exhibited Whittier's interest in early-modern Protestantism, as well over half of its pieces dealt significantly with the Puritans in some form.

10. Wood himself seems ultimately less interested in the reasons that this role should prove so influential than in critiquing a performance he finds "imaginatively, as well as politically, generally rather timid," but even "perverse" in its moral grandstanding in which "the slave was still sentimentally constructed according to a series of precepts demanding passivity and victimhood." More than any genuine concern for the slave or black citizenry, "the religious and moral corruption of the slave owner, and above all the suffering of the abolitionist, provide anti-slavery with its focus and its justification." Wood, *The Poetry of Slavery*, xv–xxxii. Here Wood builds on Wylie Sypher in *Guinea's Captive Kings*. If true in enough instances, this conclusion overreaches. Abolitionist verse was willing to grant a remarkable degree of providential power to even the bloodiest of slave rebellions and was equally capable of dramatizing the tragic and ironic facets of the struggle.

11. Cohen, "The Poetics of Reform," in *The Social Lives of Poems in Nineteenth-Century America*, 60–99.

12. Recent work influenced by the "New Formalism" has answered similar questions about antebellum poetry at large by historicizing its aesthetics, and a similar

approach to antislavery verse can illuminate its peculiar antebellum potency. Kerry Larson and Kirsten Silva Gruesz, for instance, note that antebellum poetry's "imitativeness, transparency of meaning, and overt didacticism" offered an "all-purpose template for poetic expression" that made verse more accessible to an audience that valued poetry's "democratic and equalizing aspects" above aesthetic complexity. *The Cambridge Companion to Nineteenth-Century American Poetry*, 1–2; Gruesz, *Ambassadors of Culture*, 26. As recent examples of such work, Larson names three books in particular: Mary Loeffelholz's account of a shift from domestic-pedagogical to a more consciously aesthetic framework for female poetic creativity in *From School to Salon*; Paula Bennett's argument for sentimental verse as rooted in female dissent; the emancipatory potential of an emerging periodical sphere in *Poets in the Public Sphere*; and Mary Louise Kete's account of the communal dynamics and values at the heart of antebellum verse in *Sentimental Collaboration*. To this list I would especially add Michael C. Cohen's *The Social Lives of Poems in Nineteenth-Century America*. A precursor for this approach to activist writing is Barbara Foley's "The Politics of Poetics" in Phelan, *Narrative Poetics*, 55–68, further elaborated in Foley, *Radical Representations*.

13. Robert Richardson hits upon the mixed blessing of higher criticism for American poets from more deeply religious backgrounds: "If we can approach Homeric poetry as Greek religion and Hebrew religion as Jewish poetry, the result is, on one side, skepticism about the historical reliability of either text, but on the other side, the elevation of the poet as the prophet of the present age, the truth teller, the gospel maker." Richardson, *Emerson*, 12.

14. Lowell and Parker, "Politics and the Pulpit" (1848), in *Anti-Slavery Papers*, 2:23–24.

15. Whittier, *Literary Recreations and Miscellanies.*, 329–30.

16. For instance, as the great Miltonist Barbara Lewalski noted, the Reformation's emphasis on *sola scriptura* cultivated Protestants' appreciation for the poetic qualities of the Bible as a God-ordained part of its revelation rather than ornamentation to be tolerated, and Emory Elliott noted a Puritan poetic tradition that shifted toward freer use of imagery and eloquence after 1650 (*Protestant Poetics and the Seventeenth-Century Religious Lyric*; *The Cambridge Introduction to Early American Literature*, 71–75). But both scholars likewise note how these traits were counterbalanced with caution toward artifice as spiritual artificiality.

17. Cohen, *The Social Lives of Poems in Nineteenth-Century America*, 7.

18. Haralson, *Encyclopedia of American Poetry*, 481.

19. Alonzo Lewis, *Liberator*, August 27, 1831, 4.

20. Wood, *The Poetry of Slavery*, xx–xxii.

21. James Russell Lowell, "A Word in Season," January 16, 1845. The following is an incomplete list of issues in which Ithuriel's spear appears. 1834: April 12; 1836: April 2, September 10, December 5; 1837: March 18; 1838: March 2, August 3; 1839: June 7, 21, July 19; 1840: January 3, March 20, May 15, August 21, December 18; 1841: February 5, April 30, August 13, October 1; 1842: April 8, May 20, June 3, November 11; 1843: September 15; 1845: January 3; 1846: March 6; 1847: July 23; 1848: February 11; 1849: August 24; 1852: March 5, October 1, November 19; 1853: March 25, June 10; 1854: February 3; 1855: November 6; 1856: May 30; 1857: January 9, November 6, December 18; 1858: February 12, March 12; 1859: January 7, August 26; 1860: July 6; 1862: August 29, October 3; 1863: January 23, March 6, September 4; 1864: April 8, September 23; 1865: March 24.

22. William Lloyd Garrison, "A Spur to Indolence," *Liberator*, January 22, 1831, 4.

23. Bridgenorth traces these legacies to New England, settled by "thousands of our best and most godly men," by relating the story of an Indian attack on a village and the ex nihilo appearance of a gray-haired and buck-skinned Puritan with sword and gun, commanding his countrymen, "follow me, and you shall see this day that there is a captain in Israel!" After reflecting that the man's "language, and his presence of mind" were "like the song of the inspired prophetess" in their ability to inspire attack, Bridgenorth suspects that the stranger was none other than the Puritan regicide Edward Whalley, who had been in hiding.

24. Such examples reveal a new aspect to Mark Twain's assertion that Walter Scott caused the Civil War, as potent for selective Northern readers as for Southerners.

25. Garrison, "Prison Sonnet," *Liberator*, February 5, 1831, 4.

26. Garrison, "Sonnet," *Liberator*, October 1, 1831, 4.

27. L, "Land of our Birth," *Liberator*, October 1, 1831, 4.

28. Mr. Bowring, "Sonnet," *Liberator*, February 12, 1831, 4.

29. William J. Snelling, "Song," *Liberator*, July 23, 1831, 1. Snelling's "Song" ran again in the *Liberator* on January 19, 1849, and finally on November 4, 1859—two weeks after Harper's Ferry. Snelling's poetry has largely been forgotten, rightly eclipsed by his realistic accounts of his life among Native Americans in *Tales of the Northwest*.

30. One can compare the Garrisonian poetic to average antebellum tastes in Samuel Kettell's *Specimens of American Poetry* (1829).

31. Garrison to Whittier, March 22, 1833, in Whittier and Perry, *John Greenleaf Whittier, a Sketch of His Life* , 17.

32. Whittier, *Justice and Expediency*, 54.

33. Whittier, *Justice and Expediency*, 61, 51.

34. Whittier to Lucy Hooper, August 27, 1837, in Pickard, *Life and Letters of John Greenleaf Whittier*, 213.

35. In "To George Bancroft," he urged the historian to "Speak—THUNDER in Opression's ear" and confirm that "Old Massachusetts yet / Retains her earliest fires / . . . The altars of her sires: / Her 'fierce Democracies' / Have yet their strength unshorn."

36. As Beach and Pearce note, some dismiss Whittier's abolitionist verse as "one-dimensional attacks . . . which made little attempt to nuance what had become a very complex and divisive issue," as if nuance were a goal rather than an obstacle for propaganda. Others charge that he "reinforce[s] in memorable language a noble sentiment which already exists." True enough, Whittier partly enjoyed preaching to an abolitionist choir that sang his praises, though his verse spread beyond the Garrisonian church often enough; see "John Greenleaf Whittier," in *Encyclopedia of American Poetry*, ed. Haralson, 481. A more serious critique is that Whittier's poems "do not seek to explore the institution of slavery or . . . the condition of slaves themselves" in any depth. True by today's standards, this charge is counterbalanced with Whittier's lifetime of antislavery research and certain daring poems that drew their energy from an effort to understand even the most unsettling aspects of slavery and black rebellion, as in "Toussaint L'Ouverture," a strikingly unvarnished portrait of the Haitian Revolution at a time when most white Americans either despised or sanitized the black revolutionary. Wood notes the more common antebellum trend to turn L'Ouverture into a "blancophile pacifist" in *The Poetry of Slavery*, 497. A more worthwhile critique is that Whittier's excess of New England pride amplified the abolitionist tendency to frame slavery as a threat to whites as much as blacks, though here too such choices become more understandable if evaluated as propaganda. Haralson, *Encyclopedia of American Poetry*, 481.

37. Whittier, *Poems Written During the Progress of the Abolition Question in the United States*, viii–x.
38. Lowell, *Class Poem by James Russell Lowell*, 20, 18.
39. Howard, *Victorian Knight-Errant*, 24.
40. "Superstition," the atheist Shelley wrote in "A Defence of Poetry," "would make poetry an attribute of prophecy, rather than prophecy an attribute of poetry." *Essays*, 1:7.
41. Qtd. in Howard, *Victorian Knight-Errant*, 140–44.
42. Lowell and Carter, *The Pioneer*, 25.
43. Howard, *Victorian Knight-Errant*, 144–45.
44. Howard, *Victorian Knight-Errant*, 152.
45. *Boston Courier*, March 19, 1846.
46. "Thoughts Upon the Present Crisis" was published again in the *Boston Courier* on December 11, 1845, the same day that news broke on the House Committee's favorable report on the Texas resolution.
47. Wood, *The Poetry of Slavery*, 558.
48. Buell, *New England Literary Culture from Revolution through Renaissance*, 127.
49. Lowell, "Texas," in *Anti-Slavery Papers*, 1:11–12.
50. Lowell, *Anti-Slavery Papers*, 1:40–42; Kerrigan, *The Sacred Complex*, 20.
51. Lowell, *Anti-Slavery Papers*, 1:vii. Additionally, Lowell had grown increasingly dissatisfied with Garrisonian renunciations of political strategy, both because the 1840s seemed increasingly ripe for abolitionism's shift toward party politics and because Lowell himself was growing more eager to be an active man of the world. (Even in "A Glance Behind," his Cromwell affirmed the necessity—even the excitement—of realpolitik: "Better, almost, be at work in sin, / Than in a brute inaction.")
52. "Interview" appeared in the December 30 *Courier*, "The Present Crisis" in the December 11 issue.
53. A similar growth in dramatic faculties is visible in Whittier's *Margaret Smith's Journal* (1849), his first extended work to inhabit another voice as a visitor to seventeenth-century New England.
54. Lowell, *The Biglow Papers, Second Series*, vi.
55. Marcus, Sollors, *A New Literary History of America*, 262.
56. Lowell, *The Biglow Papers, Second Series.*, viii.
57. After the first installment, Lowell set aside Hosea for fourteen months; he returned to the *Courier* on August 18, 1847, with Birdofredum Sawin, the luckless Yankee soldier. Number 3, "What Mr. Robinson Thinks," appeared on 2 November. The fifth paper, ""The Pious Editor's Creed," appeared in the May 4, 1848, *Standard*, and the final installment, a third letter from Sawin, in the September 28 issue.
58. Wood, *The Poetry of Slavery*, 559.
59. Howard, *Victorian Knight-Errant*, 240–42.
60. Lowell, *The Biglow Papers*, 31.
61. Lowell, *The Biglow Papers*, 84–85. For an invaluable digital edition of Sawin's first letter that tracks its changes from newspaper piece to single-volume chapter and "situates the poem within the context of surrounding newspaper articles," see Thompson and Showalter, "Satire in Circulation."
62. Howard, *Victorian Knight-Errant*, 232, 260.
63. Whittier, *Literary Recreations and Miscellanies*, 328–30.
64. Whittier, *Literary Recreations and Miscellanies*, 428–30.
65. Whittier, *The Panorama, and Other Poems*, 25. Whittier made a similar argument

in "What of the Day?," reasserting his Quaker preference for "the still small voice which reached the prophet's ear."

66. The latter "suggests a newfound delight in language," Christopher Beach rightly notes: "For my sport the squirrel played, / Plied the snouted mole his spade; / For my taste the blackberry cone / Purpled over hedge and stone; / Laughed the brook for my delight." Beach, "John Greenleaf Whittier," in *Encyclopedia of American Poetry*, ed. Haralson.

67. Howard, *Victorian Knight-Errant*, chap. 9.

68. Howard, *Victorian Knight-Errant*, 341.

69. Lowell, *Lectures on English Poets*, 116.

70. Lowell, "Nationality in Literature," in *The Round Table*, 15.

71. Qtd. in Bell, "The Only True Folk Songs," 138.

72. Whittier, *In War Time, and Other Poems*, 12–14.

73. Whittier, *In War Time, and Other Poems*, 16.

74. Whittier, *Snow-Bound*, 21, 37–39.

75. For a useful overview of interpretations of *Snow-Bound*, see Beach, "James Russell Lowell," in *Encyclopedia of American Poetry*, ed. Haralson.

76. Whittier's brother Matthew had two sons, Charles F. Whittier, who served in the Maine Thirteenth Infantry and died in 1909, and Joseph Poyen Whittier, who died in infancy. His sister Mary had one son, Lewis Henry Caldwell. It is unclear whether Caldwell served; born in 1832, he would have been old for a general recruit.

77. Lowell, *The Biglow Papers, Second Series*, 214.

78. Lowell, *The Biglow Papers, Second Series*, 215.

79. Lowell, *The Biglow Papers, Second Series*, 217–18.

80. Lowell, *The Biglow Papers, Second Series*, 216.

81. "New England" was written December 1864 and published the next month in the *North American Review*.

82. Lowell, *The Biglow Papers, Second Series*, 239.

83. Myerson, *Emerson and Thoreau*, 438–39.

84. Lowell, *Among My Books*, 231.

85. Lowell, *Among My Books*, 235.

86. Lowell, *Among My Books*, 236–8, 289–90. If the Salem Witch Trials were a thorn in Lowell's argument as the most frequently cited example of New England fanaticism, he downplayed their importance by arguing that they had nothing to do with Puritanism per se. Instead they were a "delusion" that "darkened the understanding of all Christendom," coming so late in New England history as to be a product more of Puritanism's decline than of its prime (236–37).

CHAPTER FIVE

1. Storrs, *The Spirit of the Pilgrims*.

2. Ward, *American Slavery, and the Means of Its Abolition*, 11–15, 21.

3. On the unstable relationship between slavery and organized Protestantism since the Reformation, see especially Davis, *The Problem of Slavery in Western Culture* and *The Problem of Slavery in the Age of Revolution, 1770–1823*. Regarding American Protestantism in the decades before the Civil War, Timothy Smith's focus on "the painful issues of revival religion's hectic youth" is invaluable in *Revivalism and Social Reform*. As will become clearer, I have also been aided by Mark Noll's account of the Civil War as a broader theological crisis and Molly Oshatz's argument for the liberalizing effects of abolitionism on Northern Protestantism; see Oshatz, *Slavery and Sin*; Noll, *The Civil War as a Theological Crisis*.

4. Beecher and Beecher, *Autobiography, Correspondence, Etc. of Lyman Beecher*, 2:122–23, 128–30.
5. Review of *Memoir of the Life and Character of Rev. Samuel Hopkins* by John Ferguson (Boston: Leonard W. Kimball, 1830), *Spirit of the Pilgrims* 3:556; "Colonization and Emancipation," *Spirit of the Pilgrims* 6:322–32. Both sources are to be found in Congregational Library & Archives.
6. "Union of Colonizationists and Abolitionists," *Spirit of the Pilgrims* 6:596–402, in Congregational Library & Archives.
7. Antipas, "Hints on the Relative Importance of New England to the Rest of the United States, in a Moral and Religious View," *Spirit of the Pilgrims* 1, no. 7 (July 1828) 337–43, in Congregational Library & Archives.
8. Crosby, letter to the editor, *Spirit of the Pilgrims* 2 (March 1829): 143–66, in Congregational Library & Archives.
9. "Discourse on the Character of the Pilgrims," *Spirit of the Pilgrims* 3:630–40, Congregational Library & Archives.
10. "Discourse on the Character of the Pilgrims," *Spirit of the Pilgrims* 3:630–40.
11. Beecher, *A Plea for the West*, 79–80.
12. Abzug, *Passionate Liberator*.
13. After Boston, Beecher evolved in the direction of what J. Earl Thomspon Jr. calls "conservative abolition," softening his Colonizationist beliefs as he assumed the role of an unofficial ambassador to the Immediatists, less loyal to either party than to his mission to unite America behind Anglo Protestantism. Thompson, "Lyman Beecher's Long Road to Conservative Abolitionism," 90–91.
14. Weld, *American Slavery, as It Is*, 112.
15. Abzug, *Passionate Liberator*, 70.
16. Volpe, "Theodore Dwight Weld's Antislavery Mission in Ohio," 12.
17. Young and Cherry, "The Secularization of Confessional Protests."
18. Qtd. in Smith, *Black Prophets of Justice*, 118.
19. I draw the term "ecclesiastical abolitionism" from Strong, *Perfectionist Politics*. Smith, *Revivalism and Social Reform*, 14–15.
20. Johnson and Whittier, *William Lloyd Garrison and His Times*, 177.
21. Applegate, *The Most Famous Man in America*, 12.
22. Beecher, *A Discourse Delivered at the Plymouth Church, Brooklyn, N.Y. Upon Thanksgiving Day*, 19–20.
23. Beecher, *Defence of Kansas*.
24. Beecher clarified that "whatever men may say, American slavery is not Hebrew slavery; it is Roman slavery," for "the fundamental feature of the Hebrew system was that the slave was a man, and not a chattel." Beecher, *Patriotic Addresses in America and England*, 255–56.
25. Beecher, *Patriotic Addresses in America and England*, 251.
26. Beecher, "Our Blameworthiness," in *Patriotic Addresses in America and England*, 248–50.
27. Beecher, "Battle Set in Array," April 14, 1861, in *Patriotic Addresses in America and England*, 273, 288.
28. Beecher, "Modes and Duties of Emancipation," November 26, 1861, in *Patriotic Addresses in America and England*, 327.
29. Beecher, "National Injustice and Penalty," September 28, 1862, in *Patriotic Addresses in America and England*, 377.

30. Beecher, "Farewell Breakfast, London," October 23, 1863, in *Patriotic Addresses in America and England*, 590.

31. Beecher, *A Discourse Delivered at the Plymouth Church, Brooklyn, N.Y. Upon Thanksgiving Day*, 21.

32. Beecher and American College and Education Society, *Man and His Institutions*, 2, 6.

33. Beecher and American College and Education Society, *Man and His Institutions*, 13–14.

34. Beecher and American College and Education Society, *Man and His Institutions*, 6.

35. Qtd. in Applegate, *The Most Famous Man in America*, 34.

36. Beecher, *Patriotic Addresses in America and England*, 762.

37. Douglas, *The Feminization of American Culture*.

38. Mayer, *All on Fire*, 421; November 1853, in *William Lloyd Garrison, 1805–1879*, 396.

39. *Liberator*, December 23, 1853, 2.

40. December 1853, Andover, in *William Lloyd Garrison, 1805–1879*, 398–400.

41. Stowe, *The Minister's Wooing*, 333.

42. Karcher, "Stowe and the Literature of Social Change"; Weinstein, *The Cambridge Companion to Harriet Beecher Stowe*.

43. Stowe, *Sunny Memories of Foreign Lands*, 2:210, 330–32.

44. Catherine de Medici in fact aimed to mediate between the Huguenots and Catholics.

45. Stowe, *Sunny Memories of Foreign Lands*, 2:392.

46. Stowe, *Sunny Memories of Foreign Lands*, 2:167.

47. Stowe, *Sunny Memories of Foreign Lands*, 2:329.

48. For recent work on *Dred* see especially Robert Levine's excellent discussion in *Martin Delany, Frederick Douglass, and the Politics of Representative Identity*, 155–65. More recently, see Pelletier, *Apocalyptic Sentimentalism*, 135–48. and Hickman, *Black Prometheus*, 365–75.

49. Stowe, *Dred*, 210.

50. Stowe, *Dred*, 211.

51. The language of individual "natures" grew increasingly frequent in Stowe's later fiction as the locus of religious sentiment, partaking in the pre-Jamesian interest in the physical and social factors that shaped spiritual experience. Adjusting for the novels' respective page lengths, *The Minister's Wooing* and *Dred* both use "nature" twice as often as *Uncle Tom's Cabin* does, and *Oldtown Folks* thrice as much. The math is as such: when we set the number of times "nature" appears in a novel over the novel's total word count, *Uncle Tom's Cabin* is .00037 (70/187914), *Dred* is .00081 (180/221170), *The Minister's Wooing* is .00102 (136/133285), and *Oldtown Folks* is .00089 (202/227153). (The same disclaimer from chapter 3 applies here: these are absolute rather than relative frequencies, sufficient for the brief point at hand.) One of Stowe's largest influence in this vein was Oliver Wendell Holmes, whose novel *Elsie Venner* ridiculed original sin by translating it from theological into physiological terms. "All your theology in that book I subscribe to with both hands," Stowe wrote to Holmes, especially "their pitiful and sympathetic vein, the pity for poor, struggling human nature." Stowe, *Life of Harriet Beecher Stowe*, 411.

52. Stowe, *Dred*, 496.

53. Smith, *The Bible Made Impossible*.

54. Stowe, *Dred*, 253.

55. Smith, "Harriet Beecher Stowe and the Sentimental Novel," Bauer and Gould, *The Cambridge Companion to Nineteenth-Century American Women's Writing*, 223.

56. Stowe, *Dred*, 185.
57. Stowe, *The Minister's Wooing*, 15, 22.
58. Stowe, *The Minister's Wooing*, 45.
59. Stowe, *The Minister's Wooing*, 88.
60. Stowe, *The Minister's Wooing*, 516–17.
61. Stowe, *The Minister's Wooing*, 17, 92.
62. Stowe, "'New England Ministers.'"
63. Stowe, *The Minister's Wooing*, 490.
64. Stowe, *The Minister's Wooing*, 50.
65. Stowe, *The Minister's Wooing*, 197.
66. Stowe, *The Minister's Wooing*, 280.
67. Stowe, *The Minister's Wooing*, 304.
68. Hedrick, *Harriet Beecher Stowe*, 300.
69. Hedrick, *Harriet Beecher Stowe*, 302.
70. Stowe, *Household Papers and Stories*, 52–53.
71. Hedrick, *Harriet Beecher Stowe*, 326.
72. Stowe to James B. Fields, August 16, 1868, Stowe Papers, qtd. in May, introduction to Stowe, *Oldtown Folks*, 29.
73. Stowe, *Oldtown Folks*, 47.
74. Sociologist Werner Stark first noted the sociological dimension of *Oldtown*. "Harriet Beecher Stowe Versus Max Weber."
75. Bushnell, *Christian Nurture*, 91.
76. Stowe, *Oldtown Folks.*, 48.
77. Stowe, *Oldtown Folks*, 52, 49.
78. Stowe, *Oldtown Folks*, 387–88.
79. Stowe was not alone in this assessment. One Presbyterian historian called the requirement of a profession of saving faith "a rejection of the judgment of charity accepted by all the Reformed churches" (see Thompson, *A History of the Presbyterian Churches*, 14), while Henry Martyn Dexter, graduate of Andover Seminary and historian of Congregationalism, wrote that early Puritan eclessiology was "a Presbyterianized Congregationalism" with "roots in the one system and its branches in the other . . . essentially Genevan within the local congregation, and essentially other outside of it" (see Dexter, *The Congregationalism of the Last Three Hundred Years, as Seen in Its Literature*, 463).
80. Buell, *New England Literary Culture*, 214–38; Stowe, *Oldtown Folk*, 258–59.
81. Bushnell, *Christian Nurture*, 218, 205.
82. "A Family Talk on Reconstruction."
83. Fredrickson, *The Black Image in the White Mind*, 27–129.
84. Qtd. in Thompson, "Lyman Beecher's Long Road to Conservative Abolitionism," 91.
85. Beecher, *New Star Papers*, 267–71.
86. Beecher, *Patriotic Addresses in America and England*, 254–55.
87. Douglas, *The Feminization of American Culture*.
88. Hedrick, *Harriet Beecher Stowe*, 345.

CHAPTER SIX

1. Though historians as early as George Bancroft in 1834 had noted that this slave ship had actually docked in 1619, the year before the *Mayflower*, many fudged the date to heighten the sense of juxtaposition.
2. *Origin Stories in Political Thought*, 10–11.

3. Winthrop's insistence that Plymouth and Jamestown had nothing in common is likely why Theodore Parker would later critique his support of the Mexican War, as noted in chapter 1, by asking where his Pilgrim blood now went. Unlike Winthrop (who was no Garrisonian), many abolitionists would have contested the simplistic sectionalism of Smith's map for overlooking the ways in which the North was complicit in slavery; yet they often evinced a similar impulse toward moral (and often sectional) binaries.

4. Winthrop, *Address*. Respected New England orators like Edward Everett and Daniel Webster had included antislavery remarks in popular Forefathers' Day addresses before Winthrop (whose invocation of the contrasting sights and sounds of the *Mayflower* and the slave ship—later used by William Wells Brown in *Clotel*—are clearly modeled on Webster's famous 1820 address). See Webster's "Plymouth Oration" from December 22, 1820, and Edward Everett's "An Oration Delivered at Plymouth" from December 22, 1824.

5. "Letter from Communipaw," *Frederick Douglass' Papers*, February 12, 1852. McCune Smith noted that filiopiety was more challenging for a group rooted in oppression and diaspora, their genealogies shrouded by slavery. "It becomes us to be meek, dear Douglass," he continued, "we of doubtful parentage, who cannot look anywhere in particular for 'forefathers' day' and 'fatherland.'" McCune Smith voiced a common black lament over what Orlando Patterson called the "social death" of slavery. Patterson, *Slavery and Social Death*.

6. Gilroy's greater aim was to challenge both nationalistic frameworks for Euro-American modernity and ethnocentric notions of blackness with "the inescapable hybridity and intermixture of ideas . . . identities which are always unfinished, always being remade" (xi).

7. On the black roots of abolition, see Quarles, *Black Abolitionists*, and Sinha, *The Slave's Cause*.

8. In vol. 1 of his *History*, Bancroft marked the 1619 docking of a slave ship at Jamestown as "the sad epoch of the introduction of negro slavery" into America (126). I am indebted to several important studies that emphasize Bancroft's centrality to American and black historical thought. In "Afro-American History" (*Key Issues*, 1:1971), Nathan I. Huggins first explored the persistence of Bancroftian myth in American historiography; Clarence Walker noted how early black historical thought was "very Bancroftian in its analysis of the race problem in that it placed great emphasis upon the role of Providence as a force of historical causation" (*Deromanticizing Black History*, 87); Leonard I. Sweet argued that Bancroft's "immensely popular writings summed up the major nineteenth century intellectual themes of the ideal image of America and the mission and destiny of America in the world" for whites (*Black Images of America*, 1–2); William L. Van Deburg is especially helpful in tracking Bancroft's mental gymnastics as he aimed to resolve his faith in Anglo-American destiny with his hatred of slavery: Bancroft, he argues, decided that "God must have had some good reason for allowing the institution"—namely, the civilizing and Christianizing of Africans—"[a] line of reasoning which profoundly misinterpreted the character of the African people" (*Slavery and Race*, 27–30). Most recently, John Ernest argues more explicitly for Bancroft's centrality to an emergent "white nationalist history" at the heart of American historiography (*Liberation Historiography*, 33–36); elsewhere Ernest has noted specific instances of black writers responding directly to Bancroft (*Resistance and Reformation*, 8). Here as elsewhere, I trace these scholars' interest in Bancroft's historiographical and racial presumptions into the

more particular stories Bancroft and black writers told about the *Mayflower* and the "Slave Ship."

9. References to the tradition of black scriptural typology are numerous, but the most important study, focused on the exodus narrative, is Glaude, *Exodus*. On the parallel between Puritan and black captivity narratives, see Saillant, *Black Puritan, Black Republican*, 152–88. Wilson Jeremiah Moses and David Howard-Pitney have built upon Bercovitch's thesis in their study of the "black jeremiad," a tradition that they trace from David Walker's "Appeal" through Douglass, Du Bois, King Jr., and more. Christopher Cameron has more recently stretched the origins of the black jeremiad into the Revolutionary period through figures like Phillis Wheatley, Caesar Sarter, Lemuel Haynes, and others. See Moses, *Black Messiahs and Uncle Toms*; Howard-Pitney, *African American Jeremiad Rev*; and Cameron, "The Puritan Origins of Black Abolitionism in Massachusetts." Cameron has even argued for the "Puritan origins of black abolitionism in Massachusetts," arguing that because the Puritans imbued their legal system with rights for slaves (redress, petition, and other Old Testament–inspired provisions), Massachusetts emerged as the center of early black activism ("The Puritan Origins of Black Abolitionism in Massachusetts").

10. The foremost studies of antebellum black historical writing come from Nathan I. Huggins, Clarence Walker, John Ernest, and Stephen G. Hall. I build upon their work in multiple respects. Following Huggins, I head his warning in "Myths, Heroes, Reality" (1971) against the dangers of Bancroftian mythmaking in history, but I also note its political potential for black Americans when reimagined (something Huggins himself did in his magnum opus *Black Odyssey* [1977], as David Blight has noted). Following Walker, I emphasize the pervasive yet complex role that Providence played as black historians attempted to understand the origins and destiny of their race within sacred time. Following Ernest, I aim to emphasize the complexity of black writers' engagement with a hegemonic white historiographical tradition as what Gilroy calls a "relationship of antagonistic indebtedness" to American culture—though I remain wary of framing these writers in the later context of liberation theology. Gilroy, *The Black Atlantic*, 191. Following Hall, I remain more interested in the immediate historical context of black historiography, though I find that his emphasis on European influences neglects American sources closer at hand, most explicitly in Bancroft, whose first volume of history, Providence-heavy and Puritancentric, as noted in the introduction, appeared just as many black writers began their historical research in the early 1840s. See Walker, "The American Negro as Historical Outsider: 1836–1935," in *Deromanticizing Black History*, 87–108; Ernest, *Liberation Historiography*; and Hall, *A Faithful Account of the Race*. Those interested in the influence of classics on early black writers should especially see Hairston's *The Ebony Column*.

11. Bruce, *The Origins of African American Literature, 1680–1865*, 8, 17.

12. Winthrop's speech appeared in the April 11, 1840, *Colored American*.

13. Garnet, "Speech at the Seventh Annual Meeting of the American Anti-Slavery Society," reprinted in the *Colored American*, May 30, 1840.

14. Garnet, "Speech at the seventh annual meeting of the American Anti-Slavery Society," reprinted in the *Colored American*, May 30, 1840.

15. On Garnet's rising militancy and its roots in family memory, see Schor, *Henry Highland Garnet*.

16. *North Star*, April 17, 1848.

17. *Past and Present Condition*, 13.

18. Joshua R. Giddings, "Speech," from *Oliver Dyer's Phonographic Report of the Proceedings of the National Free Soil Convention at Buffalo, N.Y. August 9ᵗʰ and 10ᵗʰ, 1848*, 9.

19. Delany, *The Condition, Elevation, Emigration, and Destiny of the Colored People of the United States*.

20. Brown was no simple shill for New England either, and took an opportunity to deflate its own varieties of cant through the figure of Georgiana's father, a Connecticut native who, since becoming a popular and comfortable preacher in Natchez, has fitted his theology to his lifestyle, finding no prohibition against slavery in scripture. When he boasts to a Tennessean that New Englanders "are an orderly, pious, peaceable people. Our holy religion is respected, and we do more for the cause of Christ than the whole Southern States put together," the rough white Southerner voices Brown's own wit: "I don't doubt it. . . . You sell wooden nutmegs and other spurious articles enough to do some good. You talk of your 'holy religion'; but your robes' righteousness are woven at Lowell and Manchester; your paradise is high per centum on factory stocks." *Clotel, or, The President's Daughter*, 198.

21. *Clotel, or, The President's Daughter*, 184.

22. Parker, *The Nebraska Question. Some Thoughts on the New Assault Upon Freedom in America, and the General State of the Country in Relation Thereunto, Set Forth in a Discourse Preached at the Music Hall, in Boston, on Monday, Feb. 12, 1854*, 12.

23. *Frederick Douglass' Papers*, May 11, 1855.

24. Smith, *The Works of James McCune Smith*, 116.

25. One could devote a whole chapter to black Presbygationalist ministers alone— Lemuel Haynes, Hosea Easton, Theodore Sedgwick Wright, Samuel Cornish, Amos Noë Freeman, Samuel Ringold Ward, Amos Beman, and James W. C. Pennington. In order to capture a breadth of black voices and the variety of ways they used the Puritans, I confine myself to the most explicit references to the Puritans among the most vocal antislavery activists and defer to other excellent studies on these ministers. The most comprehensive and most focused on religion is David Everett Swift's *Black Prophets of Justice*, which surveys the work of Cornish, Wright, Garnet, Beman, and Pennington, arguing that "the earliest black Presbyterian and Congregational ministers were more likely to be systematic workers for radical social reform than were black clergy of the other denominations . . . consonant with nearly two centuries of white Presbyterian and Congregational ministers' political, and even revolutionary, involvement: in the English Puritan ferment of the early 1600s, in the Cromwellian revolution, in the shaping of political institutions and practices in the new England colonies, and in the mustering of popular support for the American Revolution. Antebellum black ministers in these denominations had no monopoly on black clerical activism, but they turned a spotlight . . . on the social and political goals of the black freedom movement at large" (8–9). On Pennington, see Christopher L. Webber. On Lemuel Haynes, see John Saillant. Several of these fascinating figures await biographies.

26. Gilroy, *The Black Atlantic*, 2, 58, 30.

27. "Essay on Slavery," *Essex Journal and Merrimack Packet*, August 17, 1774. Emancipation in Massachusetts was effectively achieved seven years later when the slave Quock Walker successfully sued for his freedom on the basis on Massachusetts's new constitution.

28. "Creed of the 'Journal of Commerce,'" *Colored American*, March 9, 1839.

29. "What Places Are Sacred?" *The North Star*, January 28, 1848.

30. "American Slavery: The Tenure By Which it Exists, Letter No. 1," *North Star*, Feb-

ruary 4, 1848. British abolitionist George Thompson repeated this criticism in a speech in Toronto, printed by the *North Star* on April 17, 1851.

31. "The Fugitive Slave Law," *North Star*, October 3, 1850.

32. "Practical Abolitionism," *Frederick Douglass' Papers*, June 15, 1855.

33. "Communications," *Frederick Douglass' Paper*, November 19, 1852.

34. *North Star*, February 18, 1848; *Frederick Douglass' Papers*, December 18, 1851.

35. *Frederick Douglass' Papers*, February 26, 1852.

36. *Frederick Douglass' Papers*, August 17, 1852.

37. *Frederick Douglass' Papers*, September 7, 1854. Further examples can be found in the *Colored American* on November 4, 1837, February 2, 1839, and September 28, 1839—respectively, on Kimball's travels in the West Indies, lamenting the absence of superior New England civilization; on S. T. Armstrong's praise of the Assembly Catechism; and Edward Everett's praise of Samuel Adams as the last Puritan; in *Frederick Douglass' Papers* on June 26 and October 2, 1851, and February 17, 1854—respectively, on a meeting of US and English Congregationalists, a speech by Reverend William Henry Brisbane arguing that all reform movements require a Protestant separation, and Senator Burlingame on the superiority of New England culture.

38. From Macaulay's *Essay on Milton, Edinburgh Review* 1825, reprinted in the *Colored American* as "Puritans in the Age of Milton," November 7, 1840.

39. From Macaulay's *History of England*, vol. 1, reprinted as "Selections: Sufferings of Nonconformists in 1685," *North Star*, March 9, 1849.

40. "Selections: John Bunyan and Wm. Kiffin," *North Star*, March 16, 1849.

41. "Our Country," *Colored American*, September 22, 1838; also reprinted in the *Liberator*, September 14, 4.

42. "Infidel France—Christian America," *North Star*, April 14, 1848.

43. Maffly-Kipp, *Setting Down the Sacred Past*, 144–51.

44. John B. Russwurm, cofounder of *Freedom's Journal* with Samuel Cornish, anticipated these statements by thirty years. An initial supporter of the American Colonization Society, Russwurm noted that "when I look around and behold the Pagan darkness of the land, an aspiration rises to the Heaven that my friend may become a second Brainerd or Elliot [*sic*]," invoking the famed Presbyterian and Puritan missionaries to the Native Americans. Letter to Edward Jones, March 20, 1830, in *Black Abolitionists Papers*, 3:71. See also Holly's brother, Joseph C. Holly, who indicted the North's history of cowing to the South and forsaking its own principles and sovereignty: "Old Massachusetts, among whose granite hills are lurking whatever principle of freedom that remains to the degenerate sons of the pilgrim fathers, felt aggrieved at this treatment." *Frederick Douglass' Paper*, April 17 1848; in *Black Abolitionists Papers*, 4:21.

45. "American Colonization Society," *Frederick Douglass Papers*, February 10, 1854.

46. "An Address," *Frederick Douglass' Paper*, December 11, 1851.

47. "Letter from Samuel J. May, No. III," *Frederick Douglass' Papers*, September 10, 1852. In a second letter published the next week, May repeated the point. May rejected those who discouraged slaves from fleeing because of the hardships, for such people "know not the value of liberty." More so, such reasoning "would condemn the enterprise of the Puritan ancestors of New England, and of the generation that achieved the independence of our country. The emigration of our colored population to Canada deserves to be classed with the coming of the Puritans to the wilder-

ness of America. The latter exiles were scarcely less despised and persecuted in their decay than the former are in ours. They sought essentially the same boon, and were animated by the same spirit. And that man is very presumptuous who dares to say, that as great results may not come from the one as have come from the other enterprise." Letter from Samuel J. May, No. IV, *Frederick Douglass' Papers*, September 17, 1852.

48. For a brief historiographical overview of this idea since Du Bois, see Mount, "When Slaves Go on Strike."

49. For a detailed study of the Burns trial and its surrounding unrest, see Von Frank, *The Trials of Anthony Burns*.

50. Garnet, *The Past and the Present Condition, and the Destiny, of the Colored Race*, 8.

51. Garnet, *The Past and the Present Condition, and the Destiny, of the Colored Race*, 12. Here Garnet's source was likely Macaulay or Hume, whom William Wells Brown invoked for similar arguments in *The Black Man*, explored at present.

52. "Oration by A. H. Francis of Buffalo, on the first of August," *North Star*, August 17, 1849.

53. Garnet, "'Call to Rebellion' Address," 1843. Rev. Henry Highland Garnet, "Address to the National Convention of Negro Men, Albany, New York, August 1843."

54. Lowell et al., *American Antislavery Writings*.

55. Garnet, *The Past and the Present Condition, and the Destiny, of the Colored Race*, 26–29.

56. Baldwin, *Notes of a Native Son*, 5.

57. Qtd. in Schor, "The Rivalry between Frederick Douglass and Henry Highland Garnet," 1.

58. As with abolitionism, Benjamin Quarles was the first modern scholar to exhaustively document black war service in the Revolution and the Civil War, as well as Lincoln's relationship to black Americans. See *The Negro in the American Revolution*, *The Negro in the Civil War*, and *Lincoln and the Negro*.

59. "The Characteristics of Christian Warriors," *Frederick Douglass' Papers*, December 25, 1851.

60. William Lloyd Garrison printed the tract and next year published an essay collection, *Meditations from the Pen of Mrs. Maria W. Stewart*. He also ran transcripts of Stewart's major public speeches in the *Liberator*. Laura R. Sells, "Maria W. Miller Stewart," in *Women Public Speakers*, ed. Campbell.

61. Stewart, *Productions*, 16, 56.

62. Richardson notes that Stewart's "severe, excoriating, and denunciatory style . . . alternates with maternal and domestic appeals to solidarity"; "What If I Am a Woman?," in *Courage and Conscience*, ed. Jacobs, 198; Romero, *Home Fronts*, 68–69. Wilson J. Moses describes Stewart as both "militant and direct." Moses, *Black Messiahs*, 37.

63. Stewart, *Productions*, 18–20.

64. Brown, *The Black Man*.

65. Brown, *The Black Man*, 61–62, 97.

66. Dickerson, *Dark Victorians*, 89–90.

67. Louverture's sincerity of faith, in Brown's depiction, sparks the adoration of his follower, the two primary traits of the Carlylean hero. "The greater part of the population loved him to idolatry," Brown noted, hinting at a line of argument from *On Heroes* in which Carlyle maintains that all worship is inherently "idolatrous" in its dependence on symbols and heroes as the media of reverence (the real sin was not idolatry as such, but only its sham uses). Haitians' sincere idolization of Toussaint,

a source of revolutionary inspiration, was further evidence of his spiritual heroism. Brown, *The Black Man*, 101–5.

68. To this end, Brown also included vivid depictions of Turner's visions, filled with militant Christian imagery, as they were recorded by Thomas R. Gray in *The Confessions of Nat Turner* (1831). "The Spirit," Turner recounts, told him that "Christ had laid down the yoke . . . and that I should take it on and fight against the Serpent." Turner, *The Confessions of Nat Turner, the Leader of the Late Insurrection in Southampton, Va.*

69. Brown, *The Black Man*, 64. Turner is redeemed from fanaticism as another Carlylean hero, sincere in his religious vision and a source of reverent inspiration. "That he was sincere in all that he professed, there is not the slightest doubt," Brown remarked, and "he impressed his image upon the minds of those who once beheld him. His looks, his sermons, his acts, and his heroism live in the hearts of his race." Brown further concluded that "the present generation of slaves have a superstitious veneration for his name, and believe that in another insurrection Nat Turner will appear and take command." This served as a warning to slaveholders, for pure religion was contagious and explosive: "In every southern household there may be a Nat Turner, in whose soul God has lighted a torch of liberty that cannot be extinguished by the hand of man. The slaveholder should understand that he lives upon a volcano" (*The Black Man*, 72–73).

70. "City Items," *Christian Recorder*, April 4, 1863.

71. "Serving God in the Camp," *Christian Recorder*, May 25, 1861.

72. "Chaplains," *Christian Recorder*, June 22, 1861.

73. "The Pulpit and the Press on the War," *Christian Recorder*, August 24, 1861.

74. See Brown, *The Negro in The American Rebellion*. and Quarles, *The Negro in the Civil War*.

CONCLUSION

1. Qtd. in Milder, "Uncivil Wars," 168–91.

2. Here Melville, like Lowell, anticipates the postbellum skepticism of Menand's *Metaphysical Club*.

3. Milder, "Uncivil Wars," 184.

4. Blight, *Race and Reunion*; Foner, *Reconstruction America's Unfinished Revolution, 1863–1877*.

5. Aaron, *The Unwritten War*, xviii.

6. "The Swamp Angel" and "Formerly a Slave."

7. Stout, *Upon the Altar of the Nation*. See especially Delbanco, Stauffer, and Sinha's debate within *The Abolitionist Imagination*. Coates, "The Civil War Isn't Tragic," *Atlantic*, April 2011.

8. Williams, *Modern Tragedy*, 82.

9. Williams, *Modern Tragedy*, 83–84.

10. Williams, *Modern Tragedy*, 84.

11. Douglass's "West India Emancipation" speech at Canandaigua, New York, on the twenty-third anniversary of the event, August 3, 1857; Phillips, "Public Opinion," speech before the MA Antislavery Society, January 28, 1852.

12. Foner, *The Fiery Trial*, 20, xix. In an interview with *Jacobin*, Foner states, "I am a believer in the abolitionist concept—that the role of radicals is to stand outside of the political system . . . and if people are convinced of that, then politicians will come up with a plan to do it." "Struggle and Progress," *Jacobin*, no. 18 (Summer 2015).

13. W. James, "Lecture XIV: The Value of Saintliness"; James, *The Varieties of Religious Experience*, 358–60.
14. Fuller, *From Battlefields Rising*, 221.
15. Emerson, "Power," in *Conduct of Life*.
16. My reading of the epilogue is especially informed by Trimmer, "The Grandfather's Riddle in Ralph Ellison's Invisible Man."

BIBLIOGRAPHY

Aaron, Daniel. *The Unwritten War: American Writers and the Civil War*. New York: Alred A. Knopf / Random House, 1973.

Abzug, Robert H. *Passionate Liberator: Theodore Dwight Weld and the Dilemma of Reform*. New York: Oxford University Press, 1982.

Adams, Henry. *The Education of Henry Adams: An Autobiography*. Washington, DC, 1907.

Ahlstrom, Sydney E. *A Religious History of the American People*. New Haven, CT: Yale University Press, 2004.

American Antislavery Writings: Colonial Beginnings to Emancipation. Washington, DC: Library of America, 2012.

Andrews, William L. *Sisters of the Spirit: Three Black Women's Autobiographies of the Nineteenth Century*. Bloomington: Indiana University Press, 2000.

Anglen, Kevin P. Van. *The New England Milton: Literary Reception and Cultural Authority in the Early Republic*. University Park: Penn State Press, 1993.

Anti-Slavery Meeting and J. M. W Yerrinton, eds. *The Boston Mob of "Gentlemen of Property and Standing": Proceedings of the Anti-Slavery Meeting Held in Stacy Hall, Boston, on the Twentieth Anniversary of the Mob of October 21, 1835*. Boston: R. F. Wallcut, 1855.

Applegate, Debby. *The Most Famous Man in America: The Biography of Henry Ward Beecher*. New York: Image Books / Crown, 2006.

A Puritan. *The Abrogation of the Seventh Commandment*. New York: Ruggles, 1835.

Axelrod, Steven Gould, Camille Roman, and Thomas J. Travisano. *The New Anthology of American Poetry: Traditions and Revolutions, Beginnings to 1900*. New Brunswick: Rutgers University Press, 2003.

Baker, Dorothy Zayatz. *America's Gothic Fiction: The Legacy of Magnalia Christi Americana*. Columbus: Ohio State University Press, 2007.

Baldwin, James. *Notes of a Native Son*. New York: Dial, 1955.

Ballif, Michelle. *Theorizing Histories of Rhetoric*. Carbondale, IL: SIU Press, 2013.

Bancroft, George. *A History of the United States, from the Discovery of the American Continent*. Boston: Little, Brown, 1834. http://catalog.hathitrust.org/Record/009833192.

Baptist, Edward E. *The Half Has Never Been Told: Slavery and the Making of American Capitalism*. New York: Basic Books, 2014.

Barker-Benfield, G. J. *Portraits of American Women: From Settlement to the Present*. New York: Oxford University Press, 1998.

Bartlett, Irving H. *Wendell and Ann Phillips: The Community of Reform, 1840–1880*. New York: W. W. Norton, 1979.

Bauer, Dale M., and Philip Gould. *The Cambridge Companion to Nineteenth-Century American Women's Writing*. Cambridge: Cambridge University Press, 2001.

Baxter, Richard. *The Saints Everlasting Rest, or, A Treatise of the Blessed State of the Saints in Their Enjoyment of God in Glory Wherein Is Shewed Its Excellency and Certainty, the Misery of Those That Lose It, the Way to Attain It, and Assurance of It, and How to Live in the Continual Delightful Forecasts of It*. 2005. http://name.umdl.umich.edu/A27017 .0001.001.

Beck, Janet Kemper. *Creating the John Brown Legend: Emerson, Thoreau, Douglass, Child and Higginson in Defense of the Raid on Harpers Ferry*. Jefferson, NC: McFarland, 2009.

Beecher, Henry Ward. *Defence of Kansas*. 1856. https://territorialkansasonline.ku.edu/ index.php?SCREEN=view_image&document_id=102291&file_name=u004210.

Beecher, Henry Ward. *A Discourse Delivered at the Plymouth Church, Brooklyn, N.Y. upon Thanksgiving Day, November 25th 1847*. New York: Cady & Burgess, 1848.

Beecher, Henry Ward. *New Star Papers: Or, Views and Experiences of Religious Subjects*. New York: Derby & Jackson, 1859.

Beecher, Henry Ward, and American College and Education Society. *Man and His Institutions: An Address before the Society for the Promotion of Collegiate and Theological Education at the West, Delivered in Tremont Temple, Boston, Mass., May 28, 1856*. New York: Calkins & Stiles, 1856.

Beecher, Henry Ward, and John R. [John Raymond] Howard. *Patriotic Addresses in America and England : From 1850 to 1885, on Slavery, the Civil War, and the Development of Civil Liberty in the United States*. New York : Fords, Howard & Hulbert, 1887.

Beecher, Lyman. *A Plea for the West*. Cincinnati, OH: Truman & Smith, 1835.

Beecher, Lyman, and Charles Beecher. *Autobiography, Correspondence, Etc. of Lyman Beecher*. New York : Harper, 1865.

Bell, Michael J. "'The Only True Folk Songs We Have in English': James Russell Lowell and the Politics of the Nation." *Journal of American Folklore* 108, no. 428 (1995): 131–55. doi:10.2307/541376.

Bendroth, Margaret Lamberts. *The Last Puritans: Mainline Protestants and the Power of the Past*. Chapel Hill: University of North Carolina Press, 2015.

Benjamin, Walter. *Illuminations*. Boston: Houghton Mifflin Harcourt, 1968.

Bennett, Paula. *Poets in the Public Sphere: The Emancipatory Project of American Women's Poetry, 1800–1900*. Princeton, NJ: Princeton University Press, 2003.

Bercovitch, Sacvan. "The Problem of Ideology in American Literary History." *Critical Inquiry* 12, no. 4 (1986): 631–53. http://www.jstor.org/stable/1343431.

Bercovitch, Sacvan. *The Rites of Assent: Transformations in the Symbolic Construction of America*. New York: Routledge, 1993.

Berlin, Ira. *Generations of Captivity: A History of African-American Slaves*. Cambridge, MA: Belknap, 2004.

Berlin, Ira. *Long Emancipation: The Demise of Slavery in the United States*. Cambridge, MA: Harvard University Press, 2018.

Blight, David W. *Race and Reunion: The Civil War in American Memory*. New ed. Cambridge, MA: Belknap, 2002.

Blight, David W. "Nathan Irvin Huggins, the Art of History, and the Irony of the American Dream." *Reviews in American History* 22, no. 1 (March 1994): 174–90.

Boesky, Amy, and Mary Thomas Crane, eds. *Form and Reform in Renaissance England: Essays in Honor of Barbara Kiefer Lewalski*. Newark: University of Delaware Press, 2000.

Boston Female Anti-Slavery Society. "Annual Report of the Boston Female Anti-Slavery Society." 1836. https//catalog.hathitrust.org/Record/008637160.

Boston Female Anti-Slavery Society, ed. *Annual Report of the Boston Female Anti-Slavery Society in 1837, with a Sketch of the Obstacles Thrown in the Way of Emancipation by Certain Clerical Abolitionists and Advocates for the Subjection of Woman*. Boston: I. Knapp, 1837.

Boston Female Anti-Slavery Society and Society for the Collegiate Instruction of Women (U.S.). *Report of the Boston Female Anti-Slavery Society: With a Concise Statement of Events, Previous and Subsequent to the Annual Meeting of 1835*. Boston, 1836.

Boyers, Robert, and Peggy Boyers. *The Salmagundi Reader*. Bloomington: Indiana University Press, 1983.

Boyle, James, and William Lloyd Garrison. *A Letter to Wm. Lloyd Garrison Respecting the Clerical Appeal; Sectarianism; Also Lines on Christian Rest by Mr. Garrison*. Boston: Isaac Knapp, 1838.

Brooks, Van Wyck. *The Flowering of New England 1815—1865*. New York: E. P. Dutton, 1936.

Brown, Matthew Pentland. *The Pilgrim and the Bee: Reading Rituals and Book Culture in Early New England*. Philadelphia: University of Pennsylvania Press, 2007.

Brown, William Wells. *The Black Man: His Antecedents, His Genius, and His Achievements*. New York: T. Hamilton, 1863.

Brown, William Wells. *Clotel, or, The President's Daughter: A Narrative of Slave Life in the United States*. London: Partridge & Oakey, 1853.

Brown, William Wells. *The Negro in the American Rebellion: His Heroism and His Fidelity*. Boston: Lee & Shepard, 1867.

Bruce, Dickson D. *The Origins of African American Literature, 1680–1865*. Charlottesville: University Press of Virginia, 2001.

Buell, Lawrence. *Emerson*. Cambridge, MA: Belknap / Harvard University Press, 2003.

Buell, Lawrence. *New England Literary Culture from Revolution through Renaissance*. Cambridge: Cambridge University Press, 1986.

Buell, Lawrence. "Religion on the American Mind." *American Literary History* 19, no. 1 (2007): 32–55.

Bushnell, Horace. *Christian Nurture*. Cleveland, OH: Pilgrim, 1994.

Butler, Jon. *Awash in a Sea of Faith*. Cambridge, MA: Harvard University Press, 1990.

Cameron, Christopher. "The Puritan Origins of Black Abolitionism in Massachusetts." *Historical Journal of Massachusetts* 39, nos. 1–2 (2011).

Campbell, Karen Kohrs. *Women Public Speakers in the United States, 1925–1993*. Westport, CT: Greenwood, 1994.

Carlyle, Thomas. *The Collected Works of Thomas Carlyle*. London: Chapman; Hall, 1858.

Carlyle, Thomas. *On Heroes, Hero Worship and the Heroic in History*. New York: Charles Scribner's Sons, 1841.

Carlyle, Thomas. *On Heroes, Hero-Worship and the Heroic in History*. Edited by Michael K. Goldberg, Joel J. Brattin, and Mark Engel. Berkeley: University of California Press, 1992.

Carlyle, Thomas. *Past and Present*. Berkeley: University of California Press, 2005.

Carlyle, Thomas. *Sartor Resartus: The Life and Opinions of Herr Teufelsdröckh in Three Books*. Edited by Rodger L Tarr and Mark Engel. Berkeley: University of California Press, 2000.

Carr, Glynis. "Index to the Liberty Bell." *The Online Archive of Nineteenth-Century U.S. Women's Writings*, 1997. http://www.facstaff.bucknell.edu/gcarr/19cUSWW/LB/LBindex.html.

Casper, Scott E., ed. *Perspectives on American Book History: Artifacts and Commentary*. Amherst: University of Massachusetts Press, 2002.

Chambers, Lee V. *The Weston Sisters: An American Abolitionist Family*. Chapel Hill: UNC Press Books, 2014.

Channing, William Ellery. *Slavery*. Boston: J. Munroe, 1835.

Chapman, Maria Weston. *Right and Wrong in Massachusetts*. Boston: Dow & Jackson, 1839.

Chapman, Maria Weston. *Songs of the Free, and Hymns of Christian Freedom* . Boston: I. Knapp, 1836.

Charvat, William. *Literary Publishing in America, 1790–1850*. Amherst: University of Massachusetts Press, 1993.

Child, Lydia Maria. *An Appeal in Favor of That Class of Americans Called Africans*. Boston: Allen, Ticknor, 1833.

Child, Lydia Maria. *Autumnal Leaves: Tales and Sketches in Prose and Rhyme*. New York: C. S. Francis, 1857.

Child, Lydia Maria. *The Freedmen's Book*. Boston: Ticknor, Fields, 1865.

Child, Lydia Maria. *A Lydia Maria Child Reader*. Edited by Carolyn L Karcher. Durham, NC: Duke University Press, 1997.

Child, Lydia Maria. *Lydia Maria Child: Selected Letters, 1817–1880*. Edited by Milton Meltzer. Amherst: University of Massachusetts Press, 1983.

Child, Lydia Maria. *Letters of Lydia Maria Child*. Edited by Harriet Winslow Sewall. Introduction by John Greenleaf Whittier. Appendix by Wendell Phillips. Boston: Houghton Mifflin, 1882; rpt. Cambridge, MA: Harvard University Press, 2005.

Clapp, Elizabeth J., and Julie Roy Jeffrey. *Women, Dissent and Anti-Slavery in Britain and America, 1790–1865*. Oxford: Oxford University Press, 2011..

Cohen, Lara Langer. *The Fabrication of American Literature: Fraudulence and Antebellum Print Culture*. Philadelphia: University of Pennsylvania Press, 2011.

Cohen, Lara Langer, and Jordan Alexander Stein. *Early African American Print Culture*. Philadelphia: University of Pennsylvania Press, 2012.

Cohen, Matt. *The Networked Wilderness: Communicating in Early New England*. Minneapolis: University of Minnesota Press, 2010.

Cohen, Michael C. *The Social Lives of Poems in Nineteenth-Century America*. Philadelphia: University of Pennsylvania Press, 2015.

Cole, Phyllis. *Mary Moody Emerson and the Origins of Transcendentalism: A Family History*. New York: Oxford University Press, 1998.

Conforti, Joseph A. *Imagining New England: Explorations of Regional Identity from the Pilgrims to the Mid-twentieth Century*. Chapel Hill: University of North Carolina Press, 2001.

Cox, Samuel Sullivan. *Eight Years in Congress, from 1857–1865: Memoir and Speeches*. New York: D. Appleton, 1865.

Cox, Samuel Sullivan. *Puritanism in Politics. Speech of Hon. S. S. Cox, of Ohio, Before the Democratic Union Association, January 13, 1863*. New York: Van Evrie, Horton, 1863.

Davis, David Brion. *The Problem of Slavery in the Age of Revolution, 1770–1823*. New York: ACLS History E-Book Project, 2005.

Davis, David Brion. *The Problem of Slavery in Western Culture*. Oxford: Oxford University Press, 1998.

Davis, Jefferson. *The Papers of Jefferson Davis: 1856–1860*. Vol. 8. Edited by Lynda Lasswell Crist. Baton Rouge: Louisiana State University, 1995.

Delany, Martin Robison. *The Condition, Elevation, Emigration, and Destiny of the Colored People of the United States*. Philadelphia: Author, 1852.

Delbanco, Andrew, John Stauffer, Manisha Sinha, Darryl Pinckney, and Wilfred M McClay. *The Abolitionist Imagination*. Cambridge, MA: Harvard University Press, 2012.

Deleuze, Gilles. *Essays Critical and Clinical*. Brooklyn, NY: Verso, 1998.

Dickerson, Vanessa D. *Dark Victorians*. Urbana: University of Illinois Press, 2008.

Dijk, Teun A. van. *Ideology : A Multidisciplinary Approach*. London: Sage, 1998.

Dimock, Wai Chee. "A Theory of Resonance." *PMLA* 112, no. 5 (1997): 1060–71.

Douglas, Ann. *The Feminization of American Culture*. New York: Alfred A. Knopf, 1977.

Douglass, Frederick. *The Frederick Douglass Papers*. Edited by Peter P. Hinks, John R. McKivigan, and John W. Blassingame. New Haven, CT: Yale University Press, 1999.

Eagleton, Terry. "Capitalism, Modernism and Postmodernism." *New Left Review* 1 no. 152 (1985): 60–73.

Elliott, Emory. *The Cambridge Introduction to Early American Literature*. Cambridge: Cambridge University Press, 2002.

Emerson, Ralph Waldo. *The Collected Works of Ralph Waldo Emerson*. Edited by Robert Ernest Spiller, Alfred R Ferguson, Joseph Slater, and Jean Ferguson Carr. Cambridge, MA: Belknap / Harvard University Press, 1971.

Emerson, Ralph Waldo. *The Early Lectures of Ralph Waldo Emerson*, vol. 1, *1833–1836*. Edited by Stephen E Whicher and Robert Ernest Spiller. Cambridge, MA: Belknap / Harvard University Press, 1966.

Emerson, Ralph Waldo. *Emerson in His Journals*. Edited by Joel Porte. Cambridge, MA: Belknap / Harvard University Press, 1982.

Emerson, Ralph Waldo. *The Journals and Miscellaneous Notebooks of Ralph Waldo Emerson*. Edited by William H. Gilman. Cambridge, MA: Belknap / Harvard University Press, 1960. Emerson, Ralph Waldo. *The Later Lectures of Ralph Waldo Emerson, 1843–1871*. Edited by Ronald A. Bosco and Joel Myerson. Athens: University of Georgia Press, 2010.

Emerson, Ralph Waldo. *Emerson's Antislavery Writings*. Edited by Len Gougeon and Joel Myerson. New Haven, CT: Yale University Press, 1995.

Emerson, Ralph Waldo. *Emerson's Prose and Poetry: Authoritative Texts, Contexts, Criticism*. Edited by Joel Porte and Saundra Morris. New York: W. W. Norton, 2001.

Ernest, John. *Liberation Historiography: African American Writers and the Challenge of History, 1794–1861*. New ed. Chapel Hill: University of North Carolina Press, 2004.

Ernest, John. *Resistance and Reformation in Nineteenth-Century African-American Literature: Brown, Wilson, Jacobs, Delany, Douglass, and Harper*. Jackson: University Press of Mississippi, 1995.

Everett, Edward. *Orations and Speeches on Various Occasions*. Boston: Little, Brown, 1860.

Felker, Christopher D. *Reinventing Cotton Mather in the American Renaissance: Magnalia Christi Americana in Hawthorne, Stowe, and Stoddard*. Boston: Northeastern University Press, 1994.

Field, Peter S. *Ralph Waldo Emerson: The Making of a Democratic Intellectual*. Lanham, MD: Rowman & Littlefield, 2003.

Foley, Barbara. *Radical Representations: Politics and Form in U.S. Proletarian Fiction, 1929–41*. Durham, NC: Duke University Press, 1994.

Foner, Eric. *The Fiery Trial: Abraham Lincoln and American Slavery*. New York: W. W. Norton, 2011.

Foner, Eric. *Reconstruction America's Unfinished Revolution, 1863–1877*. New York: HarperCollins, 2015.

Forten, Charlotte L. *The Journals of Charlotte Forten Grimké*. Oxford: Oxford University Press, 1988.

Foster, Charles H. *The Rungless Ladder; Harriet Beecher Stowe and New England Puritanism.* Durham, NC: Duke University Press, 1954.

Fredrickson, George M. *The Black Image in the White Mind: The Debate on Afro-American Character and Destiny, 1817–1914.* New York: Harper & Row, 1971.

Freeden, Michael, Lyman Tower Sargent, and Marc Stears. *The Oxford Handbook of Political Ideologies.* Oxford: Oxford University Press, 2015.

Fuller, Randall. "Errand into the Wilderness: Perry Miller as American Scholar." *American Literary History* 18, no. 1 (2006): 102–28.

Fuller, Randall. *From Battlefields Rising: How the Civil War Transformed American Literature.* Reprint ed. Oxford University Press, 2014.

Fulton, Joe B. "Reason for a Renaissance: The Rhetoric of Reformation and Rebirth in the Age of Transcendentalism." *New England Quarterly* 80, no. 3 (September 2007): 383–407.

Garnet, Henry Highland. . "An Address to the Slaves of the United States of America" (1843). In *Crossing the Danger Water: Three Hundred Years of African-American Writing,* edited by Deirdre Mullane, 115–21. New York: Doubleday, 1993.Garnet, Henry Highland. *The Past and the Present Condition, and the Destiny, of the Colored Race:* Troy, NY: Steam Press of J. C. Kneeland, 1848.

Garnet, Henry Highland. "Speech at the Seventh Annual Aeeting of the American Anti-Slavery Society." *Colored American,* May 30, 1840.

Garrison, Wendell Phillips, and Francis Jackson Garrison. *William Lloyd Garrison, 1805–1879: The Story of His Life Told by His Children.* Boston: Houghton, Mifflin, 1885.

Garrison, William Lloyd. *An Address Delivered in Marlboro' Chapel, Boston.* Boston: Isaac Knapp, 1838.

Garrison, William Lloyd. *The Letters of William Lloyd Garrison, vol. 1, 1822–1835.* Edited by Walter M. Merrill. Cambridge, MA: Belknap / Harvard University Press, 1971.

Garrison, William Lloyd, ed. *A Selection of Anti-Slavery Hymns: For the Use of the Friends of Emancipation.* Boston: Garrison & Knapp, 1834.

Garrison, William Lloyd. *Selections from the Writings and Speeches of William Lloyd Garrison, with an Appendix.* Boston: R. F. Wallcut, 1852.

Giddings, Joshua R. "Speech." In *Oliver Dyer's Phonographic Report of the Proceedings of the National Free Soil Convention at Buffalo, N.Y. August 9th and 10th, 1848.* Buffalo: G. H. Derby, 1848,

Gilroy, Paul. *The Black Atlantic: Modernity and Double Consciousness.* Brooklyn, NY: Verso, 1993.

Glaude, Eddie S. *Exodus! Religion, Race, and Nation in Early Nineteenth-Century Black America.* Chicago: University of Chicago Press, 2007.

Gougeon, Len. "Militant Abolitionism: Douglass, Emerson, and the Rise of the Anti-Slave." *New England Quarterly* 85, no. 4 (November 2012): 622–57.

Gougeon, Len. *Virtue's Hero: Emerson, Antislavery, and Reform.* Athens: University of Georgia Press, 2010.

Gouldner, Alvin Ward. *The Dialectic of Ideology and Technology: The Origins, Grammar, and Future of Ideology.* New York: Seabury, 1976.

Green, Ian. *Print and Protestantism in Early Modern England.* Oxford: Oxford University Press, 2001.

Greenslade, S. L., ed. *The Cambridge History of the Bible, vol. 3, The West From the Reformation to the Present Day.* Cambridge: Cambridge University Press, 1975.

Gross, Robert A., and Mary Kelley, eds. *A History of the Book in America, vol. 2, An Extensive*

Republic: Print, Culture, and Society in the New Nation, 1790–1840. Reprint ed. Chapel Hill: University of North Carolina Press, 2014.

Gruesz, Kirsten Silva. *Ambassadors of Culture: The Transamerican Origins of Latino Writing*. Princeton, NJ: Princeton University Press, 2002.

Hahn, Steven. *A Nation under Our Feet: Black Political Struggles in the Rural South from Slavery to the Great Migration*. Cambridge, MA: Belknap / Harvard University Press, 2005.

Hahn, Steven. *The Political Worlds of Slavery and Freedom*. Cambridge, MA: Harvard University Press, 2009.

Hairston, Eric. *The Ebony Column: Classics, Civilization, and the African American Reclamation of the West*. Knoxville: University of Tennessee Press, 2013.

Hall, David D. *Cultures of Print: Essays in the History of the Book*. Amherst: University of Massachusetts Press, 1996.

Hall, David D. *Worlds of Wonder, Days of Judgment: Popular Religious Belief in Early New England*. New York: Alfred A. Knopf, 1989.

Hall, Stephen G. *A Faithful Account of the Race: African American Historical Writing in Nineteenth-Century America*. Chapel Hill: University of North Carolina Press, 2009.

Haralson, Eric L. *Encyclopedia of American Poetry*. Chicago: Fitzroy Dearborn, 1998.

Hargrove, Hondon B. *Black Union Soldiers in the Civil War*. New York: McFarland, 2003.

Harriet Beecher Stowe. "New England Ministers." *Atlantic Monthly* 1, no. 4 (February 1858): 485–95.

Hedrick, Joan D. *Harriet Beecher Stowe: A Life*. New York: Oxford University Press, 1995.

Henry Martyn Dexter, and Andover Theological Seminary. *The Congregationalism of the Last Three Hundred Years, as Seen in Its Literature*. New York: Harper & Brothers, 1880.

Hickman, Jared. *Black Prometheus: Race and Radicalism in the Age of Atlantic Slavery*. Oxford: Oxford University Press, 2016.

Howard, Leon. *Victorian Knight-Errant: A Study of the Early Literary Career of James Russell Lowell*. Westport, CT: Greenwood, 1971.

Howard-Pitney, David. *The African American Jeremiad: Appeals for Justice in America*. Philadelphia: Temple University Press, 2009.

Howe, Daniel Walker. *The Unitarian Conscience: Harvard Moral Philosophy, 1805–1861*. Cambridge, MA: Harvard University Press, 1970.

Howe, Julia Ward. *Reminiscences: 1819–1899*. Boston: Houghton Mifflin, 1899.

Hruschka, John. *How Books Came to America: The Rise of the American Book Trade*. University Park: Penn State University Press, 2013.

Huggins, Nathan I. *Black Odyssey: The African-American Ordeal in Slavery*. New York: Vintage Books, 1990.

Huggins, Nathan I. *Key Issues in the Afro-American Experience*. New York: Harcourt, Brace, Jovanovich, 1971.

Hutchinson, William R. *Transcendentalist Ministers: Church Reform in the New England Renaissance*. New Haven, CT: Yale University Press, 1959.

Jablonski, Heike. *John Foxe in America: Discourses of Martyrdom in the Eighteenth- and Nineteenth-Century United States*. Paderborn, Germany: Ferndinand Schöningh, 2017.

Jackson, Leon. "The Reader Retailored: Thomas Carlyle, His American Audiences, and the Politics of Evidence." *Book History* 2, no. 1 (August 1999): 146–72.

Jackson, Leon, and American Antiquarian Society. *The Social Construction of Thomas Carlyle's New England Reputation, 1834–36*. Worcester, MA: American Antiquarian Society, 1996.

Jacobs, Donald M. *Courage and Conscience: Black & White Abolitionists in Boston*. Bloomington: Boston Athenaeum / Indiana University Press, 1993.

James, Henry. *The Bostonians*. London: Macmillan, 1886.

James, Henry. *The Secret of Swedenborg: Being an Elucidation of His Doctrine of the Divine Natural Humanity*. Boston: Fields, Osgood, 1869.

James, William. *The Varieties of Religious Experience: A Study in Human Nature*. New York: Longmans, Green, 1917.

Jeffrey, Julie Roy. *The Great Silent Army of Abolitionism: Ordinary Women in the Antislavery Movement*. Chapel Hill: University of North Carolina Press, 2000.

Johnson, Oliver, and John Greenleaf Whittier. *William Lloyd Garrison and His Times; or, Sketches of the Anti-Slavery Movement in America, and of the Man Who Was Its Founder and Moral Leader*. Boston: Houghton Mifflin, 1881.

Johnson, Walter. *River of Dark Dreams: Slavery and Empire in the Cotton Kingdom*. Cambridge, MA: Belknap, 2013.

Kammen, Michael. *Mystic Chords of Memory: The Transformation of Tradition in American Culture*. New York: Vintage Books, 2013.

Kaplan, Amy, and Donald E. Pease, eds. *Cultures of United States Imperialism*. Durham, NC: Duke University Press Books, 1994.

Karcher, Carolyn L. *The First Woman in the Republic: A Cultural Biography of Lydia Maria Child*. Durham, NC: Duke University Press, 1994.

Kattago, Siobhan. *The Ashgate Research Companion to Memory Studies*. London: Routledge, 2016.

Kaul, Suvir. *Poems of Nation, Anthems of Empire: English Verse in the Long Eighteenth Century*. Oxford: Oxford University Press, 2001.

Kellow, Margaret M. R. "For the Sake of Suffering Kansas: Lydia Maria Child, Gender, and the Politics of the 1850s." *Journal of Women's History* 5 (Fall 1993).

Kerrigan, William. *The Sacred Complex: On the Psychogenesis of "Paradise Lost."* Cambridge, MA: Harvard University Press, 1983.

Kete, Mary Louise. *Sentimental Collaboration: Mourning and Middle-Class Identity in Nineteenth Century America*. Durham, NC; London: Duke University Press, 2000.

Kraditor, Aileen S. *Means and Ends in American Abolitionism: Garrison and His Critics on Strategy and Tactics*. New York: Pantheon Books, 1969.

Larson, Kerry C. *The Cambridge Companion to Nineteenth-Century American Poetry*. Cambridge: Cambridge University Press, 2011.

Levine, Robert S. *Martin Delany, Frederick Douglass, and the Politics of Representative Identity*. Chapel Hill: University of North Carolina Press, 2000.

Lewalski, Barbara Kiefer. *Protestant Poetics and the Seventeenth-Century Religious Lyric*. Princeton, NJ: Princeton University Press, 1979.

Leypoldt, Günter, and Bernd Engler. *American Cultural Icons: The Production of Representative Lives*. Würzburg, Germany: Königshausen und Neumann, 2010.

Liberty Bell. Edited and published by Maria [Weston] Chapman, National Anti-Slavery Bazaar, American Anti-Slavery Society, and Massachusetts Anti-Slavery Fair. 15 vols. 1839–58. http://catalog.hathitrust.org/Record/003488826.

Littell, Eliakim, and Robert S. Littell. *Littell's Living Age*. Boston: T. H. Carter, 1846.

Loeffelholz, Mary. *From School to Salon: Reading Nineteenth-Century American Women's Poetry*. Princeton, NJ: Princeton University Press, 2004.

Loughran, Trish. *The Republic in Print: Print Culture in the Age of U.S. Nation Building, 1770–1870*. New York: Columbia University Press, 2009.

Lowell, James Russell. *Among My Books*. Boston: J. R. Osgood, 1877.

Lowell, James Russell. *Anti-Slavery Papers*. Edited by William Belmont Parker. Boston: Houghton Mifflin, 1902.

Lowell, James Russell. *The Biglow Papers*. Boston: Ticknor, Fields, 1859.

Lowell, James Russell. *The Biglow Papers, Second Series*. Boston:: Ticknor and Fields, 1867.

Lowell, James Russell. "Class Poem." 1838. http://archive.org/details/aberpa.lowelljr .1838.classpoem.

Lowell, James Russell. *Lectures on English Poets*. Cleveland, OH: Rowfant Club, 1897.

Lowell, James Russell. *The Round Table*. Boston: R. G. Badger, Gorham Press, 1913.

Lowell, James Russell, and Robert Carter. *The Pioneer: A Literary and Critical Magazine*. Boston: Leland, Whiting, 1843.

Maffly-Kipp, Laurie F. *Setting Down the Sacred Past: African-American Race Histories*. Cambridge, MA: Harvard University Press, 2010.

Marcus, Greil, Werner Sollors, and Reference Collection. *A New Literary History of America*. Cambridge, MA: Belknap / Harvard University Press, 2013.

Martyn, W. Carlos. *Wendell Phillips: The Agitator*. New York: Funk & Wagnalls, 1890.

Marx, Leo. "Believing in America." *Boston Review* 28, no. 6 (2004).

Mason, Matthew. *Apostle of Union A Political Biography of Edward Everett*. Chapel Hill: University of North Carolina Press, 2016.

Mayer, Henry. *All on Fire: William Lloyd Garrison and the Abolition of Slavery*. New York: W. W. Norton, 2008.

McGill, Meredith L. *American Literature and the Culture of Reprinting, 1834–1853*. Philadelphia: University of Pennsylvania Press, 2013.

McInerney, Daniel John. *The Fortunate Heirs of Freedom Abolition and Republican Thought*. Lincoln: University of Nebraska Press, 1994.

Medico. *A Review of Garrisonian Fanaticism and Its Influence*. Boston: Ticknor, Reed & Fields, 1852..

Melish, Joanne Pope. *Disowning Slavery: Gradual Emancipation and "Race" in New England, 1780–1860*. Ithaca, NY: Cornell University Press, 2000.

Meltzer, Milton. *Tongue of Flame: The Life of Lydia Maria Child*. New York: T. Y. Crowell, 1965.

Menand, Louis. *The Metaphysical Club: A Story of Ideas in America*, New York: Farrar, Strauss, and Giroux, 2007.

Mencken, Henry Louis. *A Book of Prefaces*. New York: Alfred A. Knopf, 1917.

Milder, Robert. "From Emerson to Edwards." *New England Quarterly* 80, no. 1 (2007): 96–133.

Milder, Robert. "Uncivil Wars." In *Exiled Royalties: Melville and the Life We Imagine* (Oxford: Oxford University Press, 2006,) 168–91.

Miller, Perry. *The Transcendentalists*. Cambridge, MA: Harvard University Press, 1950.

Milton, John. "Eikonoklastes." Edited by Thomas H. Luxon. John Milton Reading Room, Dartmouth University, 1997. https://www.dartmouth.edu/~milton/reading_room/ contents/text.shtml.

Minardi, Margot. *Making Slavery History: Abolitionism and the Politics of Memory in Massachusetts*. Oxford: Oxford University Press, 2012.

Monaghan, E. Jennifer. *Learning to Read and Write in Colonial America*. Amherst, MA: University of Massachusetts Press, 2007.

Morgan, Edmund. *American Slavery, American Freedom*. New York: W. W. Norton, 2003.

Moses, Wilson Jeremiah. *Black Messiahs and Uncle Toms: Social and Literary Manipulations of a Religious Myth*. University Park: Pennsylvania State University Press, 1993.

Mount, Guy Emerson. "When Slaves Go on Strike: W. E. B. Du Bois's Black Reconstruction 80 Years Later." *Black Perspectives* (African American Intellectual History Society), December 28, 2015. https://www.aaihs.org/when-slaves-go-on-strike/.

Myerson, Joel. *Emerson and Thoreau: The Contemporary Reviews*. Cambridge: Cambridge University Press, 2009.

Noll, Mark A. *The Civil War as a Theological Crisis*. Chapel Hill: University of North Carolina Press, 2006.

Nord, David Paul. *Faith in Reading: Religious Publishing and the Birth of Mass Media in America*. New York: Oxford University Press, 2004.

Olick, Jeffrey K, Vered Vinitzky-Seroussi, and Daniel Levy. *The Collective Memory Reader*. New York: Oxford University Press, 2011.

Oshatz, Molly. *Slavery and Sin: The Fight against Slavery and the Rise of Liberal Protestantism*. New York: Oxford University Press, 2012.

Parker, Theodore. *The Nebraska Question. Some Thoughts on the New Assault Upon Freedom in America, and the General State of the Country in Relation Thereunto, Set Forth in a Discourse Preached at the Music Hall, in Boston, on Monday, Feb. 12, 1854*. Boston: B. B. Mussey, 1854.

Parker, Theodore, and Frances Power Cobbe. *Collected Works of Theodore Parker: Containing His Theological, Polemical, and Critical Writings, Sermons, Speeches, and Addresses, and Literary Miscellanies*. London: Trübner, 1876.

Parker, Theodore, James Elliott Cabot, and Ralph Waldo Emerson. *The Massachusetts Quarterly Review*. 3 vols. 1848.

Parrington, Vernon Louis. *Main Currents in American Thought*. New York: Harcourt, Brace;, 1927.

Patell, Cyrus. "Emersonian Strategies: Negative Liberty, Self-Reliance, and Democratic Individuality." *Nineteenth-Century Literature* 48, no. 4 (1994): 440–79.

Patterson, Orlando. *Slavery and Social Death: A Comparative Study*. Cambridge, MA: Harvard University Press, 1985.

Pease, Donald E. *The New American Exceptionalism*. Minneapolis: University of Minnesota Press, 2010.

Pelletier, Kevin. *Apocalyptic Sentimentalism: Love and Fear in U.S. Antebellum Literature*. Athens: University of Georgia Press, 2015.

Peterson, Carla L. *Doers of the Word: African-American Women Speakers and Writers in the North (1830–1880)*. Rutgers, NJ: Rutgers University Press, 1998.

Peterson, Merrill D. *The Great Triumvirate: Webster, Clay, and Calhoun*. New York: Oxford University Press, 1988.

Petrulionis, Sandra Harbert. *To Set This World Right: The Antislavery Movement in Thoreau's Concord*. Ithaca, NY: Cornell University Press, 2006.

Phelan, James, ed. *Narrative Poetics: Innovations, Limits, Challenges*. Columbus: Center for Comparative Studies in the Humanities, College of Humanities, Ohio State University, 1987.

Phillips, Wendell, and Theodore C. Pease. *Speeches, Lectures, and Letters*. Boston: Lee and Shepard, 1892.

Pickard, Samuel T. *Life and Letters of John Greenleaf Whittier*. London: Ardent Media, 1969.

Pizer, John David. *Toward a Theory of Radical Origin: Essays on Modern German Thought*. Lincoln: University of Nebraska Press, 1995.

Porte, Joel, and Saundra Morris. *The Cambridge Companion to Ralph Waldo Emerson*. Cambridge: Cambridge University Press, 1999.

Quarles, Benjamin. *Black Abolitionists*. New York: Da Capo, 1991.

Quarles, Benjamin. *Lincoln and the Negro*. New York: Da Capo, 1991.

Quarles, Benjamin. *The Negro in the American Revolution*. Chapel Hill: University of North Carolina Press, 1961.

Quarles, Benjamin. *The Negro in the Civil War*. New York: Da Capo, 1989.

Redpath, James, and Louisa May Alcott. *Echoes of Harper's Ferry*. Boston : Thayer, Eldridge, 1860.

Reynolds, David S. *John Brown, Abolitionist: The Man Who Killed Slavery, Sparked the Civil War, and Seeded Civil Rights*. New York: Alfred A. Knopf, 2005.

Reynolds, David S. *Mightier Than the Sword: Uncle Tom's Cabin and the Battle for America*. New York; London: W. W. Norton, 2012.

Rice, Allen Thorndike, William Hickling Prescott, Caleb Cushing, Ralph Waldo Emerson, George Bancroft, John Lothrop Motley, Washington Irving, et al. *Essays from the North American Review*. New York: D. Appleton, 1879.

Ricoeur, Paul. *Freud and Philosophy: An Essay on Interpretation*. Translated by Denis Savage. New Haven, CT: Yale University Press, 1970.

Richardson, Robert D. *Emerson: The Mind on Fire*. Berkeley: University of California Press, 1995.

Romero, Lora. *Home Fronts: Domesticity and Its Critics in the Antebellum United States*. Durham, NC: Duke University Press, 1997.

Roper, Jon. *Democracy and Its Critics: Anglo-American Democratic Thought in the Nineteenth Century*. Routledge Revivals. London: Routledge, 2013.

Russo, Peggy A., and Paul Finkelman. *Terrible Swift Sword: The Legacy of John Brown*. Athens: Ohio University Press, 2005.

Saillant, John. *Black Puritan, Black Republican: The Life and Thought of Lemuel Haynes, 1753–1833*. Oxford: Oxford University Press, 2002.

Santayana, George, and Douglas L. Wilson. *The Genteel Tradition; Nine Essays*. Cambridge, MA: Harvard University Press, 1967.

Schmidt, Leigh Eric. *Restless Souls: The Making of American Spirituality*. San Francisco: Harper, 2005.

Schor, Joel. *Henry Highland Garnet: A Voice of Black Radicalism in the Nineteenth Century*. Westport, CT: Greenwood, 1977.

Schor, Joel. "The Rivalry between Frederick Douglass and Henry Highland Garnet." *Journal of Negro History* 64, no. 1 (1979): 30–38. doi:10.2307/2717124.

Seelye, John D. *Memory's Nation: The Place of Plymouth Rock*. Chapel Hill: University of North Carolina Press, 1998.

Shelley, Percy Bysshe. "A Defence of Poetry." In *Essays, Letters from Abroad, Translations and Fragments*. London: Edward Moxon, 1840.

Showalter, Elaine. *The Civil Wars of Julia Ward Howe: A Biography*. New York: Simon & Schuster, 2016.

Siegel, Paul N. "The Style of the Communist Manifesto." *Science & Society* 46, no. 2 (1982): 222–29.

Sinha, Manisha. *The Slave's Cause: A History of Abolition*. New Haven, CT: Yale University Press, 2016.

Smith, Christian. *The Bible Made Impossible: Why Biblicism Is Not a Truly Evangelical Reading of Scripture*. Reprint ed. Grand Rapids, MI: Brazos, 2012.

Smith, James McCune, and Henry Louis Gates Jr. *The Works of James McCune Smith: Black Intellectual and Abolitionist*. Edited by John Stauffer. New York: Oxford University Press, 2007.

Smith, Steven Carl. *An Empire of Print: The New York Publishing Trade in the Early American Republic*. University Park: Penn State Press, 2017.

Smith, Timothy L. *Revivalism and Social Reform*: New York: Wipf & Stock, 2004.

Snelling, William Joseph. *Tales of the Northwest; or, Sketches of Indian Life and Character*. Boston: Hilliard, Gray, Little, Wilkins, 1830.

Stanton, Elizabeth Cady, Susan B. Anthony, and Matilda Joslyn Gage. *History of Woman Suffrage*. New York: Fowler & Wells, 1881.

Stark, Werner. "Harriet Beecher Stowe versus Max Weber." *Sociological Analysis* 42, no. 2 (1981): 173–75.

Stauffer, John. *The Black Hearts of Men: Radical Abolitionists and the Transformation of Race*. Cambridge, MA: Harvard University Press, 2004.

Stauffer, John, and Benjamin Soskis. *The Battle Hymn of the Republic: A Biography of the Song That Marches On*. Oxford: Oxford University Press, 2013.

Stavely, Keith W. F. *Puritan Legacies: "Paradise Lost" and the New England Tradition, 1630–1890*. Ithaca, NY: Cornell University Press, 1990.

Stewart, Maria. *Productions of Mrs. Maria W. Stewart presented to the First Africa Baptist Church & Society, of the City of Boston*. Boston: Friends of Freedom and Virtue, 1835.

Storrs, Richard S. *The Spirit of the Pilgrims A Sermon Delivered at Plymouth, December the Twenty-Second, 1826*. Plymouth: Allen Danforth, 1827.

Stout, Harry S. *Upon the Altar of the Nation: A Moral History of the Civil War*. Reprint ed. New York, NY: Penguin Books, 2007.

Stowe, Charles Edward. *Life of Harriet Beecher Stowe: Comp. from Her Letters and Journals*. New York: Houghton Mifflin, 1889.

Stowe, Harriet Beecher. *Dred: A Tale of the Great Dismal Swamp*. New York: Penguin Books, 2000.

Stowe, Harriet Beecher. "A Family Talk on Reconstruction." *Atlantic Monthly* 18 (1866).

Stowe, Harriet Beecher. *Household Papers and Stories*. Boston: Houghton, Mifflin, 1896.

Stowe, Harriet Beecher. *The Minister's Wooing*. New York: Penguin Books, 1999.

Stowe, Harriet Beecher. *Oldtown Folks*. Cambridge, MA: Belknap / Harvard University Press, 1966.

Stowe, Harriet Beecher. *Sunny Memories of Foreign Lands*. Boston: Phillips, Sampson, 1854.

Strong, Douglas. *Perfectionist Politics: Abolitionism and the Religious Tensions of American Democracy*. Syracuse, NY: Syracuse University Press, 1999.

Sweet, Leonard I. *Black Images of America, 1784–1870*. New York: W. W. Norton, 1976.

Swift, David Everett. *Black Prophets of Justice: Activist Clergy before the Civil War*. Baton Rouge: Louisiana State Press, 1989.

Sypher, Wylie. *Guinea's Captive Kings: British Anti-Slavery Literature of the XVIIIth Century*. New York: Octagon Books, 1969.

Tarr, Roger L. "Emerson's Transcendentalism in L. M. Child's Letter to Carlyle." *ESQ: A Journal of the American Renaissance* 73 (1973): 219–23.

Taylor, Charles. *A Secular Age*. Cambridge, MA: Belknap / Harvard University Press, 2007.

Taylor, Clare. *Women of the Anti-Slavery Movement: The Weston Sisters*. New York: Springer, 1994.

Teed, Paul E. "The Politics of Sectional Memory: Theodore Parker and the *Massachusetts Quarterly Review*, 1847–1850." *Journal of the Early Republic* 21, no. 2 (2001): 301–29.

Thompson, J. Earl. "Lyman Beecher's Long Road to Conservative Abolitionism." *Church History* 42, no. 1 (March 1973): 89–109.

Thompson, Ralph. *American Literary Annuals and Gift Books, 1825–1865*. New York: H. W. Wilson, 1939.

Thompson, R. E. *A History of the Presbyterian Churches*. American Church History Series, edited by Philip Schaff, Henry Codman Potter, and Samuel Macauley Jackson. New York: Christian Literature Company, 1895.

Thompson, Todd, and Jessica Showalter. "Satire in Circulation: James Russell Lowell's 'LETTER FROM A VOLUNTEER IN SALTILLO.'" *Scholarly Editing* 36 (2015).

Thoreau, Henry David, and Wendell Glick. *Reform Papers*. Princeton, NJ: Princeton University Press, 1973.

Tota, Anna Lisa, and Trever Hagen. *Routledge International Handbook of Memory Studies*. London: Routledge, 2015.

Trimmer, Joseph F. "The Grandfather's Riddle in Ralph Ellison's *Invisible Man*." *Black American Literature Forum* 12, no. 2 (1978): 46–50.

Turner, Nat, and Thomas R. Gray. *The Confessions of Nat Turner*. Baltimore: T. R. Gray, 1831.

Tuveson, Ernest Lee. *Redeemer Nation: The Idea of America's Millennial Role*. Chicago: University of Chicago Press, 1980.

Van Deburg, William L. *Slavery and Race in American Popular Culture*. Madison: University of Wisconsin Press, 1983.

Van Engen, Abram C. *City on a Hill: A History of American Exceptionalism*. New Haven, CT: Yale University Press, 2020.

Van Engen, Abram C. *Sympathetic Puritans: Calvinist Fellow-Feeling in Early New England*. Oxford: Oxford University Press, 2015.

Vance, William Silas. "Carlyle in America before *Sartor Resartus*." *American Literature* 7, no. 4 (1936): 363–75.

Volpe, Vernon L. "Theodore Dwight Weld's Antislavery Mission in Ohio." *Ohio History Journal* 100 (Winter-Spring 1991): 5–18.

Von Frank, Albert J. *The Trials of Anthony Burns: Freedom and Slavery in Emerson's Boston*. Cambridge, MA: Harvard University Press, 1998.

Walker, Clarence E. *Deromanticizing Black History: Critical Essays Reappraisals*. Knoxville: University of Tennessee Press, 1991.

Walzer, Michael. *The Company of Critics: Social Criticism and Political Commitment in the Twentieth Century*. New York: Basic Books, 2010.

Walzer, Michael. *Interpretation and Social Criticism*. Cambridge, MA: Harvard University Press, 1993.

Walzer, Michael. *The Revolution of the Saints: A Study in the Origins of Radical Politics*. Cambridge, MA: Harvard University Press, 1965.

Ward, Jonathan. *American Slavery, and the Means of Its Abolition*. Boston: Perkins & Marvin, 1840.

Webber, Christopher L. *American to the Backbone: The Life of James W. C. Pennington, the Fugitive Slave Who Became One of the First Black Abolitionists*. New York: Pegasus Books, 2011.

Weil, François. "John Farmer and the Making of American Genealogy." *New England Quarterly* 80, no. 3 (September 2007): 408–34.

Weinstein, Cindy, ed. *The Cambridge Companion to Harriet Beecher Stowe*. Cambridge: Cambridge University Press, 2004.

Weiss, John, Theodore Parker, and Oliver Wendell Holmes Collection (Library of Congress). *Life and Correspondence of Theodore Parker: Minister of the Twenty-Eighth Congregational Society, Boston*. New York: D. Appleton, 1864.

Weld, Theodore Dwight. *American Slavery, as It Is: Testimony of a Thousand Witnesses*. New York: American Anti-Slavery Society, 1839.

Welter, Barbara. "The Cult of True Womanhood: 1820–1860." *American Quarterly* 18, no. 2 (1966): 151–74.

Whittier, John Greenleaf. *Anti-Slavery Poems: Songs of Labor and Reform.* Cambridge, MA: Riverside, 1888.

Whittier, John Greenleaf. *In War Time, and Other Poems.* Boston: Ticknor & Fields, 1864.

Whittier, John Greenleaf. *Justice and Expediency.* Haverhill, MA: C. P. Thayer, 1833.

Whittier, John Greenleaf. *Literary Recreations and Miscellanies.* Boston: Ticknor and Fields, 1854.

Whittier, John Greenleaf. *The Panorama, and Other Poems.* Boston: Ticknor & Fields, 1856.

Whittier, John Greenleaf. *Poems Written during the Progress of the Abolition Question in the United States: Between the Years 1830–1838.* Boston: I. Knapp, 1837.

Whittier, John Greenleaf. *Snow-Bound: A Winter Idyl.* Boston: Ticknor & Fields, 1868.

Whittier, John Greenleaf, and Bliss Perry. *John Greenleaf Whittier: A Sketch of His Life with Selected Poems.* Boston: Houghton Mifflin, 1907.

Williams, Raymond. *Keywords: A Vocabulary of Culture and Society,* 2015.

Williams, Raymond. *Marxism and Literature.* Oxford: Oxford University Press, 1977.

Williams, Raymond. *Modern Tragedy.* London: Chatto & Windus, 1966.

Winthrop, Robert Charles. *An Address, Delivered Before the New England Society. December 23, 1839.* Boston: Perkins and Marvin, 1840.

Wood, Gordon S. "Struggle over the Puritans." *New York Review of Books,* November 1989.

Wood, Marcus. *The Poetry of Slavery: An Anglo-American Anthology, 1764–1866.* Oxford: Oxford University Press, 2003.

Wright, Elizur. *The Quarterly Anti-Slavery Magazine.* Boston: American Anti-Slavery Society, 1836.

Wright, Joanne Harriet. *Origin Stories in Political Thought: Discourses on Gender, Power, and Citizenship.* Toronto: University of Toronto Press, 2004.

Yellin, Jean Fagan. *Women and Sisters: Antislavery Feminists in American Culture.* New Haven, CT: Yale University Press, 1992.

Yellin, Jean Fagan, and John C. Van Horne. *The Abolitionist Sisterhood: Women's Political Culture in Antebellum America.* Ithaca, NY: Cornell University Press, 1994.

Young, Alfred F. *The Shoemaker and the Tea Party: Memory and the American Revolution.* Boston: Beacon, 1999.

Young, Michael P., and Stephen M. Cherry. "The Secularization of Confessional Protests: The Role of Religious Processes of Rationalization and Differentiation." *Journal for the Scientific Study of Religion* 44, no. 4 (December 2005): 373–95.

INDEX

Aaron, Daniel, 3, 177

abolitionism, 3, 4, 10–12, 18, 25–27, 34, 44, 46–47, 50–51, 56, 60, 62–63, 72, 75, 79, 81, 90, 101, 105, 114, 120, 121, 129, 149, 157, 159, 190n43, 193n29, 209n3; ecclesiastical, 129, 210n19; Garrisonian, 7, 13–14, 21, 25, 33, 37–38, 45–46, 52–54, 63–64, 69–70, 84–95, 98, 102–3, 105, 108, 110, 113, 124–25, 132, 134–36, 146, 149, 154, 158–59, 162, 169, 171, 191n63, 197n27, 203n40, 205n8, 208n51; and the imagination, 7–8, 10, 12, 14, 97–98, 105, 151, 190n53

Adams, Charles Francis, 53

Adams, Henry, 4, 7–8, 16, 42, 53, 88, 92, 123, 163

Adams, John Quincy, 53, 163, 194n50

Adams, Samuel, 216n37

aesthetics, 13, 55, 63, 84, 98–100, 103, 105, 112, 115, 137, 141, 143–44, 193n18, 205n12

affections, 19, 60, 63, 91, 112, 141, 189n26, 200n94

Africa, 61, 147–48, 153–57, 160, 166, 172, 188n18, 198n52, 213n8; civilization, 168; and the slave trade, 126

African Americans, 15, 38–39, 149, 153–59, 168, 177; abolitionism, 97, 158, 167, 173–74, 213n8, 214n9; activism, 14, 70, 161, 165, 168; clergy, 215n25; community, 74, 80, 160; destiny, 168–70; emigration, 154,

158, 165, 171; enfranchisement, 56; enlistment, 174; heroes, 169; historical writing, 214n10; jeremiad, 154, 214n9; literature, 2, 14–15, 56, 60–62, 71, 154–55, 164, 167–68, 171, 174; newspapers, 14, 80, 155, 163–65; origins, 153, 155, 168–70; Protestantism, 166, 215n25; regiments in the Civil War, 38–40, 173, 177 (*see also* Massachusetts Fifty-Fourth Regiment); revolutionaries, 2, 135, 169, 172, 207; troops in the Civil War, 15, 40–41, 70, 171–73; women, 57, 81

African Methodist Episcopal Church, 15, 173

agitation, 21–22, 34, 49, 79, 84, 179

America, 4–5, 8, 10, 14, 26, 29, 32, 35, 41–42, 55, 79, 81, 90, 119, 120, 123, 125, 127–28, 130, 134, 137, 142, 144, 153–56, 158–60, 162, 165, 166, 169, 170, 175, 176, 187, 188n17, 213n6; culture, 12, 60, 112, 136; destiny, 154; exceptionalism, 175–76, 188; history, 24, 84, 129, 188, 190n53; identity, 153–54, 160–61, 174, 180; ideology, 91; liberty, 127; materialism, 10; myth, 160; nationalism, 56; origins, 153; principles, 158, 163; society, 3, 41, 45, 105, 156

American Revolution, 5–6, 24, 32, 38, 76, 85, 179, 195, 215n25, 217n58

anarchism, 8, 17–18, 24, 91, 135–37, 139, 140